Good Housekeeping Cookery Club

COLLECTION

Good Housekeeping Cookery Club
COLLECTION

Delicious recipes for all kinds of occasions

BCA

LONDON NEW YORK SYDNEY TORONTO

First published 1996

1 3 5 7 9 10 8 6 4 2

This edition published in 1996 by BCA by arrangement with Ebury Press
Random House, 20 Vauxhall Bridge Road,
London, SW1V 2SA

Random House Australia (Pty) Limited
20 Alfred Street, Milsons Point, Sydney,
New South Wales, 2061 Australia

Random House New Zealand Limited
18 Poland Road, Glenfield,
Auckland 10, New Zealand

Random House South Africa (Pty) Limited
PO Box 337, Bergvlei, South Africa

Random House UK Limited Reg. No. 954009

A catalogue record for this book is available from the British
Library

CN 2735

Managing Editor: JANET ILLSLEY
Design: SARA KIDD
Photography: KARL ADAMSON, LAURIE EVANS, KEN FIELD,
GUS FILGATE, GRAHAM KIRK, JAMES MURPHY,

Printed and bound in Italy by New Interlitho Italia S.p.a.

CONTENTS

COOKERY NOTES

- Both metric and imperial measures are given for the recipes. Follow *either* metric or imperial throughout.
- All spoon measures are level unless otherwise stated. Sets of measuring spoons are available in metric and imperial for accurate measurement of small quantities.
- Ovens should be preheated to the specified temperature. Grills should also be preheated. The cooking times given in the recipes assume that this has been done.
- Where a stage is specified under freezing instructions, the dish should be frozen at the end of that stage.
- Size 2 eggs should be used unless otherwise specified.

SOUPS AND STARTERS

GARLIC, BEAN AND TOMATO SOUP WITH PESTO

This is a soup for confirmed garlic lovers – a caramelised garlic broth forms the basis of the stock, and a garlic pesto sauce is served as a garnish. Caramelising raw garlic changes its character dramatically, giving it a far sweeter and milder flavour. Cooking it in this way also makes garlic more digestible.

SERVES 4

125 g (4 oz) dried borlotti beans, soaked overnight in cold water (see note)

1.2 litres (2 pints) vegetable stock (see page 5)

1 head of garlic

30 ml (2 tbsp) olive oil

450 g (1 lb) ripe tomatoes

15 ml (1 tbsp) lemon juice

salt and pepper

PESTO

1 garlic clove, chopped

2.5 ml ($\frac{1}{2}$ tsp) sea salt

25 g (1 oz) basil leaves

25 g (1 oz) pine nuts

125 ml (4 fl oz) extra-virgin olive oil

30 ml (2 tbsp) freshly grated Parmesan cheese

PREPARATION TIME
15 minutes, plus overnight soaking
COOKING TIME
1 hour
FREEZING
Suitable: Without the pesto

530 CALS PER SERVING

1. Preheat the oven to 200°C (400°F), Mark 6. Drain and rinse the beans and place in a saucepan with the stock. Bring to the boil and boil rapidly for 10 minutes. Reduce the heat, cover and simmer for 40-45 minutes until the beans are tender.

2. Meanwhile, separate and peel the garlic cloves. Place them in a roasting tin, drizzle with the oil and bake near the top of the oven for 15 minutes. Meanwhile, roughly chop the tomatoes. Add to the garlic, stir to mix and bake for a further 10-15 minutes until the garlic is lightly browned and the tomatoes are soft. Set aside.

3. Transfer the cooked beans and their liquid to a blender or food processor, then add the tomato and garlic mixture, salt and pepper. Purée until fairly smooth, then return to the pan. Add the lemon juice and check the seasoning. Heat through for 5 minutes.

4. Meanwhile, make the pesto. Place the garlic, salt, basil and pine nuts in a food processor and blend until fairly smooth. Gradually blend in the oil. Stir in the cheese and salt and pepper to taste.

5. Ladle the soup into warmed bowls and top each serving with a spoonful of pesto.

NOTE: To save time, use a 400 g (14 oz) can borlotti or haricot beans rather than dried beans and reduce the stock to 900 ml (1$\frac{1}{2}$ pints). Rinse the beans before puréeing them with the stock and tomato mixture in step 3.

VARIATION

Add 225 g (8 oz) button mushrooms to the tomato and garlic mixture with an extra 15 ml (1 tbsp) olive oil. Bake as above, stir into the cooked beans and add 125 g (4 oz) each of peas, broad beans and diced broccoli. Cook until tender and serve topped with the pesto.

TECHNIQUE

Bake the garlic and tomatoes until soft and lightly browned.

OXTAIL AND ONION SOUP WITH CAMEMBERT TOASTS

The rich depth of flavour derived from the oxtail makes the advance preparation of the stock for this soup well worthwhile. Be sure to get your butcher to cut the oxtail into chunks for you as the bone that runs through the centre is very hard indeed. Garlic and Camembert topped croûtons are an unusual garnish, but the creamy, gooey texture of the melted cheese is quite wonderful.

SERVES 4

900 g (2 lb) oxtail, in chunks
   (see above)
1 small leek, trimmed
2 carrots, peeled
2 celery sticks
1 bouquet garni
1.75 litres (3 pints) water
1 large head of garlic
30 ml (2 tbsp) olive oil
900 g (2 lb) red onions
50 g (2 oz) unsalted butter
15 ml (1 tbsp) chopped fresh
   thyme
5 ml (1 tsp) sugar
5 ml (1 tsp) salt
150 ml (¼ pint) red wine
pepper
TO SERVE
125 g (4 oz) Camembert
   cheese
4 slices French stick

PREPARATION TIME
30 minutes, plus overnight chilling
COOKING TIME
2¾ hours
FREEZING
Suitable: Without toasts

605-405 CALS PER SERVING

1. Wash the oxtail chunks and pat dry. Chop the leek, carrots and celery, and place in a large pan with the oxtail, bouquet garni and water. Bring to the boil, skim the surface to remove any scum, cover and simmer for 2 hours. Strain the stock into a clean pan. Leave to cool and chill overnight.

2. The following day, preheat the oven to 200°C (400°F) Mark 6. Cut a thin slice from the top of the garlic and sit on a double piece of foil. Drizzle over the oil and fold over the foil to seal in the garlic. Bake for 45-50 minutes until the garlic cloves are tender. Remove from the oven and leave to cool slightly.

3. Meanwhile, remove the fat from the surface of the stock. Bring the stock to the boil and simmer to reduce to about 900 ml (1½ pints).

4. Peel and thinly slice the onions. Melt the butter in a large heavy-based pan, add the onions and fry over a medium heat for 20-25 minutes until caramelised. Stir in the thyme, sugar and salt and continue to fry for a further 5 minutes.

5. Pour in the red wine and boil rapidly until well reduced, then add the stock. Bring to the boil, cover and simmer for 20 minutes. Season with salt and pepper to taste and keep warm.

6. Preheat the grill. Squeeze the garlic cloves from their skins and mash to a paste. Cut the Camembert into thin slices. Lightly toast the French stick slices on one side, then spread the garlic paste over the untoasted side and top each one with a slice of Camembert. Grill for 1-2 minutes until bubbling and golden.

7. Divide the soup between warmed serving bowls and top with the toasts. Serve at once.

TECHNIQUE

Squeeze out the softened garlic cloves from their skins and spread onto the slices of French bread.

SPICY PARSNIP AND CARROT SOUP WITH CUMIN

A wonderfully warming vegetarian soup, with a delicious hint of spicy cumin seeds. As the parsnip and carrot purée is sufficient to thicken the soup, there are no added calories in the form of flour – making it an ideal recipe for slimmers. For optimum flavour, use homemade vegetable stock. Serve the soup as a sustaining lunch, accompanied by wholemeal bread or crusty rolls.

SERVES 4

1 onion
450 g (1 lb) parsnips
225 g (8 oz) carrots
30 ml (2 tbsp) olive oil
15 ml (1 tbsp) curry powder
350 ml (¾ pint) vegetable
   stock
300 ml (½ pint) semi-
   skimmed milk
salt and pepper
TO GARNISH
10 ml (2 tsp) cumin seeds

PREPARATION TIME
15 minutes
COOKING TIME
15-20 minutes
FREEZING
Suitable

200 CALS PER SERVING

1. Peel and finely chop the onion. Peel the parsnips, cut in half and remove the woody stems. Peel the carrots. Cut the parsnips and carrots into even-sized pieces.

2. Heat the olive oil in a heavy-based saucepan, add the vegetables and stir to lightly coat in the oil. Cover and cook for a few minutes until the vegetables are slightly softened. Sprinkle in the curry powder and cook, stirring, for 1 minute.

3. Stir in the vegetable stock and milk, and season with salt and pepper. Bring to the boil, then reduce the heat to a gentle simmer and cook for 15-20 minutes until the vegetables are soft.

4. Allow the soup to cool a little, then transfer to a blender or food processor and work until smooth. If the consistency is a little too thick for your liking, add a dash more milk or vegetable stock.

5. Toast the cumin seeds by gently frying them in a non-stick pan, or spread on a baking sheet and grill under a medium heat. Meanwhile, return the soup to the saucepan and reheat gently. Serve the soup in warmed soup bowls, garnished with a sprinkling of cumin seeds.

VARIATIONS

Use pumpkin in place of carrots for a vibrant soup with an excellent flavour. Alternatively, use a mixture of root vegetables, such as swede, parsnip and potato.

TECHNIQUE

Purée the soup in a blender or food processor, then return to the saucepan and reheat gently.

THAI SHELLFISH SOUP

With many of the exotic ingredients used in oriental dishes now readily available in our stores, authentic Thai dishes are far easier to achieve. Red curry paste provides the main flavouring for this tasty soup. For optimum flavour, make your own paste (see below); use the remainder in other Thai dishes, such as curries and stir-fries. Alternatively you can buy jars of ready-made Thai red curry paste.

SERVES 4

8 large raw prawns in shells

20 fresh mussels

4-8 small squid, cleaned

4 large cooked crab claws

900 ml (1½ pints) fish or
vegetable stock (see
page 5-6)

15 ml (1 tbsp) groundnut or
sunflower oil

15-30 ml (1-2 tbsp) Thai red
curry paste (see below)

300 ml (½ pint) coconut
milk

30 ml (2 tbsp) light soy
sauce

salt and pepper

coriander leaves, to garnish

PREPARATION TIME
30 minutes
COOKING TIME
1 hour
FREEZING
Not suitable

350 CALS PER SERVING

1. Prepare the shellfish. Peel the prawns and place the heads and shells in a large saucepan. Scrub the mussels thoroughly in plenty of cold water and remove the beards. Discard any mussels which do not close when tapped firmly. Slice the squid into rings and halve the tentacles, if large. Separate the crab claws at the joints and crack the shells slightly with a mallet or nut crackers. Set all the shellfish aside.

2. Add the stock to the prawn shells, bring to the boil, cover the pan and simmer gently for 30 minutes. Strain and reserve the stock.

3. Meanwhile, place the mussels in a large saucepan with a little water. Cover with a tight-fitting lid and cook over a high heat for 3 minutes until the shells are steamed open. Drain the mussels and discard any that remain closed. Refresh the mussels immediately under cold running water and set aside.

4. Heat the oil in a clean pan, add the Thai curry paste and fry, stirring, over a gentle heat for 2 minutes. Stir in the reserved prawn stock, coconut milk, and soy sauce. Bring to the boil, cover and simmer gently for 20 minutes.

5. Add the prawns and crab claws to the soup. Simmer for 5 minutes, then add the squid and mussels. Heat through

for a further 3-4 minutes and check the seasoning. Serve at once, garnished with the coriander leaves.

THAI RED CURRY PASTE: To make your own version you will need 8 dried red chillies, seeded; 8 coriander roots, scrubbed; 2.5 cm (1 inch) piece fresh root ginger, peeled and chopped; 4 kaffir lime leaves, shredded; 2 lemon grass stalks, peeled and chopped; 4 garlic cloves, peeled and chopped; 2 shallots, peeled and chopped; 5 ml (1 tsp) black pepper; and 15 ml (1 tbsp) sunflower oil. Place all the ingredients in a blender or food processor and work to a smooth paste. Store in a screw-topped jar in the refrigerator for up to 1 week.

NOTE: Cracking the crab claws prior to cooking makes getting into the flesh easier. So don't forget the finger bowls!

TECHNIQUE

Separate the crab claws at the joints and crack the shells slightly.

JERUSALEM ARTICHOKE AND PARMESAN SOUP

An unusual combination of mild Jerusalem artichokes with a hint of spice and the nutty taste of Parmesan cheese. The flavour of fresh Parmesan makes this soup really special. Don't be tempted to use the dry cheese sold in cartons – it bears no comparison to the real thing!

SERVES 6

450 g (1 lb) Jerusalem
   artichokes
2 shallots
50 g (2 oz) butter
5 ml (1 tsp) mild curry paste
900 ml (1½ pints) chicken or
   vegetable stock
150 ml (¼ pint) single
   cream (or milk for a less
   rich soup)
freshly grated nutmeg, to
   taste
pinch of cayenne pepper
60 ml (4 tbsp) freshly grated
   Parmesan cheese
salt and pepper
MELBA TOAST
3-4 slices day-old softgrain
   white bread
a little freshly grated
   Parmesan cheese, for
   sprinkling
1.25 ml (¼ tsp) paprika

PREPARATION TIME
15 minutes
COOKING TIME
25 minutes
FREEZING
Suitable

190 CALS PER SERVING

1. Scrub the Jerusalem artichokes thoroughly to remove any dirt. Pat dry, then slice thinly. Peel and dice the shallots.

2. Melt the butter in a large saucepan and add the shallots. Cook gently for 5 minutes until soft and golden. Stir in the curry paste and cook for 1 minute. Add the sliced artichokes and stock; stir well. Bring to the boil, cover and simmer for about 15 minutes or until the artichokes are tender.

3. Meanwhile, make the Melba toast. Preheat the oven to 180°C (350°F) Mark 4. Toast the bread lightly on both sides. Quickly cut off the crusts and split each slice in two. Scrape off any doughy bits, then sprinkle with Parmesan and paprika. Place on a baking sheet and bake in the oven for 10-15 minutes or until uniformly golden.

4. Add the cream, nutmeg and cayenne to the soup. Transfer to a blender or food processor and work until smooth, then pass through a sieve into a clean saucepan. Reheat the soup and stir in the Parmesan cheese. Taste and adjust the seasoning. Serve at once, with the hot Melba toast.

NOTE: If preferred the Melba toast can be prepared ahead, allowed to cool, then stored in an airtight tin. Warm through in the oven before serving.

VARIATION

Replace the Jerusalem artichokes with 1 large cauliflower. Cut away the leaves and core, and discard. Divide the cauliflower into florets. Add to the shallots with the stock and bring to the boil. Simmer for about 10 minutes or until very soft, then continue as in step 4.

TECHNIQUE

To make the Melba toast, carefully split each slice of toast horizontally in two. On baking these fine slices will curl.

GRILLED PEPPER AND AUBERGINE SOUP

Peppers and aubergine become sweet as their flesh caramelises under the grill, giving this soup an intensity of flavour that is hard to surpass. The saffron cream garnish is similar to *rouille*.

SERVES 4-6

2 large red peppers
1 large aubergine
90 ml (3 fl oz) olive oil
1 large onion
2 garlic cloves
5 ml (1 tsp) grated lemon
  rind
15 ml (1 tbsp) chopped fresh
  thyme
5 ml (1 tsp) dried oregano
400 g (14 oz) can chopped
  tomatoes
900 ml (1½ pints) vegetable
  or chicken stock
1 bay leaf
30 ml (2 tbsp) chopped fresh
  basil
salt and pepper
SAFFRON CREAM
small pinch of saffron strands
1 egg yolk
1 garlic clove, crushed
2.5 ml (½ tsp) cayenne
  pepper
10 ml (2 tsp) lemon juice
150-175 ml (5-6 fl oz) olive oil

PREPARATION TIME
25 minutes
COOKING TIME
45-50 minutes
FREEZING
Suitable: Without saffron cream

390-300 CALS PER SERVING

1. Preheat the grill. Quarter, core and deseed the red peppers. Brush with a little olive oil and grill for 3-4 minutes on each side until charred and tender. Transfer to a plate, cover with a cloth and leave until cool enough to handle. Peel the peppers and roughly chop the flesh.

2. Thinly slice the aubergine lengthways. Brush with oil and grill for 4-5 minutes on each side until charred and tender. Leave until cool enough to handle, then chop roughly.

3. Peel and chop the onion and garlic. Heat the remaining oil in a large pan, add the onion, garlic, lemon rind, thyme and oregano and fry, stirring, for 10 minutes until browned. Add the peppers, aubergine, tomatoes, stock and bay leaf. Bring to the boil, cover and simmer for 20 minutes. Discard the bay leaf.

4. Meanwhile, make the saffron cream. Put the saffron in a small bowl, pour on 15 ml (1 tbsp) boiling water and leave to soak for 5 minutes. In a bowl, whisk the egg yolk with the garlic, cayenne, lemon juice and seasoning until pale and slightly thickened. Gradually whisk in the oil, until thick. Stir in the saffron liquid and seasoning to taste.

5. Transfer the soup to a blender or food processor. Add the basil and work until smooth. Return to the pan and heat through. Adjust the seasoning and pour into warmed soup bowls. Spoon a little saffron cream onto each portion, garnish with basil leaves and serve at once.

VARIATION

Replace the aubergine with 2 yellow peppers and grill as above. Divide all other ingredients in half and cook in separate pans, adding the red peppers to one and the yellow peppers to the other. Cook until tender and purée separately to give two different coloured pepper soups. Serve half and half in each bowl, swirling them attractively, and garnish with saffron cream.

TECHNIQUE

For the saffron cream, whisk in the oil a little at a time, beating well between each addition.

CHILLED BEETROOT AND APPLE SOUP

A cool, deep crimson soup that's as wonderfully refreshing to eat as it looks. Serve it topped with a dollop of minted cucumber cream – to mix in at the table. Grissini bread sticks are an ideal accompaniment.

SERVES 4

350 g (12 oz) cooked, peeled
   beetroot
juice of ½ lemon
600 ml (1 pint) unsweetened
   apple juice, chilled
200 g (7 oz) Greek-style
   yogurt, chilled
salt and pepper
cayenne pepper
10 cm (4 inch) piece
   cucumber
6 fresh mint leaves
6-8 fresh chives
TO SERVE
chives and mint sprigs, to
   garnish
grissini bread sticks

PREPARATION TIME
10 minutes
COOKING TIME
Nil
FREEZING
Not suitable

160 CALS PER SERVING

1. Slice the beetroot and place in a food processor or blender. Add the lemon juice, half the apple juice and half the yogurt. Process for 1-2 minutes until smooth.

2. Pour the beetroot mixture into a mixing bowl, stir in the rest of the apple juice and season with salt, pepper and cayenne pepper to taste. Chill until you are ready to serve, then pour into individual soup bowls.

3. To make the cucumber cream, grate the cucumber and stir into the remaining yogurt. Chop the mint and stir into the mixture. Spoon some cucumber cream into the middle of each serving and sprinkle with a little cayenne pepper. Snip some chives over the top and garnish with mint. Serve at once, accompanied by the bread sticks.

NOTE: If there is time, pass the puréed beetroot through a sieve to yield a smoother soup.

VARIATION

For the cucumber cream, use crème fraîche instead of Greek-style yogurt.

TECHNIQUE

For the cucumber cream, grate the cucumber into the yogurt.

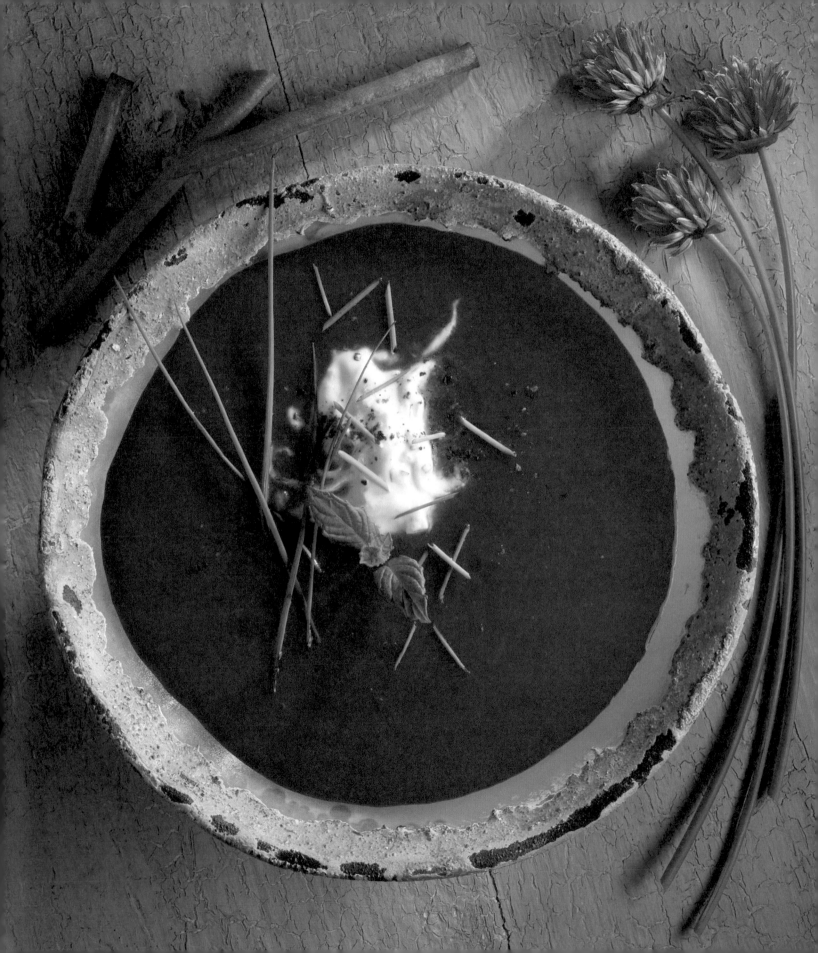

CURRIED MUSSEL SOUP

It is best to buy mussels several hours before cooking and soak them in cold water with a little wholemeal flour or oatmeal added to the water. This helps clean out their digestive systems and rids them of excess grit. After soaking, scrub the mussels to remove the grit and pull out the "beards" that remain attached to the shells. Discard any that are cracked or wide open.

SERVES 4

900 g (2 lb) fresh mussels

pinch of saffron strands

600 ml (1 pint) fish or
vegetable stock
(see page 5)

2 small leeks, trimmed

30 ml (2 tbsp) olive oil

1 garlic clove, crushed

30 ml (2 tbsp) mild curry
paste

2.5 ml (½ tsp) mustard
powder

150 ml (¼ pint) dry cider

150 ml (¼ pint) double
cream

15 ml (1 tbsp) chopped fresh
chervil or parsley

salt and pepper

PREPARATION TIME
20 minutes
COOKING TIME
20 minutes
FREEZING
Not suitable

320 CALS PER SERVING

1. Preheat the oven to its lowest setting. Clean the mussels thoroughly under cold running water, removing their beards and discarding any with open or cracked shells. Put the saffron strands in a bowl. Heat the stock, pour over the saffron and leave to soak for 10 minutes.

2. Meanwhile, slice the leeks. Heat the oil in a large saucepan, add the garlic and leeks and fry gently for 5 minutes until soft but not coloured. Stir in the curry paste, mustard powder and cider. Boil rapidly until the cider is almost completely reduced.

3. Add the mussels, stir once and pour in the saffron stock. Bring to the boil, cover and simmer gently for 6-8 minutes until the mussels have opened. Discard any that remain closed.

4. Carefully strain the liquid through a fine sieve into a clean saucepan. Transfer the mussels to warmed soup bowls and keep warm in the oven.

5. Bring the liquid to a simmer and whisk in the cream and chervil or parsley. Bring to the boil and boil steadily for 5 minutes. Season with salt and pepper to taste and pour immediately over the mussels. Serve at once.

VARIATION

For a coconut curry soup, replace the double cream with the same amount of coconut milk. Bring to a gentle simmer and immediately pour over the mussels.

TECHNIQUE

Scrub the mussels thoroughly under cold running water and pull away the beard from each shell.

MARINATED PEPPERS WITH ARTICHOKES AND ANCHOVIES

There is nothing more evocative of sunny, warm Mediterranean meals than sweet roasted red peppers marinated in golden, garlicky olive oil with artichoke hearts and anchovies to add extra bite. Left overnight for the flavours to mature, the peppers release a sweet juice into the oil, making a delicious sauce – perfect for mopping up with copious amounts of bread.

SERVES 6

6 red, orange or yellow
   peppers (or a mixture)
12 artichoke hearts in oil,
   drained
24 salted anchovies (see
   below), or canned
   anchovy fillets
salt and pepper
4 garlic cloves
30 ml (2 tbsp) chopped fresh
   oregano
extra-virgin olive oil, for
   marinating

PREPARATION TIME
20 minutes, plus overnight
marinating
COOKING TIME
10-15 minutes
FREEZING
Not suitable

300 CALS PER SERVING

1. Preheat the grill to high. Place the whole peppers in the grill pan and grill, turning occasionally, until the skins are evenly charred all over. Place in a covered bowl for 1-2 minutes until cool enough to handle.

2. Slip off the skins while the peppers are still warm, then cut in half lengthways and scrape out the seeds. Place the peppers cut-side up in a shallow dish.

3. Cut the artichoke hearts in half and place two halves in each pepper half. Lay the anchovy fillets on top. Season well with salt and pepper. Peel and slice the garlic. Scatter the garlic and chopped oregano over the peppers.

4. Pour over enough olive oil to cover the peppers (see note). Cover the dish and leave to marinate in the refrigerator overnight to permit the flavours to blend. Allow to come to room temperature before serving, with crusty Italian bread.

NOTE: Use the leftover flavoured olive oil again and again to make more of the same dish, or in salad dressings.

SALTED ANCHOVIES: These have a much better flavour than canned anchovy fillets. They are available in jars from Italian delicatessens and larger supermarkets. Usually salted anchovies are whole and have to be rinsed, split open and the backbone and other small bones removed.

VARIATION

Fill the peppers with grilled thin lengthwise slices of courgette and top with cubed mozzarella cheese.

TECHNIQUE

Place two artichoke halves in each grilled pepper half. Top with the anchovy fillets.

GRILLED AVOCADO STUFFED WITH CRAB

Soft goat's cheese lends a mild, fresh taste and creamy texture to the crab meat. If available, choose small Hass avocados for their nutty flavour. Serve the stuffed avocados, thickly sliced, on a bed of crisp colourful salad leaves, lightly dressed with olive oil and lemon juice.

SERVES 4

125 g (4 oz) white crab meat
125 g (4 oz) fresh soft goat's cheese
5 ml (1 tsp) chopped fresh tarragon
salt and pepper
15 ml (1 tbsp) lemon juice
2 ripe avocados
50 g (2 oz) brown crab meat
2 plum tomatoes
DRESSING
15 ml (1 tbsp) walnut oil
30 ml (2 tbsp) olive oil
15 ml (1 tbsp) lemon juice
TO SERVE
salad leaves

PREPARATION TIME
10 minutes
COOKING TIME
10 minutes
FREEZING
Not suitable

390 CALS PER SERVING

1. In a bowl, loosen the white crab meat with a fork, removing any pieces of shell. Add 50 g (2 oz) of the goat's cheese and the chopped tarragon. Mix together with a fork, seasoning with salt and pepper to taste.

2. Cut the avocados in half and remove the stones. Brush the cut surfaces with lemon juice to prevent discolouration. Divide the brown crab meat between the four avocado halves, spooning it into the cavities.

3. Divide the white crab meat mixture between the avocados, mounding it over the brown meat and spreading it over the avocado.

4. Slice the tomatoes thinly and arrange over the crab. Crumble the remaining goat's cheese on top of the tomatoes and season with pepper.

5. Preheat the grill to medium. Place the avocados on a baking sheet or in an ovenproof dish and grill for about 10 minutes, until the cheese has browned and the avocado is warm.

6. Whisk together the ingredients for the dressing in a small bowl, seasoning with salt and pepper to taste.

7. To serve, cut the avocados crosswise into thick slices and arrange on a bed of salad leaves. Drizzle with the dressing. Serve warm or cold.

TECHNIQUE

Spoon the white crab meat mixture on top of the brown meat and spread it over the avocado.

GRILLED TOMATO AND MOZZARELLA SALAD

This hot salad starter can be prepared ahead, chilled, then grilled just before serving. Make sure you use tomatoes which are ripe and have plenty of flavour – it does make a difference. If you are buying from a supermarket, look for the packs marked 'grown for flavour'.

SERVES 4

175 g (6 oz) aubergine
45 ml (3 tbsp) olive oil
450 g (1 lb) tomatoes
150 g (5 oz) mozzarella
  cheese
60 ml (4 tbsp) torn fresh
  basil leaves
finely grated rind of 1 lemon
5 ml (1 tsp) lemon juice
salt and pepper
TO GARNISH
basil leaves

PREPARATION TIME
10 minutes
COOKING TIME
About 10 minutes
FREEZING
Not suitable

240 CALS PER SERVING

1. Preheat the grill. Cut the aubergine into thin slices. Brush very lightly with some of the olive oil and place on the grill rack. Grill the aubergine slices on both sides until they are crisp and golden brown; do not let them turn too dark at this stage.

2. Thinly slice the tomatoes. Cut the mozzarella cheese into thin slices.

3. In a bowl, whisk together the remaining olive oil, torn basil, lemon rind and juice. Season with salt and pepper.

4. Arrange the tomato, aubergine and mozzarella slices, overlapping in a single layer, in a large shallow flameproof dish. Spoon the dressing evenly over the top.

5. Place under a hot grill for 3-4 minutes or until the mozzarella begins to melt. Sprinkle with salt and pepper and garnish with basil leaves. Serve immediately, accompanied by warm crusty bread.

VARIATION

Instead of basil, flavour the salad with 45 ml (3 tbsp) snipped chives or chopped coriander leaves.

TECHNIQUE

Layer the aubergine, tomato and mozzarella slices in the dish, overlapping them.

ROASTED VEGETABLES IN GARLIC BREAD BASKETS

Wholemeal bread baskets are rubbed with garlic, baked until crisp, then filled with a selection of roasted Mediterranean vegetables to delicious effect. Drizzling the baskets with a little balsamic vinegar lifts the flavour and a pretty garnish of basil and black olive slivers adds the finishing touch. An attractive starter to complement any meal.

SERVES 6

2 red onions

2 garlic cloves, peeled

1 yellow pepper

1 red pepper

1 small aubergine

2 courgettes

15 ml (1 tbsp) olive oil

pinch of sea salt

4 fresh rosemary sprigs

12 slices wholemeal bread

15 ml (1 tbsp) black olive
   paste

15 ml (1 tbsp) balsamic
   vinegar

TO GARNISH

12 basil sprigs

few black olives, stoned and
   sliced

PREPARATION TIME
30 minutes
COOKING TIME
20-30 minutes
FREEZING
Not suitable

215 CALS PER SERVING

1. Preheat the oven to 230°C (450°F) Mark 8. Peel the onions and slice lengthwise. Halve one of the garlic cloves and set aside; crush the other garlic clove. Halve the peppers, then remove the core and seeds. Cut the peppers, aubergine and courgettes into 2.5 cm (1 inch) chunks.

2. Place all the vegetables in a roasting tin, drizzle over the olive oil and sprinkle with the sea salt, rosemary and crushed garlic. Bake in the oven for 20-30 minutes, turning occasionally until just tinged brown at the edges.

3. Remove the crusts from the bread and roll out each slice lightly. Cut a 9 cm (3½ inch) circle from each slice using a plain cutter, and rub with the halved garlic clove. Line a 12-hole deep bun tin or muffin tin with the bread rounds.

4. Place in the oven for 5 minutes. Carefully remove the bread baskets from the tin and return to the oven for 5 minutes to allow the bread to crisp.

5. Spread a little olive paste over the base of each basket. Remove the roasted vegetables from the oven and divide between the toasted bread baskets. Just before serving, drizzle a little balsamic

vinegar over each basket. Garnish with sprigs of basil and slivers of black olive. Serve warm.

VARIATIONS

Use the bread baskets as containers for other combinations of vegetables, such as lightly roasted leeks, courgettes and cauliflower.

TECHNIQUE

To shape the bread baskets, line a 12-hole deep bun tin with the bread slices.

POTTED MIXED SEAFOOD WITH HERB SODA BREAD

Sweet, meaty prawns are flavoured with a hint of garlic, and packed into little pots with moist flakes of poached trout. Serve the accompanying soda bread very fresh – preferably still warm from the oven.

SERVES 8

POTTED SEAFOOD

2 large trout

300 g (10 oz) lightly salted butter

700 g (1½ lb) large raw prawns (see note)

2 garlic cloves, crushed

1.25 ml (¼ tsp) ground mace

pepper

SODA BREAD

600 ml (1 pint) milk

15 ml (1 tbsp) lemon juice

225 g (8 oz) plain wholemeal flour

375 g (13 oz) strong white flour

10 ml (2 tsp) salt

5 ml (1 tsp) bicarbonate of soda

25 g (1 oz) butter

1 spring onion, chopped

45 ml (3 tbsp) chopped herbs (parsley, tarragon, chervil)

50 g (2 oz) medium oatmeal

extra oatmeal, for sprinkling

PREPARATION TIME
35 minutes, plus chilling
COOKING TIME
Potted Seafood: 20 minutes; Bread 25 minutes
FREEZING Not suitable

720 CALS PER SERVING`

1. To make the potted seafood, wrap the trout in buttered foil, seal tightly and lower into a saucepan containing 2.5 cm (1 inch) depth of boiling water. Cover and steam for about 20 minutes until the thickest area of the fish flakes easily. Remove and leave to cool.

2. Flake the trout into small pieces, discarding skin and bones. Heat 50 g (2 oz) butter in a frying pan. Add the prawns with the garlic and mace; cook for 2 minutes until pink on the underside. Turn and cook for a further 1-2 minutes until pink all over. Remove with a slotted spoon, reserving the butter in the pan.

3. Peel the prawns and pack with the trout into 8 small ramekins. Cut the remaining butter into pieces and add to the pan. Stir until melted and add a little pepper.

4. Turn the melted butter into a jug and pour over the ramekins until the fish is just submerged. Leave to cool, then chill for several hours until firm.

5. For the soda bread, preheat the oven to 220°C (425°F) Mark 7. Mix together the milk and lemon juice. Sift the flours, salt and bicarbonate of soda into a bowl, adding any bran left in the sieve. Rub in the butter. Add the spring onion, herbs and oatmeal.

6. Add most of the milk and mix to a dough with a round-bladed knife, adding the remaining milk as necessary. Turn out onto a floured surface and knead lightly.

7. Divide the mixture in half and shape each piece into a round. Place slightly apart on a lightly greased large baking sheet. Score with the back of a knife, then sprinkle generously with oatmeal. Bake for about 25 minutes until risen and browned. Transfer to a wire rack.

8. Loosen the potted seafood and turn out onto serving plates. Surround with a herb salad and serve with the warm soda bread.

NOTE: If raw prawns are unobtainable, use 575 g (1¼ lb) cooked shelled prawns instead. Heat through for 1 minute only.

TECHNIQUE

Pour the melted butter over the fish in each ramekin until just covered.

TOMATO AND MOZZARELLA SALAD ON BRUSCHETTA

A classic mozzarella and cherry tomato salad, which is marinated in olive oil, then piled onto garlic-scented toasted country bread and served surrounded with rocket and basil leaves. Bruschetta (pronounced *bruce-ketta*) is a popular snack all over Italy, served in bars and at home. The best bruschetta is toasted on the barbecue or over a wood fire, rubbed with garlic and drizzled with olive oil. The toppings are infinite – the simplest being a perfectly ripe tomato crushed onto the toast. Serve as a substantial starter, snack or lunch.

SERVES 4

12 boconcini (baby
   mozzarelle) or 375 g
   (12 oz) mozzarella
20 cherry tomatoes
45 ml (3 tbsp) olive oil
5 ml (1 tsp) balsamic or
   sherry vinegar
salt and pepper
4 thick slices of Italian
   country bread
2 garlic cloves, peeled
125 g (4 oz) rocket or
   watercress
extra olive oil, to serve
a generous handful of basil
   leaves, to garnish

PREPARATION TIME
15 minutes
COOKING TIME
Nil
FREEZING
Not suitable

590 CALS PER SERVING

1. Cut baby mozzarelle in half, or cut whole mozzarella into large cubes; place in a bowl. Halve the cherry tomatoes and add to the cheese.

2. Whisk together the olive oil and balsamic vinegar. Season with salt and pepper, then pour over the cheese and tomatoes. Stir well.

3. Preheat the grill and toast the slices of bread until golden on both sides. Halve the garlic cloves and rub over each slice of hot toasted bread.

4. Place a slice of toast on each serving plate and surround with the rocket. Pile the mozzarella and tomato mixture on the toast and drizzle the olive oil over the rocket. Garnish with basil leaves and serve at once.

NOTE: Baby mozzarelle are sold in tubs, immersed in water. They look very pretty in this salad, but ordinary mozzarella will do. Try to buy the round-shaped cheese, or even the expensive *mozzarella di bufala* (made with water-buffalo milk); these are superior in flavour and texture to the mozzarella bricks which are best used for pizzas.

VARIATION

Replace the mozzarella with chopped avocado.

TECHNIQUE

Rub the garlic cloves all over the hot toast to impart flavour.

HERBED MUSHROOM RAVIOLI

These pretty green herb-speckled ravioli are filled with a delicious mixture of wild mushrooms. Serve them simply topped with melted butter and freshly pared Parmesan cheese. A pasta machine gives excellent results, rolling the dough very finely – so that you may only need to use about two thirds of the quantity.

SERVES 6

PASTA

200 g (7 oz) type '00' pasta flour, or strong white bread flour

pinch of salt

2 (size 2) eggs

15 ml (1 tbsp) olive oil

45 ml (3 tbsp) mixed chopped fresh tarragon, marjoram and parsley

MUSHROOM FILLING

2 shallots

225 g (8 oz) mixed wild mushrooms or 175 g (6 oz) dark flat mushrooms, _plus_ 40 g (1½ oz) dried porcini

25 g (1 oz) black olives

4 sun-dried tomatoes in oil

50 g (2 oz) butter

15 ml (1 tbsp) dry sherry

salt and pepper

freshly grated nutmeg

beaten egg, for brushing

TO SERVE

50 g (2 oz) butter, melted

few sautéed wild mushrooms

Parmesan cheese

PREPARATION TIME
55 minutes, plus resting
COOKING TIME
5 minutes
FREEZING
Suitable

550 CALS PER SERVING

1. To make the pasta, sift the flour and salt into a mound on a clean work surface and make a well in the centre. Beat the eggs and oil together, then pour into the well. Sprinkle in the herbs. Gradually mix the liquid into the flour using one hand, then bring the dough together.

2. On a clean surface, with clean hands, knead the pasta for 5-10 minutes until smooth and elastic. Wrap in cling film and allow to rest at room temperature for 30 minutes.

3. For the filling, peel and finely chop the shallots. Wipe or brush the fresh mushrooms clean, then chop finely. If using dried mushrooms, soak in hot water to cover for 10-15 minutes. Remove and chop finely. Strain the soaking liquid through a filter paper and reserve. Stone and finely chop the olives. Drain and finely chop the sun-dried tomatoes.

4. Melt the butter in a pan, add the shallots and cook for 5 minutes until soft and golden. Add all the mushrooms, olives and dried tomatoes; cook, stirring, over a high heat for 1-2 minutes. Add the sherry and reserved liquid; cook for 1 minute. Season well with salt, pepper and nutmeg. Transfer to a bowl; cool.

5. If using a pasta machine, roll manageable portions of dough into strips. If rolling out by hand, divide in half and roll into 2 sheets on a very lightly floured surface. Either way, roll out as thinly as possible and keep covered with a slightly damp tea towel.

6. Place 18 heaped spoonfuls of filling on one half of the pasta, spacing them at 4 cm (1½ inch) intervals. Brush the dough in between with beaten egg. Lift the other sheet(s) of pasta over the top. Press down firmly between the pockets of filling and cut into 7.5 cm (3 inch) squares. Transfer to a floured tea towel and leave to rest for 1 hour.

7. Bring a large pan of salted water to the boil, with a dash of oil added. Carefully add the ravioli, bring back to the boil, turn off the heat and cover with a tight-fitting lid. Leave for 5 minutes, then drain well. Serve immediately, on warmed plates, topped with the melted butter, sautéed mushrooms and shavings of Parmesan cheese.

TECHNIQUE

Lift the plain pasta over the ravioli filling, taking care to avoid tearing the dough.

SPICED PORK WONTONS

These powerfully flavoured meatballs are wrapped in a casing of shredded wonton pastry. Look for wonton wrappers in good Chinese supermarkets where they are invariably sold both fresh and frozen, or scour the 'ethnic' section of your local supermarket. Alternatively, try making your own wrappers (see note). Serve these wontons as cocktail nibbles or as a prelude to a stir-fried main course, accompanied by a soy sauce dip, flavoured with chopped chilli and sesame oil, if you like.

MAKES 20-24

2.5 cm (1 inch) piece fresh
    root ginger
2 garlic cloves
1 small onion
2 hot chillies
5 ml (1 tsp) Chinese five-
    spice powder
90 ml (6 tbsp) chopped fresh
    coriander
700 g (1½ lb) lean minced
    pork
salt and pepper
20-24 wonton wrappers
1 egg, beaten
oil for deep-frying

PREPARATION TIME
30 minutes
COOKING TIME
About 15 minutes
FREEZING
Not suitable

100 CALS PER WONTON

1. Peel the ginger and cut in half. Peel the garlic. Peel and quarter the onion. Remove the stems from the chillies and, if a milder flavour is preferred, discard the seeds. Put all of these ingredients in a food processor or blender and process until finely chopped.

2. Add the five-spice powder, coriander and pork. Process again until evenly mixed. Season generously with salt and pepper.

3. Using floured hands, shape the mixture into walnut-sized balls.

4. Wrap each one in a wonton wrapper, sealing the edges with beaten egg. Alternatively, stack the wonton wrappers in a neat pile and cut into thin shreds, using a large sharp knife. Spread them in a single layer on a plate. Dip the pork balls into the beaten egg then drop onto the shredded wontons and roll around on the plate until coated on all sides. The wonton strips should stick out, rather than lie flat.

5. Heat the oil in a deep-fat fryer to 175°C (345°F). Test the temperature by dropping in a cube of bread – it should turn golden brown in about 1 minute. Deep-fry the wontons, in batches, for about 4 minutes until golden brown on all sides and the pork is cooked right through. Drain on crumpled kitchen paper. Serve warm.

NOTE: To make your own wonton wrappers, put 225 g (8 oz) plain white flour in a bowl with a large pinch of salt. Beat 1 egg with 60 ml (4 tbsp) cold water and stir into the flour. Knead together with your fingers, adding a little more water if necessary to make a smooth dough. Cover with a damp cloth and leave to rest for 30 minutes. Roll out the dough *very* thinly and cut into 7.5 cm (3 inch) squares.

VARIATIONS

Replace the pork with minced lamb or chicken. Replace the fresh coriander with 4 finely chopped spring onions.

TECHNIQUE

Roll the pork balls around on the shredded wonton wrappers until coated on all sides.

DIVINE SPARE RIBS

In this recipe the ribs are first simmered to tenderise the meat before being roasted with a tangy Chinese-style glaze – resulting in succulent, tender ribs. Remember to give each guest a finger bowl of warm water – eating ribs can be a messy business!

SERVES 4

900 g (2 lb) pork spare ribs
30 ml (2 tbsp) malt vinegar
30 ml (2 tbsp) sesame oil
90 ml (3 fl oz) rice or wine
   vinegar
60 ml (2 fl oz) dark soy
   sauce
10 ml (2 tsp) grated fresh
   root ginger
1 garlic clove, crushed
grated rind of 1 lime
60 ml (4 tbsp) soft brown
   sugar
2.5 ml (½ tsp) Chinese five-
   spice powder
90 ml (3 fl oz) water
TO GARNISH
coriander sprigs
lime wedges

PREPARATION TIME
15 minutes
COOKING TIME
1½ hours
FREEZING
Suitable: For up to 1 month.
Thaw at room temperature;
reheat in a covered dish in a
moderate oven for 20 minutes.

280 CALS PER SERVING

1. Wash and dry the spare ribs and place in a saucepan. Cover with plenty of cold water and add the malt vinegar. Bring to the boil and simmer for 20 minutes, skimming the surface from time to time to remove the scum.

2. Preheat the oven to 220°C (425°F) Mark 7. Meanwhile, place all the remaining ingredients in a small pan, bring to the boil and simmer for 5 minutes until reduced and thickened slightly.

3. Drain the ribs and transfer to a roasting dish that will hold the ribs in a single layer. Pour over the soy mixture and toss the ribs to coat evenly.

4. Cover loosely with foil and roast in the oven for 30 minutes. Remove the foil and cook for a further 30 minutes, turning and basting the ribs every 5 minutes. Leave to cool slightly for about 10 minutes before serving.

5. Garnish with coriander and lime wedges, and provide finger bowls and plenty of napkins.

VARIATION

Barbecued chicken wings make a tasty alternative to the pork ribs. Omit the par-boiling stage. Roast as above, coated with the glaze, for the same time or until glazed and tender.

TECHNIQUE

Turn the ribs and baste with the glaze every 5 minutes during the second half of roasting.

BEEF SATAY

This Thai snack is very simple to make and quite delicious to eat. Strips of beef are marinated for several hours, threaded onto bamboo skewers and grilled until charred and tender. They are served with a peanut dipping sauce and cubes of chilled cooked rice which provide a cool, refreshing balance to the spicy beef.

350 g (12 oz) fillet steak

2 garlic cloves, peeled

2.5 cm (1 inch) piece fresh
   root ginger, peeled

30 ml (2 tbsp) dark soy sauce

30 ml (2 tbsp) sweet sherry

15 ml (1 tbsp) rice or wine
   vinegar

10 ml (2 tsp) sesame oil

2.5 ml (½ tsp) chilli powder

RICE CUBES

50 g (2 oz) Thai fragrant rice

salt

PEANUT SAUCE

60 ml (4 tbsp) chopped
   peanuts

1.25 ml (¼ tsp) crushed chilli
   flakes

1 garlic clove, crushed

15 ml (1 tbsp) dark soy sauce

15 ml (1 tbsp) lime juice

5 ml (1 tsp) thin honey

½ x 200 g (7 oz) packet
   creamed coconut

PREPARATION TIME
30 minutes, plus freezing and
marinating
COOKING TIME
20 minutes
FREEZING
Not suitable

1. Place the beef in the freezer for 30 minutes until firm (to make it easier to slice).

2. Using a sharp knife, slice the beef across the grain into thin strips. Place in a shallow non-reactive dish. Crush the garlic and grate the ginger; place in a bowl with the soy sauce, sherry, vinegar, sesame oil and chilli powder. Pour over the beef, stir well, cover and leave to marinate in a cool place for 2-4 hours.

3. Cook the rice in boiling salted water for 15 minutes until very soft. Drain and refresh under cold water. Drain thoroughly. Press the rice into a small oiled dish and smooth the surface. Chill in the refrigerator until required.

4. Preheat the grill. Remove the beef from the marinade and thread onto bamboo skewers in a zig-zag fashion. Place the beef skewers on the grill rack and grill as close to the heat as possible for 4-5 minutes until tender, turning halfway through cooking.

5. Meanwhile make the peanut sauce. Put the peanuts, chilli flakes, garlic, soy sauce, lime juice and honey in a small pan and heat gently. Add the creamed coconut and cook, stirring, until smooth. Remove from the heat. Unmould the rice and cut into cubes. Serve the beef satay with the peanut dipping sauce and rice cubes.

For a vegetarian alternative, choose a selection of root vegetables and cut into small, equal-sized cubes. Marinate as above, thread the vegetables alternately onto the skewers and grill until golden and tender. Serve with the peanut sauce and rice cubes.

TECHNIQUE

Thread the marinated beef strips onto the skewers in a zig-zag fashion.

THAI FISH CAKES

Bursting with the flavours of chillies, kaffir lime and lemon grass, these bear absolutely no resemblance to the traditional British fish cake and are definitely not for serving with chips and tartare sauce! Serve them on a bed of salad leaves as a starter or snack, accompanied by a crunchy salad of shredded cabbage, beansprouts and pepper strips, tossed in a soy-based dressing and sprinkled with toasted sesame seeds.

MAKES ABOUT 10

450 g (1 lb) white fish fillets, such as cod or haddock

4 kaffir lime leaves

30 ml (2 tbsp) chopped fresh coriander

15 ml (1 tbsp) nam pla (Thai fish sauce)

15 ml (1 tbsp) lime juice

30 ml (2 tbsp) Thai Red Curry Paste (see page 7)

salt and pepper

flour, for coating

oil for shallow-frying

TO SERVE

salad leaves

shredded spring onion

1 mild red chilli, sliced

lime halves

PREPARATION TIME
25 minutes
COOKING TIME
About 20 minutes
FREEZING
Suitable

100 CALS PER FISH CAKE

1. Remove any skin from the fish, then place the fish in a food processor or blender and work until smooth.

2. Finely chop the lime leaves and add to the fish with the coriander, nam pla, lime juice and red curry paste. Season with salt and pepper. Process until well mixed.

3. Using lightly floured hands, divide the mixture into about 10 pieces and shape each one into a cake, about 6 cm (2½ inches) in diameter.

4. Shallow-fry the fish cakes in batches. Heat a 1 cm (½ inch) depth of oil in a frying pan. Cook the fish cakes, a few at a time, for about 4 minutes each side. Drain on crumpled kitchen paper and keep hot while cooking the remainder.

5. Serve the fish cakes as soon as they are all cooked, on a bed of salad leaves scattered with shredded spring onion and chilli slices. Serve with lime halves.

NOTE: If you don't have time to make your own curry paste use ready-made Thai red curry paste, which is available in jars from large supermarkets and delicatessens.

TECHNIQUE

With lightly floured hands, shape the mixture into cakes, each about 6 cm (2½ inches) in diameter.

Deep-Fried Whitebait with Hot Sauce

Whitebait are the young of herrings or sprats. Usually no more than about 5 cm (2 inches) long, they are eaten head, bones and all. Here they are deep-fried – always the best way to cook whitebait – and partnered by a fiery paprika and chilli sauce. Serve as a starter or lunch dish, or as part of a mezze or tapas-style meal comprising a variety of savoury dishes.

SERVES 4

700 g (1½ lb) whitebait
60 ml (4 tbsp) plain white flour
oil for deep-frying
HOT SAUCE
25 g (1 oz) ground hazelnuts
2-3 hot red chillies
1 small onion
3 garlic cloves
1 ripe tomato
15 ml (1 tbsp) mild paprika
salt and pepper
10 ml (2 tsp) balsamic or red wine vinegar
about 60 ml (4 tbsp) virgin olive oil
TO SERVE
chopped parsley, to garnish
paprika, for sprinkling
lime or lemon wedges

PREPARATION TIME
20 minutes
COOKING TIME
About 15 minutes
FREEZING
Not suitable

790 CALS PER SERVING

1. First make the sauce. Preheat the grill to medium. Spread the hazelnuts in the grill pan and toast until golden brown, shaking the pan occasionally to ensure that they brown evenly. Remove the stems from the chillies. Peel and quarter the onion; peel the garlic. Immerse the tomato in a bowl of boiling water for 15-30 seconds, then remove and peel away the skin.

2. Put all the sauce ingredients, except the olive oil, in a food processor or blender and process until smooth. Add a little of the olive oil if the mixture gets stuck around the blades. With the machine running, gradually add the olive oil in a thin stream through the feeder tube, to make a fairly thick sauce. Season with salt and pepper to taste.

3. Put the flour in a bowl and season generously with salt and pepper. Add the whitebait and toss to coat in the flour.

4. Heat the oil in a deep-fat fryer to 190°C (380°F). Test the temperature by dropping a cube of stale bread into the oil – the bread should sizzle immediately on contact with the oil, rise to the surface and become golden brown in about 30 seconds.

5. Deep-fry the fish in the hot oil in batches for about 3 minutes or until golden brown. Drain on crumpled kitchen paper and keep hot while cooking the remainder.

6. Serve the whitebait as soon as they are all cooked, garnished with chopped parsley and a sprinkling of paprika, and accompanied by lime wedges and the sauce.

VARIATION

If you're short of time, serve the whitebait with a spiced mayonnaise instead of the hot sauce. Flavour some homemade or good bought mayonnaise with grated lime rind, chopped chilli and chopped basil to taste.

TECHNIQUE

Toss the whitebait in the well-seasoned flour to coat evenly.

MUSHROOM PÂTÉ WITH MADEIRA

This is a rich mushroom pâté, flavoured with dried porcini and a variety of fresh mushrooms. You can use any combination of mushrooms, but try to include some flavourful wild ones or cultivated dark field mushrooms. Don't be tempted to use all button mushrooms as the end result will lack colour and flavour. Serve the pâté with hot olive bread, ciabatta, French bread or toast.

SERVES 6

15 g (½ oz) dried porcini
   mushrooms (see note)
150 ml (¼ pint) milk
1 small onion
1 garlic clove (optional)
25 g (1 oz) butter
coarse sea salt and pepper
350 g (12 oz) mushrooms
125 g (4 oz) ricotta cheese
15 ml (1 tbsp) Madeira
2.5 ml (½ tsp) balsamic
   vinegar or lemon juice
5 ml (1 tsp) mushroom
   ketchup
freshly grated nutmeg, to
   taste
15-30 ml (1-2 tbsp) chopped
   fresh parsley or coriander
   (optional)
TO GARNISH
chopped parsley or
   coriander

PREPARATION TIME
15 minutes, plus soaking
COOKING TIME
20-25 minutes
FREEZING
Not suitable

100 CALS PER SERVING

1. Rinse the porcini under cold running water to wash away the grit, then place in a bowl. Pour on the warm milk and leave to soak for 20 minutes. Drain the porcini and chop finely.

2. Peel and finely chop the onion and garlic, if using. Melt the butter in a saucepan, add the onion and garlic and fry gently for 5-10 minutes until softened and transparent. Season with salt and pepper.

3. Meanwhile, wipe the fresh mushrooms with a damp cloth to clean them. then chop finely.

4. Add the porcini and fresh mushrooms to the onion and garlic, increase the heat a little and cook, stirring occasionally, for about 15 minutes until the mushrooms are tender and reduced to a thick pulp. Leave to cool slightly.

5. Transfer the mushroom mixture to a food processor or bowl. Add the ricotta, Madeira, balsamic vinegar, mushroom ketchup and nutmeg and process very briefly or stir until evenly mixed; the pâté should retain a coarse texture. Stir in the chopped parsley or coriander if using. Adjust the seasoning.

6. Turn into a serving dish or individual ramekins and garnish with parsley or coriander. Serve with olive bread, ciabatta, French bread or toast.

NOTE: If dried porcini are unobtainable, use an extra 125 g (4 oz) flavourful fresh mushrooms.

TECHNIQUE

Rinse the porcini under cold running water to wash away the grit.

CHICKEN LIVER AND PISTACHIO PÂTÉ

This tasty pâté is blended with cream cheese rather than butter to give a lighter, less calorific result. If you are concerned about calories you could omit the butter seal altogether and instead decorate it simply with chopped herbs. As a starter which can be prepared well ahead and doesn't require last minute titivation, it is ideal if you are entertaining. If you haven't enough suitable individual dishes, set it in one large serving dish.

SERVES 8-10

2 rashers of streaky bacon,
  derinded
700 g (1½ lb) chicken livers
1-2 garlic cloves
about 225 g (8 oz) butter
large pinch of ground
  allspice
125 g (4 oz) flat
  mushrooms
1 medium onion, peeled
200 g (7 oz) low-fat soft
  cheese
30 ml (2 tbsp) double cream
40 g (1½ oz) shelled
  pistachio nuts
45 ml (3 tbsp) chopped
  mixed fresh parsley,
  chives and thyme
salt and pepper
TO GARNISH
parsley or other herb leaves
few shelled pistachio nuts

PREPARATION TIME
20 minutes, plus overnight
chilling
COOKING TIME
15 minutes
FREEZING
Suitable

435-350 CALS PER SERVING

1. Chop the bacon finely. Place in a heavy-based frying pan and heat gently until the fat starts to run, then increase the heat and cook until lightly browned.

2. Meanwhile, trim the chicken livers and remove any membranes and the white fibrous bits in the middle. Roughly chop the livers. Peel and chop the garlic.

3. Add 50 g (2 oz) of the butter to the pan and heat until just melted. Add the livers to the pan with the garlic and all-spice, and cook briskly over a high heat until the livers are sealed and browned on the outside but still a little pink (but not bloody) on the inside. Remove the bacon and livers from the pan with a slotted spoon and set aside.

4. Finely chop mushrooms and onion. Add to the pan and cook gently until the onion is softened. Remove from the heat.

5. Transfer the livers and bacon to a blender or food processor. Add the onion and mushrooms, along with any butter remaining in the pan. Add the soft cheese and cream and work until smooth. Turn into a mixing bowl.

6. Roughly chop the nuts and herbs, then fold into the pâté. Season with salt and

pepper to taste. Spoon the pâté into small individual dishes and level the tops.

7. Melt the remaining butter in a small saucepan over a very low heat. Slowly pour into a jug, leaving the milky sediment behind. Slowly pour the clarified butter onto the pâtés to cover them completely. (Depending on the size of your dishes you may need to melt a little more.) Immerse herbs and pistachios in the butter to garnish. Chill overnight to set. Serve with plenty of good bread or toast.

VARIATION

To make a milder pâté, increase the cream cheese to 400 g (14 oz).

TECHNIQUE

Slowly and carefully pour the melted butter into a measuring jug, leaving the milky sediment behind.

SMOKED FISH PÂTÉ WITH MELBA TOAST

A pretty, chunky, smoked fish mousse combining pale pink trout with flakes of white smoked cod. Try other combinations such as kipper with smoked haddock, or Scottish smokie (hot-smoked haddock) with cubes of smoked salmon for real luxury!

SERVES 4-6

125 g (4 oz) smoked cod
2 large hot-smoked pink
   trout (in skins), each
   about 200 g (7 oz)
150 ml (¼ pint) soured
   cream
150 ml (¼ pint) fromage
   frais
2.5 ml (½ tsp) hot paprika
lemon juice, to taste
salt and pepper
MELBA TOAST
3-4 slices day-old softgrain
   white bread
TO GARNISH
paprika, for sprinkling

PREPARATION TIME
20 minutes, plus chilling
COOKING TIME
5 minutes
FREEZING
Not suitable

365-245 CALS PER SERVING

1. Place the smoked cod, skin uppermost, in a pan and cover with water. Simmer for 5 minutes until the fish is opaque and flakes easily. Lift out the fish, remove the skin and flake roughly. Set aside in a bowl to cool.

2. Peel the skin from the trout and flake the flesh into a food processor or blender. Add the soured cream, fromage frais and paprika; process until smooth. Taste and add lemon juice, salt and pepper to taste.

3. Scrape the trout out into the bowl containing the cod and mix gently but thoroughly, taking care to avoid breaking up the flakes of cod. Spoon into a serving dish or individual dishes and smooth the tops. Chill in the refrigerator for at least 3 hours.

4. Meanwhile, make the Melba toast. Preheat the oven to 180°C (350°F) Mark 4. Toast the bread lightly on both sides. Quickly cut off the crusts and split each slice in two. Scrape off any doughy bits. Place on a baking sheet and bake in the oven for 10-15 minutes or until uniformly golden.

5. Serve the smoked fish pâté sprinkled with a little paprika and accompanied by the hot Melba toast.

NOTE: For convenience the Melba toast can be prepared well ahead, then cooled and stored in an airtight tin. Warm through in a moderate oven just before serving.

TECHNIQUE

Using two forks, divide the poached smoked cod into flakes.

FISH AND SHELLFISH

SALMON EN PAPILLOTE WITH LIME BUTTER SAUCE

Salmon steaks – scented with lime and ginger – are gently cooked in paper parcels, then served with a rich butter sauce flavoured with lime and dry sherry. The sauce can be made in advance and gently reheated in a bain-marie as the fish is cooking, making this recipe a perfect dinner party dish.

SERVES 4

75 g (3 oz) unsalted butter
2 limes
15 g (½ oz) fresh root
   ginger
4 salmon steaks, each about
   175 g (6 oz)
salt and pepper
4 spring onions, trimmed
pinch of sugar
45 ml (3 tbsp) dry sherry
   (preferably Manzanilla)
45 ml (3 tbsp) double cream

PREPARATION TIME
20 minutes
COOKING TIME
12-15 minutes
FREEZING
Not suitable

635 CALS PER SERVING

1. Preheat the oven to 200°C (400°F) Mark 6. Cut 4 baking parchment or greaseproof paper rectangles, measuring 30 x 20 cm (12 x 8 inches). Using 25 g (1 oz) of the butter, grease the paper.

2. Grate the rind from 1 lime and squeeze the juice. Peel the ginger, then cut into very fine slices or julienne strips.

3. Place a salmon steak on one half of each paper rectangle. Season with salt and pepper. Scatter the lime rind and ginger on top, then sprinkle with the lime juice. Fold the other half of the paper over the top, brushing the edges together. Make small overlapping folds along the edges to seal. Place on a baking sheet and set aside.

4. To make the sauce, chop the spring onions. Heat 15 g (½ oz) butter in a small pan, add the spring onions and cook until softened. Squeeze the juice from the remaining lime. Add to the onions with the sugar and sherry. Increase the heat and boil steadily until the liquid is reduced by half.

5. Place the fish papillotes in the oven and cook for 12-15 minutes; the parcels will puff up.

6. Add the cream to the sauce and allow to bubble for a few seconds. Gradually whisk in the remaining butter, a piece at a time, taking the pan off the heat occasionally to prevent the sauce from splitting. The sauce should be smooth and slightly thickened. Season with salt and pepper.

7. Serve the papillotes at the table, allowing each person to enjoy the fragrance as they open their own parcel. Serve the sauce separately.

NOTE: Manzanilla sherry has a dry, almost salty tang which complements the fish well. If unavailable, fino sherry could be used instead.

TECHNIQUE

Fold the paper to enclose the salmon steak, bringing the edges together, then seal.

GRILLED SALMON FILLETS WITH CAPERS

These salmon fillets are sprinkled with capers and cooked on a bed of lemon and dill-flavoured leeks. The pretty pink flesh of salmon will often appeal to those who are not so keen on fish, and the wide availability of farmed salmon – now at reasonable prices – enables this 'king of fish' to be served more often.

SERVES 6

4 leeks
salt and pepper
1 lemon
15 ml (1 tbsp) snipped fresh
    dill
6 salmon fillets, each about
    150 g (5 oz)
25 g (1 oz) capers, drained
    and rinsed
**ORANGE AND DILL
SAUCE**
1 orange
15 ml (1 tbsp) low-fat
    mayonnaise
30 ml (2 tbsp) low-fat bio
    yogurt
15 ml (1 tbsp) chopped fresh
    dill
15 ml (1 tbsp) chopped fresh
    parsley
TO GARNISH
orange slices
flat-leaf parsley sprigs

PREPARATION TIME
15 minutes
COOKING TIME
About 10 minutes
FREEZING
Not suitable

310 CALS PER SERVING

1. Trim leeks, wash thoroughly and slice thinly. Blanch in a pan of boiling salted water for 2 minutes; drain.

2. Finely grate the rind from the lemon and squeeze the juice. Mix 15 ml (1 tbsp) lemon juice, the lemon rind and dill with the leeks. Lay a thin layer over the base of a shallow flameproof dish, about 20 cm (8 inches) square.

3. Skin the salmon: place a sharp knife between the flesh and skin and, with a sawing action, cut across the fish pulling the skin away.

4. Preheat the grill to high. Place the salmon on top of the leeks. Divide the capers between the fillets, pressing down well. Sprinkle with salt and pepper and drizzle over 30 ml (2 tbsp) of the lemon juice. Grill for 5-8 minutes, until the fish is just firm to the touch. (The timing will depend on the thickness of the fillets.)

5. Meanwhile, prepare the orange and dill sauce. Grate the rind from the orange and squeeze the juice. Mix the mayonnaise and yogurt together, then stir in the orange rind, juice and herbs.

6. To serve, lift the salmon fillets and leeks with a fish slice onto warmed serving plates. Garnish with orange slices and parsley, and serve with the orange and dill sauce.

VARIATION

Replace the salmon fillets with cod steaks and serve on a bed of sautéed chopped red onion.

TECHNIQUE

Place a sharp knife between the flesh and skin of the salmon and cut across the fish with a sawing action to remove the skin.

TROUT WITH DILL AND HORSERADISH MAYONNAISE

Each pink-fleshed trout lies on a long leaf of Cos lettuce, making a simple, elegant dish – perfect for a supper party. The cooking is beautifully simple too, for the fish complete their cooking in the cooling poaching liquor. Serve with a potato salad, ideally in a hazelnut oil dressing and finished with a scattering of nuts.

SERVES 4

4 gutted trout, each about 200 g (7 oz)

100 ml (3½ fl oz) white wine vinegar

10 ml (2 tsp) black peppercorns

10 ml (2 tsp) dill seeds (optional)

3 bay leaves

5 ml (1 tsp) salt

MAYONNAISE

1 Bramley apple, about 150 g (5 oz)

150 ml (¼ pint) good-quality mayonnaise

45 ml (3 tbsp) chopped fresh dill leaves

10 ml (2 tsp) grated horseradish or horseradish sauce

TO SERVE

8 long Cos lettuce leaves

dill sprigs, bay leaves and lime wedges, to garnish

PREPARATION TIME
15 minutes
COOKING TIME
35-40 minutes, including cooling
FREEZING
Not suitable

560 CALS PER SERVING

1. Wash the fish inside and out under cold running water. Fill a large roasting tin with boiling water. Add the wine vinegar, peppercorns, dill seeds if using, bay leaves and salt. Immerse the fish in the liquid and bring back to the boil. As soon as it reaches the boil, turn off the heat and leave the fish undisturbed in the liquid for at least 20 minutes.

2. For the mayonnaise, peel, quarter, core and slice the apple. Place in a small pan with 45 ml (3 tbsp) water. Cover and cook until the apple is softened to a purée. Beat until smooth and allow to cool, then mix with the mayonnaise, chopped dill and horseradish.

3. Lift the trout from the poaching liquor, remove the skin, and their heads if preferred. Lay each fish in a long lettuce leaf on a serving plate and spoon some of the dill and apple mayonnaise alongside. Garnish with dill sprigs, bay leaves and lime wedges.

NOTE: Trout are often sold ready-gutted, but if they are whole allow a little extra weight and ask the fishmonger to gut them for you.

VARIATION

Use the same poaching method for a whole salmon, bringing to the boil then leaving to cool in the liquor, but put the salmon into *cold* seasoned water and raise the liquid to boiling point slowly.

TECHNIQUE

Carefully remove the skin from each trout to reveal the pink flesh.

SOLE FLORENTINE

Rolled sole fillets are baked on layers of fresh tomatoes, garlic and fresh spinach, beneath a creamy cheese sauce. This is another perfect supper dish, which can be prepared in advance. Ring the changes with other varieties of fish – cod, haddock or any other white fish would do. Serve with sauté potatoes – the other vegetables are already there!

SERVES 4

6 ripe tomatoes
25 g (1 oz) butter
1 garlic clove, crushed
1 kg (2¼ lb) fresh spinach
salt and pepper
pinch of freshly grated
    nutmeg
8 single sole fillets
CHEESE SAUCE
20 g (¾ oz) butter
20 g (¾ oz) plain flour
300 ml (½ pint) milk
50 g (2 oz) Gruyère cheese,
    grated
TOPPING
15 ml (1 tbsp) dried bread-
    crumbs
15 ml (1 tbsp) freshly grated
    Parmesan cheese

PREPARATION TIME
30 minutes
COOKING TIME
10-15 minutes
FREEZING
Not suitable

385 CALS PER SERVING

1. First make the cheese sauce. Melt the butter in a saucepan and stir in the flour. Cook, stirring, for 1 minute. Remove from the heat and gradually stir in the milk. Return to the heat and bring to the boil, stirring. Simmer for 2 minutes. Remove from the heat, add the cheese and mix until smooth. Season with salt and pepper. Cover the surface with a buttered piece of greaseproof paper to prevent a skin forming.

2. Preheat the oven to 180°C (350°F) Mark 4. Plunge the tomatoes into a bowl of boiling water for 30 seconds, refresh in cold water, then peel away the skins. Thickly slice the tomatoes. Melt 15 g (½ oz) butter in a frying pan and add the garlic. Add the tomatoes and fry briefly; don't let them become too soft. Transfer to a buttered ovenproof dish.

3. Clean the spinach thoroughly and remove any tough stalks. Place in a large saucepan with just the water clinging to the leaves after washing. Cover and cook for 5 minutes, shaking the pan. (You may need to cook it in two batches.) Drain the spinach well, squeezing out as much moisture as possible. Chop roughly, then return to the pan with the remaining 15 g (½ oz) butter. Season with salt, pepper and nutmeg. Cook, stirring, for 1 minute. Spread the spinach over the tomatoes.

4. Lay the sole fillets on a board, skinned-side up, and season with salt and pepper. Roll up from the tail end, then place on top of the spinach.

5. Reheat the cheese sauce and pour evenly over the fish and spinach. Sprinkle with the breadcrumbs and Parmesan and bake for 10-15 minutes until hot and bubbling. Meanwhile, preheat the grill. When the fish is cooked, place the dish under the grill to brown the topping.

NOTE: Frozen spinach can be used in place of fresh, although the colour and texture won't be quite as good.

TECHNIQUE

Drain the spinach in a sieve, pressing out as much liquid as possible with the back of a wooden spoon.

FRIED SKATE WINGS WITH OLIVE AND HERB SAUCE

Skate wings have a wonderful texture and are surprisingly easy to eat, as the flesh just falls away from the bones. This is a relatively quick and easy dish, although you may need two frying pans to cook the fish. Serve with boiled new potatoes and lightly cooked fresh spinach.

SERVES 4

4 skate wings, each
   300-350 g (10-12 oz)
salt and pepper
60 ml (4 tbsp) plain flour
50 g (2 oz) butter
30 ml (2 tbsp) oil
SAUCE
2 garlic cloves
8 anchovy fillets
30 ml (2 tbsp) capers,
   drained and rinsed
10 ml (2 tsp) black olive
   paste
15 ml (1 tbsp) sun-dried
   tomato paste
60 ml (4 tbsp) chopped
   fresh parsley
15 ml (1 tbsp) chopped
   fresh chives
60 ml (4 tbsp) extra-virgin
   olive oil
juice of 1 lemon
TO GARNISH
few chives

PREPARATION TIME
10 minutes
COOKING TIME
12 minutes
FREEZING
Not suitable

600 CALS PER SERVING

1. First make the sauce. Crush the garlic cloves and place in a bowl. Drain the anchovy fillets on kitchen paper, chop finely and add to the garlic. Add the capers, olive paste, sun-dried tomato paste, parsley, chives, olive oil and lemon juice. Mix thoroughly.

2. If the skate wings are very large, cut them into more manageable pieces. Season with salt and pepper and dust with flour.

3. Heat the butter and oil in a very large frying pan, or two smaller ones. When the butter begins to foam, add the skate wings and fry gently for about 5 minutes on each side or until just cooked. To test, prise a little of the flesh away from the bone with the tip of a knife: if it comes away easily the fish is cooked.

4. Pour the sauce around the fish and heat through for 1-2 minutes. Serve immediately, garnished with chives.

NOTE: Both olive and sun-dried tomato pastes are available from larger supermarkets and good delicatessens. If unavailable, or if you prefer a coarse textured sauce, use chopped pitted olives and sun-dried tomatoes instead.

TECHNIQUE

To check if the fish is cooked, prise a little of the flesh away from the bone with the tip of a knife. If it comes away easily the skate is cooked.

COD CUTLETS PROVENÇALE

Robust flavours and bright colour contrasts characterise this southern treatment of fish from northern waters. Scarlet tomatoes, shiny black olives and vivid green basil leaves offset the white fish perfectly, and a splash of aniseed liqueur gives the dish resonant depth.

SERVES 4

4 cod cutlets, each about
   150 g (5 oz)
1 Spanish onion
75 ml (5 tbsp) olive oil
5 ml (1 tsp) dried oregano
3 garlic cloves
400 g (14 oz) can peeled
   plum tomatoes
15 ml (1 tbsp) tomato purée
10 ml (2 tsp) pastis, ouzo or
   other aniseed liqueur
salt and pepper
12 small black olives
1-2 fresh basil sprigs
extra basil sprigs, to garnish

PREPARATION TIME
10 minutes
COOKING TIME
About 25 minutes
FREEZING
Not suitable

325 CALS PER SERVING

1. Rinse the fish cutlets and pat dry with kitchen paper; set aside.

2. Peel and chop the onion very finely. Heat the olive oil in a large shallow frying pan. Add the onion with the oregano and cook over a very low heat for 10 minutes, stirring frequently. Meanwhile, peel and finely chop or crush the garlic; add to the pan and cook for a further 2-3 minutes until the onion is translucent and beginning to turn pale golden.

3. Add the tomatoes to the pan, mashing with a fork to break them down. Add the tomato purée, bring to the boil and stir in the liqueur. Season with salt and pepper to taste.

4. Bury the fish cutlets in the tomato sauce and scatter the olives between them. Cover and cook gently for 6 minutes, then turn the fish cutlets over and continue cooking for a further 4-5 minutes, until you can just pull the flesh from the bone with the tip of a knife.

5. Check the seasoning of the sauce. Tear the basil leaves over the dish and serve immediately, garnished with extra basil sprigs.

NOTE: Ricard is the best-known brand of pastis. Pernod is similarly flavoured with anise and has the same effect in cooking.

VARIATIONS

Use other white fish steaks – such as swordfish or haddock. If you have no aniseed-flavoured liqueur, fry a teaspoonful of fennel seeds with the onion.

TECHNIQUE

Add the fish cutlets to the pan, burying them in the sauce.

GRILLED PLAICE WITH RED PEPPER SALSA

Plaice is a good value fish to use, but often forgotten in place of more exotic species. Served like this – on a split pea purée with a red pepper salsa – it makes an unusual and tasty dish.

SERVES 4

125 g (4 oz) split yellow peas
1 onion
2 garlic cloves, crushed
1 bay leaf
6 fresh thyme sprigs
salt and pepper
30 ml (2 tbsp) plain flour
45 ml (3 tbsp) finely
   chopped fresh parsley
4 plaice fillets
15-30 ml (1-2 tbsp) olive oil
SALSA
1 red pepper
1 plum tomato
½ red onion
2.5 ml (½ tsp) mustard
   seeds
pinch of sugar
TO GARNISH
watercress sprigs

PREPARATION TIME
10 minutes
COOKING TIME
40-45 minutes
FREEZING
Not suitable

390 CALS PER SERVING

1. Rinse the split yellow peas in a sieve under running cold water, then place in a saucepan.

2. Peel and finely chop the onion and add to the split peas with the garlic, herbs and seasoning. Pour on 450 ml (¾ pint) cold water, bring to the boil, then simmer for 35-40 minutes, until soft and mushy. Drain, and remove the herb sprigs. Check the seasoning and beat to form a rough-textured purée.

3. Meanwhile, prepare the salsa. Place the pepper under a preheated hot grill and cook, turning, until blackened. Cover with a damp tea-towel and leave until cool enough to handle, then remove the skin. Cut the pepper in half and remove the core and seeds. Finely dice the pepper and place in a small bowl. Finely dice the tomato. Peel and finely chop the onion. Add the tomato and onion to the red pepper with the mustard seeds and sugar. Stir well and set aside.

4. Preheat the grill to medium. Season the flour with salt and pepper and mix in the parsley. Dip the flesh side of each plaice fillet in the mixture to coat evenly, then lay skin-side down on the grill rack. Drizzle each fillet with about 1.25 ml (¼ tsp) of the olive oil. Grill for about 5 minutes, depending on the thickness

of the fillets, until the flesh turns white and is just firm to the touch.

5. To serve, place a spoonful of the split pea mixture on each warmed serving plate. Lay a fish fillet on top and spoon over 2-3 teaspoons of the salsa. Garnish with watercress.

VARIATION

Replace the plaice fillets with lemon sole fillets. Replace the grilled pepper with tomato.

TECHNIQUE

Dip the flesh side of each plaice fillet in the flour mixture to coat evenly.

ROASTED MONKFISH TAILS WITH ROCKET PESTO ON A BED OF SHALLOTS

A wonderfully tender and flavoursome fish dish. Roasting the fish at a high temperature ensures it cooks quickly and is succulent. Rocket gives the pesto a good flavour as well as an intense green colour.

SERVES 4

225 g (8 oz) shallots
4 garlic cloves (unpeeled)
30 ml (2 tbsp) cider vinegar
30 ml (2 tbsp) olive oil
900 g (2 lb) monkfish tails
  (on the bone)
salt and pepper
4 fresh rosemary sprigs
4 fresh thyme sprigs
4 fresh oregano sprigs
ROCKET PESTO
50 g (2 oz) rocket leaves
15 g ($\frac{1}{2}$ oz) fresh Parmesan
  cheese
15 ml (1 tbsp) olive oil
30 ml (2 tbsp) apple juice

PREPARATION TIME
30 minutes
COOKING TIME
35-45 minutes
FREEZING
Not suitable

320 CALS PER SERVING

1. Preheat the oven to 220°C (425°F) Mark 7. Peel the shallots and cut in half. Place in a roasting pan with the garlic, sprinkle with the cider vinegar and oil and cook for 15-20 minutes.

2. Meanwhile, make the pesto. Wash the rocket, removing any bruised leaves. Place in a blender or food processor. Grate the Parmesan cheese and add to the blender with the oil. With the machine running, pour the apple juice through the feeder tube in a steady stream. Blend until a smooth paste is formed.

3. Remove any skin and membrane from the monkfish: cut around the membrane, pull back and tear off using your fingers.

4. Cut along one side of the centre bone, as close to the bone as possible, and remove the fillet. Repeat on the other side.

5. Lay one fillet, cut side up, on a board and spread with the pesto. Place the other fillet on top, cut side down, to sandwich the pesto. Tie the two pieces together at regular intervals with string.

6. Remove the roasting pan from the oven, push the shallots and garlic to the sides, and lay the monkfish parcel in the centre of the pan. Sprinkle with salt and pepper and add the herb sprigs. Cook for 20-25 minutes, until the monkfish turns opaque.

7. To serve, remove the string and lift the fish onto a serving platter, discarding any milky residue. Place the shallots and garlic around the fish. Serve with boiled new potatoes or simmered wild rice and steamed mangetouts.

VARIATION

Use a tail end of salmon instead of monkfish. For speed, use ready-made pesto.

TECHNIQUE

To fillet the fish, cut along both sides of the central bone, placing the knife as close as possible to the bone.

BAKED RED MULLET WITH ROSEMARY AND LEMON

Rosy-skinned and white-fleshed, the handsome red mullet is a favourite Mediterranean fish. In Greece it is typically seasoned with rosemary, lemon and a drizzle of olive oil, then baked in a hot oven to crisp perfection and served with skordalia – a pungent garlicky sauce. Make the sauce first to allow time for the flavours to develop.

SERVES 4

8 small or 4 large red mullet
8 fresh rosemary sprigs, halved
1 lemon, thinly sliced
120 ml (8 tbsp) dry white wine
60 ml (4 tbsp) olive oil
salt and pepper
SKORDALIA
3 garlic cloves
40 g (1½ oz) crustless white bread
125 g (4 oz) ground almonds
coarse sea salt
100 ml (3½ fl oz) light olive oil, or olive oil and sunflower oil mixed
juice of ½ lemon
TO GARNISH
lemon wedges

PREPARATION TIME
15 minutes
COOKING TIME
20 minutes
FREEZING
Not suitable

680 CALS PER SERVING

1. First make the skordalia. Crush the garlic cloves and place in a blender or food processor. Moisten the bread with a little cold water and squeeze out the excess by hand to give a sticky paste. Add to the food processor with the ground almonds and a little sea salt. Process briefly, then with the motor running, slowly drizzle in the oil, as for making mayonnaise, to give a smooth sauce. Add the lemon juice and check the seasoning. Set aside.

2. Preheat the oven to 220°C (425°F) Mark 7. With a sharp knife make slashes in the sides of each fish. Tuck a rosemary sprig and a slice of lemon into the cavity of each fish and season with salt and pepper.

3. Arrange the fish, head to tail, in a large baking dish or roasting tin. Tuck the rest of the lemon slices in between the fish. Scatter over the remaining rosemary sprigs. Drizzle over the white wine and olive oil. Bake for about 20 minutes until the fish flakes easily, basting halfway through cooking.

4. Serve the red mullet with the garlic sauce, accompanied by a crisp salad and some good bread.

VARIATION

Flavour the fish with oregano or thyme sprigs instead of rosemary.

TECHNIQUE

Using a sharp knife, make three diagonal slashes in the side of each fish.

BRAISED COD BOULANGÈRE

Thick cod fillets are pan-fried briefly to give them a golden hue, then baked on a bed of sliced potatoes and onions, flavoured with herbs and moistened with stock. This is the perfect supper dish – easy to prepare and cook, and can be brought to the table in the dish it's cooked in. Serve with a green vegetable; fresh peas, when in season, are the perfect accompaniment.

SERVES 4

700 g (1½ lb) potatoes
1 onion
75 g (3 oz) butter
salt and pepper
few fresh thyme sprigs
300 ml (½ pint) chicken
    stock
4 thick cod fillets, each
    about 150 g (5 oz)
snipped chives, to garnish

PREPARATION TIME
10 minutes
COOKING TIME
1 hour
FREEZING
Not suitable

395 CALS PER SERVING

1. Preheat the oven to 190°C (375°F) Mark 5. Peel the potatoes and onion, then slice both thinly and as evenly as possible.

2. Use 25 g (1 oz) of the butter to grease an ovenproof dish. Layer the potatoes and onion alternately in the dish, sprinkling each layer with salt, pepper and thyme. Dot with half of the remaining butter. Pour in the stock and bake in the oven for 40-50 minutes.

3. Melt the remaining butter in a non-stick frying pan, add the cod fillets and fry briefly until golden on both sides.

4. Place the fish on top of the potatoes. Cover the dish and return to the oven for a further 10-15 minutes. The fish should be firm, but tender; check by prising the flesh away from the bone – if it comes away easily, the fish is ready.

5. Sprinkle the dish with the chives and serve immediately.

VARIATION

Use fillets of haddock, sole or whiting instead of cod.

TECHNIQUE

Layer the potatoes and onions in a greased ovenproof dish, sprinkling each layer with salt, pepper and thyme.

COD IN CRISP BATTER WITH LEMON AND PARSLEY SAUCE

There is nothing quite like crispy battered fresh white fish, served with a generous portion of chips. The homemade version is invariably far better than anything you buy from the local fish and chip shop. A creamy, yet tangy lemon and parsley sauce is the ideal accompaniment.

SERVES 4

700 g (1 ½ lb) cod or
   haddock fillet
30 ml (2 tbsp) plain flour
salt and pepper
oil for deep-frying
BATTER
200 g (7 oz) self-raising flour
2.5 ml (½ tsp) baking
   powder
2.5 ml (½ tsp) salt
SAUCE
25 g (1 oz) butter
15 ml (1 tbsp) plain flour
250 ml (8 fl oz) milk
60 ml (4 tbsp) chopped fresh
   parsley
finely grated rind of 1 lemon
juice of ½ lemon
45 ml (3 tbsp) double cream
TO GARNISH
lemon wedges

PREPARATION TIME
15 minutes, plus standing
COOKING TIME
About 15 minutes
FREEZING
Not suitable

655 CALS PER SERVING

1. First make the batter. Sift the flour, baking powder and salt into a bowl. Gradually whisk in 300 ml (½ pint) water to make a smooth batter. Leave to stand for 30 minutes to 1 hour.

2. Skin the fish if necessary and remove any small bones. Cut the fillets into slightly smaller pieces. Season the flour with salt and pepper and use to coat the fish pieces evenly.

3. To make the sauce, melt the butter in a small saucepan. Add the flour and cook, stirring, for 1 minute. Remove from the heat and gradually blend in the milk. Return to the heat and cook gently, stirring, until thickened. Stir in the parsley, lemon rind and juice, cream and seasoning.

4. Half fill a large deep saucepan or deep-fat fryer with oil and heat to 190°C (375°F). Cook the fish pieces in three batches. Coat them in the batter, lower into the oil and deep-fry for about 5 minutes until golden and crisp.

5. Lift the fish out with a slotted spoon and drain on kitchen paper. Keep warm while frying the remainder.

6. Meanwhile, gently reheat the sauce. Place the fish on warmed serving plates and garnish with lemon wedges. Serve with the lemon and parsley sauce, and vegetables of your choice.

NOTE: It's worth making chips to serve with the fish while you're using the deep fryer. Peel and cut the potatoes into chips. Put into the frying basket and lower into the oil. Deep-fry at 200°C (400°F) for 6-7 minutes until starting to colour. Lift the basket and drain the chips, then deep-fry for a further 3 minutes until golden and crisp. Drain, season and keep warm, while frying the fish.

TECHNIQUE

Carefully lower the pieces of battered fish into the oil and fry until golden.

PRAWNS FRIED WITH GREENS

This is a good way to use those interesting greens sold in Chinese food stores. Pak choi is the one with the long, ribbed white stalks and dark green leaves which grow from a central root, rather like a head of celery. Baby pak choi – the mini variety – is good in this dish as it can be left whole for maximum visual impact. Chinese flowering cabbage has thin white stems, bright green leaves and tiny yellow flowers. Some supermarkets now stock Dutch-grown varieties of these Chinese vegetables.

SERVES 4-6

2 garlic cloves
1 lemon grass stalk
2 kaffir lime leaves
2 red shallots, or 1 small red onion
1-2 hot red chillies
4 cm (1½ inch) piece fresh root ginger
15 ml (1 tbsp) coriander seeds
75 g (3 oz) green beans
175 g (6 oz) mangetouts
450 g (1 lb) large raw prawns (see note)
1 small head of pak choi or Chinese flowering cabbage, or 2-3 baby pak choi (or a mixture)
30 ml (2 tbsp) vegetable oil
juice of 1 lime, or to taste
30 ml (2 tbsp) nam pla (Thai fish sauce)
lime halves, to garnish

PREPARATION TIME
20 minutes
COOKING TIME
About 10 minutes
FREEZING
Not suitable

195-130 CALS PER SERVING

1. Peel the garlic and slice thinly. Cut the lemon grass in half and bruise with a rolling pin. Tear the kaffir lime leaves into small pieces. Peel and thinly slice the shallots or onion. Slice the chillies, discarding the seeds if a milder flavour is preferred. Peel the ginger and cut into long, thin shreds. Crush the coriander seeds. Trim the beans and mangetouts.

2. Peel the prawns, leaving the tail end attached. Using a small sharp knife, make a shallow slit along the outer curve from the tail to the head end and remove the dark intestinal vein. Rinse under cold running water, drain and pat dry with kitchen paper.

3. Trim the pak choi or Chinese flowering cabbage, removing any discoloured leaves or damaged stems. Leave baby pak choi whole; tear other leaves into manageable pieces.

4. Heat the oil in a wok or large frying pan. Add the garlic, lemon grass, lime leaves, shallots, chillies, ginger and coriander seeds, and stir-fry for 2 minutes. Add the green beans and cook for 2 minutes. Add the prawns, mangetouts and pak choi or Chinese flowering cabbage and stir-fry for 2-3 minutes, until

the vegetables are cooked but still crisp and the prawns are pink and opaque.

5. Add the nam pla and lime juice, and heat through for 1 minute. Serve immediately, while the vegetables are crisp.

NOTE: If raw prawns are unobtainable, use cooked ones instead. Add with the lime juice; heat through for 1 minute only.

VARIATION

Replace the prawns with skinned chicken breast fillets, cut into wafer-thin slices. Stir-fry with the beans at stage 4.

TECHNIQUE

Using a small sharp knife, make a shallow slit along the outer curve of each prawn from tail to head end and remove the dark intestinal vein.

PAELLA

Paella, a traditional Spanish dish, is a typical example of the good balance of food found in the Mediterranean diet. A colourful all-in-one dish, it is excellent for an informal dinner party: easy to serve; a good combination of taste and texture; and nutritious, providing carbohydrate, protein and fibre.

SERVES 6

2 skinless chicken breast
   fillets
15-30 ml (1-2 tbsp) olive oil
225 g (8 oz) cleaned squid
125 g (4 oz) scallops
225 g (8 oz) mussels in shells
1 large onion
225 g (8 oz) plum tomatoes
3 garlic cloves, crushed
5 ml (1 tsp) paprika
salt and pepper
600 ml (1 pint) chicken
   stock
15 ml (1 tbsp) tomato purée
350 g (12 oz) risotto rice
   (eg Arborio)
150 ml (¼ pint) dry white
   wine
pinch of saffron threads
2 red peppers
125 g (4 oz) shelled peas
30 ml (2 tbsp) chopped fresh
   parsley

PREPARATION TIME
30 minutes
COOKING TIME
40 minutes
FREEZING
Not suitable

405 CALS PER SERVING

1. Cut each chicken breast crosswise into 4 pieces. Heat 15 ml (1 tbsp) of the oil in a paella pan, large non-stick frying pan or flameproof casserole. Toss the chicken pieces quickly in the oil to brown. Set aside.

2. Pull the ink sac from the squid and discard. Cut off the tentacles and slice the squid into thin rings. Slice each scallop into 2 or 3 rounds, depending on their thickness. Set both aside.

3. Wash the mussels thoroughly in plenty of cold water, scrubbing well, and remove the beards. Discard any which do not close when tapped firmly. Place in a large pan with about 90 ml (6 tbsp) water. Bring to the boil, then cover tightly and cook for 3-4 minutes until the shells have opened; discard any that do not open. Set aside.

4. Peel and finely chop the onion. Immerse the tomatoes in a bowl of boiling water for 1 minute. Remove from the water and pull away the skins. Chop the flesh into 1 cm (½ inch) pieces.

5. Heat the remaining oil in the same pan. Add the onion, tomatoes, garlic, paprika, salt and pepper. Stir well and cook gently for 7-10 minutes, until softened.

6. In another pan, heat the chicken stock to just below boiling point, then stir in the tomato purée.

7. Add the rice to the tomato mixture and cook, stirring, for 1 minute. Pour in 300 ml (½ pint) of the hot stock and the wine. Cook, stirring, for about 7 minutes, until the liquid has been absorbed.

8. Meanwhile, soak the saffron threads in the remaining stock. Add to the rice with the squid, scallops and chicken. Cover and simmer gently for 15 minutes.

9. Meanwhile, preheat the grill and grill the red peppers, turning, until blackened. Cover with a damp tea-towel, leave until cool enough to handle, then remove the skins. Cut the peppers in half, remove the core and seeds, then cut into thin strips.

10. Stir the peppers into the paella with the mussels, peas and parsley. Cook for a further 5 minutes. Check the seasoning and serve immediately, with a salad.

TECHNIQUE

Cut off the tentacles and slice the squid into thin rings.

PAN-FRIED HERRING ROES WITH POTATO PANCAKES

For this quick supper dish all the components can be cooked in the same pan, one after another. Firstly, the pancakes are fried until crisp and golden, then apple slices are sautéed until soft and melting, and finally the herring roes are cooked in butter and lightly seasoned with cayenne pepper. The combination of tastes and textures is quite delicious!

SERVES 4

POTATO PANCAKES

450 g (1 lb) potatoes
½ onion
2 eggs, beaten
30 ml (2 tbsp) plain flour
5 ml (1 tsp) salt
pepper
oil for frying
PAN-FRY
2 eating apples (preferably
  red-skinned)
75 g (3 oz) butter
575 g (1¼ lb) fresh herring
  roes
1.25 ml (¼ tsp) cayenne
  pepper
30 ml (2 tbsp) chopped
  fresh parsley

PREPARATION TIME
10 minutes
COOKING TIME
20 minutes
FREEZING
Not suitable

525 CALS PER SERVING

1. To make the potato pancakes, grate the potatoes fairly coarsely, then squeeze out as much moisture as possible (see technique).

2. Peel and finely chop the onion. Place the grated potatoes in a bowl and add the onion, eggs, flour and salt. Season with pepper and mix well.

3. Heat enough oil in a frying pan (preferably a non-stick one) to cover the base with a thin layer. Put large spoonfuls of the potato mixture into the pan, flattening them down as you do so; they should be roughly 7.5 cm (3 inches) in diameter. Fry for about 3 minutes on each side until golden and crisp. Repeat to make 8 pancakes in total. Remove from the pan and drain on kitchen paper; keep hot.

4. Wipe the frying pan out with kitchen paper. Core the apples and cut into thickish slices. Melt 25 g (1 oz) butter in the pan and when foaming, add the apple slices. Sauté until softened, but still retaining their shape. Remove from the pan and keep warm.

5. Melt the remaining butter in the pan. When it is beginning to turn brown, add the herring roes and sauté for about 5 minutes until lightly golden. Sprinkle with the cayenne and a little salt and pepper.

6. Put two potato pancakes on each warmed serving plate and divide the fried herring roes between the plates. Spoon the pan juices over the roes. Garnish with the apple slices and a sprinkling of chopped parsley.

VARIATION

Cod's roe can be used in place of the herring roe. However, it must be gently poached first, left to cool, then sliced and fried as directed.

TECHNIQUE

To extract as much moisture as possible from the grated potatoes, place them on a clean piece of muslin, bring the corners together and squeeze tightly.

SAFFRON SEAFOOD RISOTTO

A wonderful seafood and wine risotto, bright yellow and fragrant with saffron. The risotto takes a little time to make, but emerges deliciously creamy and packed with all manner of delights from the sea.

SERVES 6

2 sachets of saffron threads
350 g (12 oz) raw prawns in
   shell
1.4 litres (2½ pints) fish
   stock
300 ml (½ pint) dry white
   wine
6 baby squid, cleaned
6 fresh scallops, shelled
600 ml (1 pint) fresh
   mussels in shells
300 ml (½ pint) fresh venus
   clams in shells
1 onion
75 g (3 oz) butter
500 g (1 lb 2 oz) packet
   risotto rice
45 ml (3 tbsp) chopped fresh
   parsley

PREPARATION TIME
20 minutes
COOKING TIME
30 minutes
FREEZING
Not suitable

690 CALS PER SERVING

1. Place the saffron threads in a small bowl, cover with a little boiling water and leave to infuse.

2. Twist the heads off the prawns and put them in a saucepan with the stock and wine. Bring to the boil, cover and simmer for 10 minutes. Set aside the prawns.

3. Meanwhile, cut the squid pouches into rings and cut the tentacles from the heads, discarding the heads. Remove the hard white muscle from one side of each scallop, then separate the white meat from the orange roe. Scrub the mussels well and pull off any beards; discard any that do not close when sharply tapped. Scrub the clams, discarding any open ones.

4. Strain the stock into a clean pan and bring to simmering point. Add the prawns and cook for 2 minutes. Add the squid, white scallop meat and roe; cook for a further 2 minutes. Remove all these shellfish with a slotted spoon and set aside. Add the mussels and clams to the stock and bring to the boil. Cover with a tight-fitting lid and cook for 5 minutes or until the shellfish have opened. Remove with a slotted spoon and set aside. Discard any with unopened shells.

5. Meanwhile, peel and chop the onion. Melt the butter in a large saucepan, add the onion and cook gently for about 5 minutes until soft but not coloured.

Add the rice and stir to coat with the butter. Add the saffron and soaking water, plus a ladleful of the stock. Simmer, stirring until absorbed. Continue adding the stock, a ladleful at a time until only 2 ladlefuls remain, and the rice is tender but still has some bite to it. This should take about 20 minutes. Season generously with salt and pepper to taste.

6. Stir in the remaining stock with the seafood, cover and cook gently for 5 minutes or until piping hot. Transfer to a large warmed bowl and sprinkle with the parsley. Serve immediately.

VARIATION

Use ready-prepared frozen mixed seafood. Allow to thaw thoroughly, then add at stage 6, making sure the seafood is thoroughly heated through.

TECHNIQUE

Remove the tough white muscle from one side of each scallop, then separate the orange roe from the white meat.

MEAT

GRILLED STEAKS WITH SHALLOTS AND WINE

An old-fashioned French classic for hurried cooks in search of a treat. Croûtes of French bread are used to mop up the delicious juices from the grill pan and served on the side. A green salad and a bottle of good red wine from Bordeaux are the only other accompaniments you'll need.

SERVES 4

225 g (8 oz) shallots
50 g (2 oz) chilled butter
350 ml (12 fl oz) red
   Bordeaux wine
4 sirloin steaks, each about
   175-200 g (6-7 oz)
30 ml (2 tbsp) vegetable oil
8 slices French bread
10-15 ml (2-3 tsp) Dijon
   mustard
30 ml (2 tbsp) chopped fresh
   parsley
parsley sprigs, to garnish

PREPARATION TIME
15 minutes while grill preheats
COOKING TIME
4-12 minutes
FREEZING
Not suitable

555 CALS PER SERVING

1. Preheat the grill. Peel and chop the shallots. Melt 15 g (½ oz) of the butter in a saucepan. Add the shallots and sauté for a few minutes until slightly softened. Add the wine and bring to the boil. Simmer, uncovered, until the wine is reduced by half and the shallots are soft.

2. Smear the steaks on both sides with the oil and arrange on the grill rack. Cook, as close to the heat as possible, turning the steaks every 2 minutes. Allow 4 minutes (one turn) for very rare steaks; 8 minutes (three turns) for medium. For well-done steaks allow 12 minutes, increasing the time between turns to 3 minutes. Season the steaks with salt and pepper as you make the final turn.

3. Meanwhile, cut the remaining butter into 6 cubes and beat one at a time into the shallot sauce, making sure each one is totally absorbed before adding the next.

4. Transfer the steaks to warmed serving plates and keep warm. Press the bread slices onto the grill pan to soak up the juices, then spread each lightly with Dijon mustard. Put 2 slices beside each steak. Pour the sauce over the steaks, sprinkle with chopped parsley and serve garnished with sprigs of parsley.

NOTE: The technique of beating cold diced butter into a hot wine-based sauce is called 'mounting'. It thickens the sauce slightly and gives a glossy finish.

VARIATIONS

Use rump rather than sirloin steaks. Use a hot griddle pan to cook the steaks, rather than grill them.

TECHNIQUE

After cooking the steaks, rub the slices of French bread around the grill pan to gather up the pan juices.

ORIENTAL BEEF STIR-FRY

Stir-frying is a favourite Chinese cooking method. Here tender strips of beef are stir-fried in an oriental sauce of black and yellow bean sauce, which combines well with the rich earthy flavour of beef. Using lots of vegetables in your cooking increases the amount of fibre, vitamins and minerals in your diet.

SERVES 4-6

350 g (12 oz) fillet steak

2 bunches of spring onions

2 orange peppers

1 red chilli

225 g (8 oz) broccoli

175 g (6 oz) spinach (or pak choi or choi sam)

15 ml (1 tbsp) chilli or stir-fry oil

MARINADE

30 ml (2 tbsp) sherry vinegar

30 ml (2 tbsp) black bean sauce

30 ml (2 tbsp) yellow bean sauce

2.5 cm (1 inch) piece fresh root ginger

15 ml (1 tbsp) dark soy sauce

PREPARATION TIME
20 minutes, plus marinating beef
COOKING TIME
10-15 minutes
FREEZING
Not suitable

200-135 CALS PER SERVING

1. First, prepare the marinade. Mix the sherry vinegar with the black and yellow bean sauces. Peel and crush the ginger and add to the mixture with the soy sauce.

2. Slice the fillet steak into thin strips, about 5 cm (2 inches) long and 1 cm (½ inch) wide. Stir into the marinade. Cover and leave to marinate in a cool place for at least 30 minutes or up to 12 hours in the refrigerator.

3. Trim the spring onions and cut into diagonal strips about 5 cm (2 inches) long. Cut the peppers and chilli in half, remove and discard the seeds. Slice the peppers into thin strips; cut the chilli into very fine strips. Cut the broccoli into small even florets. Shred the spinach.

4. Drain the meat from the marinade, using a draining spoon. Heat the oil in a large non-stick frying pan or wok, add the meat and cook for 3-4 minutes, stirring. Stir in the vegetables and cook for 3-4 minutes. Stir in the marinade and heat through for 3-4 minutes. Serve immediately, with noodles.

NOTE: Stir-fried food is cooked in minutes in very little oil, so the natural flavours and textures are retained. Swirling the hot oil over the surface of the pan just before adding the food produces an even heat.

TECHNIQUE

Marinate the strips of fillet steak in the sherry vinegar, bean sauce, ginger and soy sauce mixture before stir-frying.

SPICED BEEF AND COCONUT CURRY

The combination of different spices gives this robust curry its distinctive flavour. Beef, potatoes, onions and chillies are simmered in a spiced coconut broth, and cashew nuts are added to the stew just before serving. Accompany the curry with plain boiled Thai rice.

450 g (1 lb) sirloin steak
4 cloves
5 ml (1 tsp) coriander seeds
5 ml (1 tsp) cumin seeds
seeds from 3 cardamom pods
2 garlic cloves, peeled
2.5 cm (1 inch) piece fresh
   root ginger, peeled
1 small onion, peeled
30 ml (2 tbsp) sunflower oil
15 ml (1 tbsp) sesame oil
15 ml (1 tbsp) Indian curry
   paste
5 ml (1 tsp) turmeric
225 g (8 oz) potatoes,
   peeled
4 tomatoes
5 ml (1 tsp) sugar
15 ml (1 tbsp) light soy sauce
300 ml (½ pint) coconut milk
150 ml (¼ pint) beef or
   chicken stock
4 fresh red chillies, bruised
50 g (2 oz) cashew nuts

PREPARATION TIME
30 minutes
COOKING TIME
40-45 minutes
FREEZING
Not suitable

505 CALS PER SERVING

1. Cut the steak into 3 cm (1¼ inch) cubes.

2. Place the cloves and coriander, cumin and cardamom seeds in a small heavy-based frying pan. Roast over a high heat for 1-2 minutes until the spices are golden and release their aroma. Cool slightly, then grind to a powder in a spice grinder or blender.

3. Roughly chop the garlic, ginger and onion, then purée in a food processor to form a smooth paste. Heat the two oils together in a deep frying pan. Add the onion purée with the curry paste and stir-fry for 5 minutes, then add the roasted ground spices and turmeric and fry for a further 5 minutes.

4. Add the beef to the pan and fry for a further 5 minutes until browned on all sides. Quarter the potatoes and tomatoes and add to the pan with all the remaining ingredients, except the cashews. Bring to the boil, lower the heat and simmer, covered, for 20-25 minutes until the beef is tender and the potatoes are cooked.

5. Stir in the cashew nuts and serve the curry with plain boiled rice or noodles and stir-fried vegetables.

For a vegetable curry, replace the steak with 450 g (1 lb) of your favourite root vegetables. Celeriac and sweet potato, for example, make a particularly delicious combination. Add to the sauce along with the potatoes and cook for 25-30 minutes until tender.

TECHNIQUE

Dry roast the whole spices in a small heavy-based pan until they release their aroma.

BRAISED HAM WITH MADEIRA MUSTARD SAUCE

This beautiful ham braised in Madeira is served with a piquant creamy mustard sauce, made with the cooking juices. It is large enough to serve 6-8 as a hot main course and leave sufficient to serve cold over the festive holiday. If preferred, you could of course buy a smaller joint.

SERVES 12-16

3.7 kg (6 lb) piece of gammon
½ bottle medium white wine
6 cloves
8 peppercorns
½ bottle Madeira
SAUCE
8 shallots
300 ml (½ pint) dry white
   wine
about 300 ml (½ pint) light
   stock
75 g (3 oz) butter
40 g (1½ oz) plain flour
6 juniper berries, crushed
6 dried green peppercorns,
   crushed
120 ml (4 fl oz) white wine
   vinegar
30 ml (2 tbsp) Dijon
   mustard
120 ml (4 fl oz) crème
   fraîche or soured cream
salt and pepper

PREPARATION TIME
30 minutes, plus overnight
soaking
COOKING TIME
About 3¼-3½ hours
FREEZING
Suitable: Sauce only

625-515 CALS PER SERVING

1. Cover the gammon with cold water and leave to soak overnight. Scrub the skin and drain and dry well. Weigh the gammon and calculate the poaching time, allowing 25 minutes per 450 g (1 lb).

2. Place the gammon in a large pan and cover with cold water. Bring slowly to the boil, then drain off the water. Pour the wine into the pan and add the cloves and peppercorns and enough hot water to cover. Cover and simmer very gently for the calculated time. Allow the gammon to cool in the liquid, then drain.

3. Preheat the oven to 180°C (350°F) Mark 4. Strip the rind off the gammon and score the fat into a diamond pattern. Place the gammon in a roasting tin and pour over the Madeira. Braise in the oven for 45 minutes to 1 hour, basting frequently, until golden brown.

4. Meanwhile, peel and chop the shallots. Transfer the gammon to a platter, cover loosely and keep warm while making the sauce.

5. Pour off the juices from the roasting tin into a measuring jug and wait for the fat to rise to the surface. Skim off the fat and reserve 30 ml (2 tbsp). Make the braising liquid up to 1.2 litres (2 pints) with the wine and stock.

6. Melt the butter and reserved ham fat in a saucepan. Add the flour and cook, stirring, for 3-4 minutes until foaming. Whisk in the wine and stock mixture. Add the juniper berries and half the shallots. Bring to the boil and simmer for 10 minutes.

7. Meanwhile, put the green peppercorns, remaining shallots and vinegar in a saucepan and reduce to 10 ml (2 tsp). Dip the base of the pan into cold water to stop the reduction. Stir the Madeira sauce into the reduced vinegar with the mustard and simmer for at least 15 minutes. Stir in the crème fraîche or cream and bring to the boil. Check the seasoning. Pour into a warmed sauceboat.

8. Slice the ham and serve with the sauce and seasonal vegetables.

TECHNIQUE

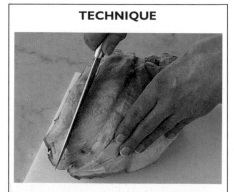

Before braising, score the gammon fat in a diamond pattern, using a sharp knife.

Bacon, potato and MUSHROOM GRATIN

A satisfyingly self-indulgent supper dish for two, simple to knock together late in the evening when you've been busy with other things. Serve with a crisp leafy salad and a glass of wine.

SERVES 2

250 g (9 oz) small new
  potatoes
salt and pepper
1 small onion
125 g (4 oz) bacon, derinded
30 ml (2 tbsp) olive oil
125 g (4 oz) mushrooms
125 g (4 oz) Cheddar cheese

PREPARATION TIME
5 minutes
COOKING TIME
20 minutes
FREEZING
Not suitable

595 CALS PER SERVING

1. Wash the potatoes and halve them (unless they are very small). Cook in salted water until tender. Drain thoroughly.

2. In the meantime, peel and chop the onion; dice the bacon. Heat the olive oil in a frying pan and add the onion and bacon. Cook gently, stirring frequently, to soften the onion and crisp the bacon. Meanwhile, wipe the mushrooms. Leave very small button mushrooms whole; halve or slice larger ones. Add them to the bacon towards the end of cooking and stir-cook for 2-3 minutes. Preheat the grill.

3. Transfer the bacon, onion and mushrooms to a flameproof gratin dish and stir in the potatoes. Season with pepper only, and grate the cheese all over the surface. Grill until the cheese is bubbling, then serve immediately.

NOTE: It's important to cook the diced bacon and onion slowly and to stir frequently.

VARIATION

For a vegetarian version, replace the bacon with sliced leeks, increasing the olive oil by 15 ml (1 tbsp) and adding a sprinkling of thyme.

TECHNIQUE

Add the mushrooms to the fried onion and bacon mixture towards the end of cooking and stir-cook for 2-3 minutes.

GLAZED PORK LOIN WITH FIG STUFFING

A tender loin of pork rolled around a tasty fig, apple and rosemary stuffing, then roasted until the crackling is a deep mahogany brown and deliciously crisp. It is important to score the crackling deeply to ensure a crisp result. The crackling bastes the meat during cooking and keeps it moist.

SERVES 6

1.4 kg (3 lb) boned loin of
    pork, skin well scored
salt and pepper
FIG STUFFING
4 shallots
1 garlic clove
225 g (8 oz) no-need-to-soak
    dried figs
1 eating apple
2 fresh rosemary sprigs
50 g (2 oz) butter
finely grated rind and juice
    of 1 lemon
45 ml (3 tbsp) dry sherry
GLAZE
60 ml (4 tbsp) thin honey
10 ml (2 tsp) mustard
    powder
finely grated rind of 1 lemon
TO GARNISH
rosemary sprigs
few fresh figs

PREPARATION TIME
30 minutes
COOKING TIME
2 hours
FREEZING
Not suitable

480 CALS PER SERVING

1. For the stuffing, peel and finely chop the shallots. Crush the garlic. Roughly chop the figs. Peel, core and finely chop the apple. Chop the rosemary.

2. Melt the butter in a saucepan and add the shallots and garlic. Cook for 5-10 minutes until soft and golden. Stir in the figs, apple, rosemary, lemon rind and juice, and sherry. Cook, stirring, for 5 minutes until slightly softened and most of the liquid has evaporated. Cool.

3. Preheat the oven to 190°C (375°F) Mark 5. Lay the pork loin, skin-side down, on a clean surface. Season well with salt and pepper and spread the stuffing along the middle. Roll up and tie at intervals with fine string. Place in a roasting tin and roast in the oven for 1 hour.

4. Meanwhile, make the glaze. Place the honey, mustard and lemon rind in a saucepan and heat gently, stirring. Brush over the pork skin and roast for a further 45 minutes, basting every 15 minutes with the glaze.

5. Leave the meat to rest in a warm place for 15 minutes. Carve into thick slices and serve garnished with sprigs of rosemary. Accompany with a gravy made from the pan juices if wished, and seasonal vegetables.

NOTE: If you buy a pork loin without crackling, brown it all over in butter after stuffing, before roasting.

Any leftover stuffing can be used to fill halved and cored eating apples. Roast around the joint for the last 20 minutes and serve as an accompaniment.

VARIATION

Replace the figs with no-need-to-soak stoned prunes or apricots. Use thyme instead of rosemary.

TECHNIQUE

Tie the stuffed pork loin at regular intervals with fine cotton string to secure the stuffing.

ITALIAN SAUSAGES

Real sausages – made with pure pork and highly seasoned with black pepper – are easy to make. Certain recipes call for Italian sausages, and these fit the bill if you haven't access to an Italian delicatessen. The secret lies in mincing or hand-chopping the meat coarsely, and using a proportion of gammon to give the right salty taste. The mixture can be filled into sausage skins, made into meatballs or patties, or used as sausagemeat.

SERVES 6

450 g (1 lb) shoulder of pork
225 g (8 oz) piece unsmoked
  gammon
225 g (8 oz) belly of pork
2 large garlic cloves, peeled
  (optional)
15 ml (1 tbsp) coarse sea
  salt
15 ml (1 tbsp) granulated
  sugar
30 ml (2 tbsp) coarsely
  crushed black pepper
sausage casings (optional)

PREPARATION TIME
45 minutes
COOKING TIME
10-15 minutes
FREEZING
Suitable: Up to 3 months

340 CALS PER SERVING

1. Trim the shoulder of pork, gammon and belly pork of any skin or connective tissue, then cut into rough chunks.

2. Pass through the coarse blade of a mincer or chop with a large sharp knife or cleaver (see note).

3. Place the meat in a large bowl. Crush the garlic, if using, and add to the meat with the sea salt, sugar and pepper. Mix thoroughly.

4. Shape the mixture into patties or roll into balls and dust with flour before cooking. Alternatively use to fill sausage casings as follows. Spoon the sausage-meat into a large piping bag fitted with a large plain plastic nozzle. Rinse the casings in cold water and roll the open end over the nozzle. Hold the first 5 cm (2 inches) casing closed and squeeze the filling into the casing to form the first sausage, easing the casing from the nozzle as it fills. Stop when the sausage is big enough and twist gently before filling the next one. Tie the loose end of the casing on the first sausage. Continue until all the filling is used up. If you like, tie the sausages at two points between the links with fine string, then cut into individual sausages.

5. To cook, heat a little oil in a frying pan and gently fry the sausages for 10-15 minutes, turning once or twice until cooked through. Alternatively cook under a preheated grill for 5 minutes on each side. Serve with fresh tomato sauce or grilled polenta.

NOTE: Large food mixers have a mincer attachment, and small hand-cranked ones are available. Do not use a food processor as this gives a poor texture.

Any good butcher who makes his own sausages should be able to supply sausage skins or casings.

VARIATIONS

Salsicce Genovese: Add 45 ml (3 tbsp) chopped fresh basil, 45 ml (3 tbsp) freshly grated Parmesan and 30 ml (2 tbsp) pine nuts to the mixture.
Salsicce Finocchio: Add 30 ml (2 tbsp) fennel seeds and 5 ml (1 tsp) dried chilli flakes to the meat mixture.

TECHNIQUE

With clean hands, mix all the sausage ingredients together thoroughly.

ROAST LAMB WITH GARLIC AND MUSHROOM STUFFING

As with most great British roasts, lamb is traditionally cooked with little embellishment, to allow the flavour of the meat to dominate. To impart extra flavour, a robust garlic, mushroom and leek stuffing is included here. To save yourself time order a boned leg of lamb from the butcher several days in advance and use the bone to make the stock for the gravy.

SERVES 8

225 g (8 oz) brown
   mushrooms
6 large cloves garlic
1 leek
60 ml (4 tbsp) olive oil
45 ml (3 tbsp) chopped fresh
   oregano
salt and pepper
2.3 kg (5 lb) boned leg of
   lamb
45-60 ml (3-4 tbsp)
   redcurrant jelly
10 ml (2 tsp) wine vinegar
150 ml (¼ pint) red wine
300 ml (½ pint) lamb stock
TO GARNISH
herb sprigs

PREPARATION TIME
20 minutes, plus cooling
COOKING TIME
2½-3 hours
FREEZING
Not suitable

560 CALS PER SERVING

1. Wipe the mushrooms and peel the garlic. Place both in a food processor and work briefly until finely chopped. Trim and chop the leek. Heat the oil in a frying pan. Add the mushrooms, garlic and leek and fry for about 10 minutes until the mushroom juices have evaporated and the mixture has the consistency of a thick paste. Stir in the oregano and season with salt and pepper. Leave to cool.

2. Preheat the oven to 180°C (350°F) Mark 4. Open out the lamb and pack the stuffing down the centre. Fold the meat over the stuffing to enclose and tie with string. Place the lamb, joined-side down, in a roasting tin.

3. Roast the lamb for 25 minutes per 450 g (1 lb) plus 25 minutes for medium; 30 minutes per 450 g (1 lb) plus 30 minutes for well done.

4. Melt the redcurrant jelly in a small saucepan with the wine vinegar. Thirty minutes before the end of the roasting time, brush the lamb with the redcurrant glaze. Repeat several times before the end of the cooking time.

5. Remove the lamb from the tin and transfer to a warmed serving platter.

Keep warm. Drain off the fat from the pan and stir in the wine and stock. Bring to the boil and boil until slightly reduced. Strain the gravy, if preferred, into a warmed sauceboat.

6. Remove the string from the lamb. Surround with herbs and serve accompanied by the gravy, and vegetables of your choice.

VARIATION

Whole roasted garlic bulbs make an attractive and delicious garnish. Roast them in their skins around the meat in the roasting tin.

TECHNIQUE

Spread the stuffing down the centre of the meat, then bring the meat over the stuffing and tie with string.

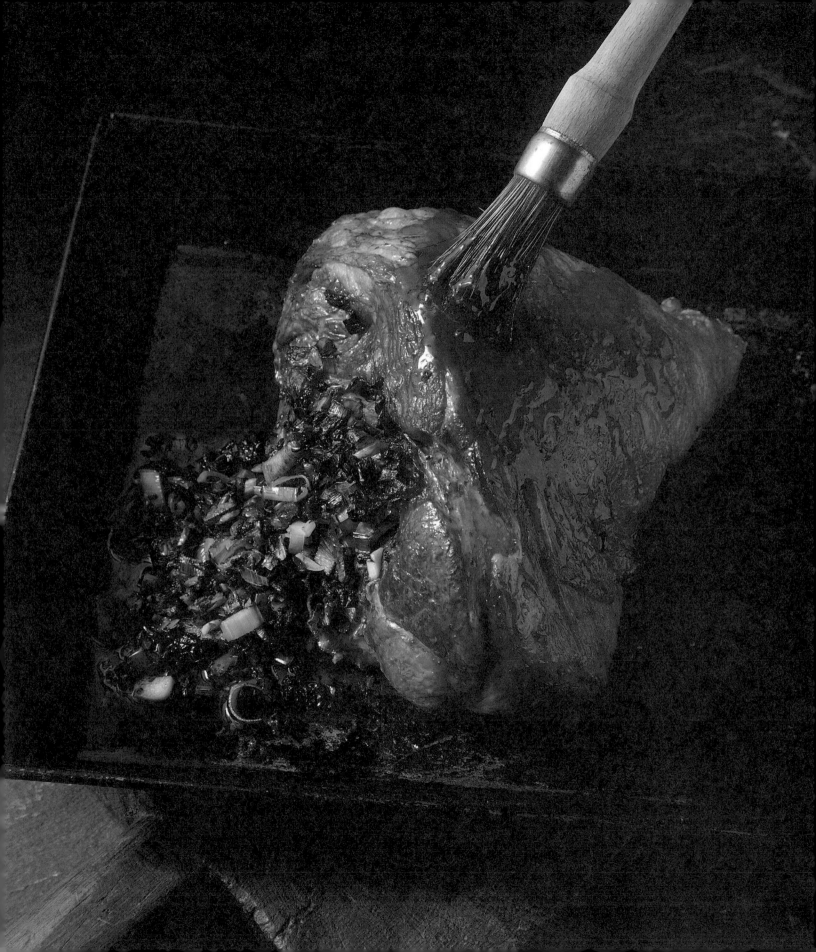

SPICED LAMB WITH SPINACH AND POTATO

Lean and tender lamb leg steaks cook quickly under the grill. Here they are finished with a creamy topping that bathes the meat in spices as it melts to a rich golden sauce. Spicy vegetables are the perfect complement.

SERVES 4

4 boneless leg steaks of lamb, each about 150-175 g (5-6 oz)
juice of 1 lemon
3 garlic cloves, crushed
15 ml (1 tbsp) chilli oil (see note)
1 onion
575 g (1¼ lb) small new potatoes
10 ml (2 tsp) mustard seeds
60 ml (4 tbsp) vegetable oil
300 g (10 oz) packet frozen leaf spinach
salt and pepper
5 ml (1 tsp) ground cumin
5 cm (2 inch) piece fresh root ginger
7.5 ml (1½ tsp) turmeric
60 ml (4 tbsp) crème fraîche or Greek yogurt
few mint leaves, shredded
cayenne pepper, to taste
mint sprigs, to garnish

PREPARATION TIME
15 minutes
COOKING TIME
25 minutes
FREEZING
Not suitable

545 CALS PER SERVING

1. Lay the lamb steaks in a shallow dish and sprinkle with half of the lemon juice. Spread half of the garlic over the meat, then sprinkle a few drops of chilli oil onto both sides of each steak. Rub the garlic, oil and lemon juice well into the meat.

2. Peel and chop the onion. Wash the potatoes and halve any larger ones. Preheat the grill.

3. Put the mustard seeds in a dry heavy-based pan over a medium heat, cover and shake the pan until the popping dies down. Add 45 ml (3 tbsp) of the oil and the chopped onion. Cook, stirring frequently, over a low heat for 5 minutes. Add the potatoes and remaining garlic. Cook for a further 2 minutes.

4. Add the spinach, remaining lemon juice and 5 ml (1 tsp) each of salt and ground cumin. Stir until the spinach thaws, then cover and leave to cook for 15 minutes.

5. Meanwhile, peel and grate the ginger and mix with the turmeric and remaining 15 ml (1 tbsp) oil. Stir in the crème fraîche or yogurt. Season with salt and pepper.

6. Line the rack of the grill pan with foil, lay the lamb steaks on top and grill for 5 minutes on one side. Turn and spread the cream or yogurt mixture over the uncooked side of the meat and return to the grill for 5 minutes.

7. Uncover the vegetables towards the end of the cooking time if there is too much liquid, to allow the excess to evaporate. Just before serving, add the shredded mint, black pepper, and more salt if necessary.

8. Divide the vegetables between warmed serving plates and place the lamb steaks alongside. Sprinkle a little cayenne over each one. Garnish with extra mint sprigs to serve.

NOTE: If you haven't any chilli-flavoured oil, use ordinary vegetable oil adding a dash of Tabasco.

TECHNIQUE

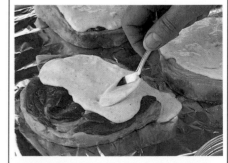

Spread the spiced yogurt over the turned leg steaks.

MINTED LAMB ESCALOPES

Extra-lean, wafer-thin lamb escalopes are flavoured with a fresh-tasting minted yogurt marinade, then grilled to perfection. A colourful salad of baby spinach leaves, tomatoes and onion is the ideal accompaniment. Serve with some warm pitta bread, too.

SERVES 4

450 g (1 lb) lamb escalopes
  (see note)
MARINADE
90 ml (6 tbsp) Greek-style
  yogurt
1 garlic clove, crushed
60 ml (4 tbsp) chopped fresh
  mint
30 ml (2 tbsp) lemon juice
salt and coarsely ground
  black pepper
TO GARNISH
mint sprigs

PREPARATION TIME
10 minutes, plus marinating
COOKING TIME
6 minutes
FREEZING
Not suitable

210 CALS PER SERVING

1. For the marinade, mix the yogurt, crushed garlic, chopped mint and lemon juice together in a shallow non-metallic dish. Season with salt and pepper. Add the lamb escalopes and turn to coat evenly in the yogurt mixture. Cover the dish and leave to marinate in a cool place for 2-3 hours.

2. Preheat the grill to high. Place the lamb escalopes on the grill rack in a single layer. Grill for 3 minutes on each side or until golden brown and cooked through, basting occasionally with the marinade.

3. Transfer the lamb to warmed serving plates and garnish with mint sprigs. Serve with a spinach, tomato and onion salad, and warm pitta bread.

NOTE: For this recipe, you need very thin lean escalopes cut from the leg. These are sold ready-prepared in some supermarkets; alternatively ask your butcher to prepare them for you.

VARIATION

For spiced lamb escalopes, replace the mint with 5 ml (1 tsp) each ground cumin and turmeric, and 2.5 cm (1 inch) piece fresh root ginger, grated.

TECHNIQUE

Add the lamb escalopes to the minted yogurt marinade and turn to coat evenly.

LAMB PASANDA

This deliciously rich creamy curry is thickened with ground nuts and cream. It is important to ensure that the meat, nuts and onions are thoroughly browned, or the sauce will have an insipid colour. As this dish is very rich, it is best served with plain boiled rice and a simple vegetable accompaniment.

SERVES 4

50 g (2 oz) blanched
   almonds
50 g (2 oz) unsalted cashew
   nuts
30 ml (2 tbsp) sesame seeds
2.5 cm (1 inch) piece fresh
   root ginger
2 garlic cloves
2 onions
30 ml (2 tbsp) ghee or
   vegetable oil
10 ml (2 tsp) ground cumin
10 ml (2 tsp) ground
   coriander
2.5 ml (½ tsp) ground
   turmeric
2.5 ml (½ tsp) ground
   cardamom
2.5 ml (½ tsp) ground cloves
750 g (1½ lb) lean boneless
   lamb, cubed
150 ml (¼ pint) double
   cream
150 ml (¼ pint) coconut
   milk
30 ml (2 tbsp) lemon juice
salt

PREPARATION TIME
20 minutes
COOKING TIME
1½ hours
FREEZING
Suitable

865 CALS PER SERVING

1. Put the nuts in a heavy-based frying pan and dry-fry over a gentle heat until just golden brown. Remove from the pan and leave to cool. Toast the sesame seeds in the same way; allow to cool.

2. Peel and roughly chop the ginger. Peel the garlic. Peel and thinly slice the onions.

3. Tip the nuts into a blender or food processor and process briefly until finely chopped. Add the sesame seeds, ginger, garlic and 15 ml (1 tbsp) water and work to a purée.

4. Heat the ghee or oil in a large saucepan or flameproof casserole, add the onions and cook over a fairly high heat until tinged with brown. Add the nut mixture and cook over a moderately high heat for 2 minutes.

5. Add the ground spices and cook, stirring, for 2 minutes. Add the meat and cook over a high heat, turning constantly until browned and sealed on all sides.

6. Add the cream, coconut milk and 150 ml (¼ pint) water. Stir in the lemon juice and season with salt to taste. Bring slowly to the boil, then lower the heat and simmer very gently for about 1½ hours or until the lamb is tender. Serve with rice.

VARIATIONS

• Replace the lamb with beef. Use lean braising steak and cook for about 2 hours.
• Use chicken instead of lamb. Either joint a 1.4 kg (3 lb) chicken or use 4 chicken quarters, halved. Cook as above for about 45 minutes.

TECHNIQUE

Dry-fry the almonds and cashew nuts in a heavy-based frying pan over a low heat until tinged golden brown.

Lamb meatballs with dill sauce

Cinnamon adds a hint of spice to these delicate fine-textured meatballs, which are served with a creamy wine and dill-flavoured sauce. If fresh dill is unobtainable you will find that dried dill weed – with its concentrated flavour – is an excellent substitute.

6 spring onions

175 g (6 oz) unsmoked rindless streaky bacon

1 garlic clove

pinch of ground cinnamon

700 g (1½ lb) lean minced lamb

salt and pepper

45 ml (3 tbsp) olive oil

450 ml (¾ pint) dry white wine

60 ml (4 tbsp) chopped fresh dill *or* 20 ml (2 tsp) dried dill weed

300 ml (½ pint) double cream

2 egg yolks

TO GARNISH

dill sprigs and lemon wedges

PREPARATION TIME
30 minutes
COOKING TIME
1 hour 10 minutes
FREEZING
Suitable, without cream. Stir in cream just before serving

650 CALS PER SERVING

1. Trim the spring onions; roughly chop the bacon; peel the garlic. Place the spring onions, bacon, garlic and cinnamon in a food processor and blend until almost smooth. Add the minced lamb and plenty of salt and pepper. Process until well mixed and smooth.

2. With wet hands, shape the mixture into 30-36 even-sized balls. Keep wetting your hands to prevent sticking.

3. Preheat the oven to 180°C (350°F) Mark 4. Heat the oil in a large frying pan and brown the meatballs in batches, then transfer to a shallow ovenproof dish. Pour the wine into the frying pan and bring to the boil, scraping up any sediment from the bottom of the pan. Pour over the meatballs, cover and bake in the preheated oven for 1 hour.

4. Pour the cooking liquid into a saucepan; cover the meatballs and keep warm. Bring the liquid to the boil and boil rapidly until reduced to 300 ml (½ pint). Lower the heat and stir in the dill, cream and egg yolks. Stir over a gentle heat for about 10 minutes or until slightly thickened; do not allow to boil. Taste and adjust the seasoning.

5. Transfer the meatballs to warmed serving plates and spoon the sauce over them. Garnish with dill sprigs and lemon wedges. Serve with boiled new potatoes or buttered noodles.

Use lean minced pork instead of lamb and tarragon in place of the dill.

With dampened hands, roll each piece of mixture in the palm of your hand to form an even-shaped ball.

OSSO BUCCO WITH RISOTTO MILANESE

This easy Milanese dish of veal in a rich tomato sauce is perfect for a winter's dinner party and tastes even better if cooked the day before and reheated. Gremolata — an aromatic mixture of parsley, garlic and lemon rind — is always sprinkled over the finished dish and a saffron risotto is the classic accompaniment.

4 thick slices shin of veal for 'osso bucco'
salt and pepper
flour, for coating
30 ml (2 tbsp) olive oil
150 ml (¼ pint) dry white wine
400 g (14 oz) can chopped tomatoes (see note)
about 450 ml (¾ pint) veal or chicken stock
GREMOLATA
1 garlic clove
60 ml (4 tbsp) chopped fresh parsley
15 ml (1 tbsp) finely grated lemon rind
RISOTTO
1 onion
50 g (2 oz) butter
150 ml (¼ pint) dry white wine
275 g (10 oz) arborio rice
1 packet saffron threads
1 litre (1¾ pints) veal or chicken stock
50 g (2 oz) freshly grated Parmesan cheese

PREPARATION TIME
20 minutes
COOKING TIME
About 2 hours

FREEZING Suitable: Stage 2

705 CALS PER SERVING

1. Dip the veal in seasoned flour to coat evenly, shaking off excess. Heat the oil in a flameproof casserole (into which the meat fits snugly in one layer). Add the meat and brown on all sides.

2. Stir in the wine and tomatoes. Bring to the boil and simmer, uncovered, for 10 minutes. Pour in enough stock to cover the meat and add seasoning. Cover tightly and simmer gently for 1¾-2 hours until the veal is very tender. (Alternatively bake in a preheated oven at 170°C (325° F) Mark 3.)

3. Check the sauce: it should be quite thick. If not, transfer the meat to a warmed dish; boil the sauce rapidly to reduce, then return the meat to the casserole.

4. Meanwhile, make the gremolata. Peel and crush the garlic and mix with the chopped parsley and lemon rind.

5. To make the risotto, peel and chop the onion. Melt half the butter in a large saucepan, add the onion and cook gently for 5 minutes until soft but not coloured. Pour in the wine and boil rapidly until almost totally reduced.

6. Add the rice and stir to coat with the butter. Add the saffron and a ladleful of stock and simmer, stirring, until absorbed. Continue adding the stock ladle by ladle until the rice is tender and creamy but still has some bite to it. This should take about 20 minutes; it may not be necessary to add all of the stock.

7. About 5 minutes before serving, sprinkle the gremolata over the meat. Stir the remaining butter and the Parmesan into the risotto and season with salt and pepper to taste. Serve immediately, with the Osso Bucco.

NOTE: When ripe flavourful tomatoes are available, use 450 g (1 lb), skinned and chopped, in place of the canned tomatoes.

TECHNIQUE

Add the stock a ladleful at a time, making sure each addition is absorbed before you add the next.

SAUSAGE COILED IN A CAKE TIN

The sausage has risen to new heights of respectability recently, due to a proliferation of specialist shops making worthy bangers on the premises, and the supermarket response with new premium sausages. Serve your sausage proudly in a sauce chunky with vegetables – and if you are opening a bottle of wine to drink with it, as this dish certainly deserves, add a splash to the pan too.

SERVES 4

450 g (1 lb) Cumberland or
   other high-quality sausage
   (preferably unlinked)
12 shallots
30 ml (2 tbsp) vegetable oil
400 g (14 oz) can peeled
   plum tomatoes
5 ml (1 tsp) dried oregano
200 g (7 oz) frozen peas
10 ml (2 tsp)
   Worcestershire sauce
30 ml (2 tbsp) red wine
   (optional)
salt and pepper

PREPARATION TIME
20 minutes while oven preheats
COOKING TIME
25 minutes
FREEZING
Not suitable

540 CALS PER SERVING

1. Preheat the oven to 220°C (425°F) Mark 7. If the sausage you are using is twisted in links, untwist between each sausage and gently massage the meat towards the middle to form an even cylinder. Twist the skin at the ends and trim off surplus skin.

2. Peel the shallots; if large, cut in half. Oil a 20 cm (8 inch) shallow cake tin (with a solid base). Coil the sausage in the middle of the tin and arrange the shallots around the edge. Brush both sausage and shallots with more oil. Bake in the oven for about 25 minutes until the sausage is a deep brown colour and shiny on top.

3. Meanwhile, drain the tomatoes, tip them into a saucepan and mash roughly. Add the oregano, peas, Worcestershire sauce and red wine if using. Cook gently until the peas are tender. Season with salt and pepper.

4. Cut the cooked sausage into wedges. Transfer the sausage and shallots to warmed serving plates and spoon on the tomatoes and peas. Serve with mashed potatoes or hot French bread.

NOTE: Cumberland sausage is traditionally sold untwisted in a continuous coil. If your sausages are linked, you will first need to untwist them.

VARIATION

Vary the dish with any of the new flavours of sausage now available.

TECHNIQUE

Coil the sausage in a solid-based 20 cm (8 inch) shallow cake tin, arranging the shallots around the edge.

STEAK AND KIDNEY PUDDING

Of all British favourites, this dish seems to win the greatest acclaim as we remember the inviting aroma and rich meaty gravy seeping into the suety pastry case. Fresh oysters, once the food of the poor, were frequently used to stretch the meat. Here a few canned oysters are included instead to impart a delicious smoky flavour.

SERVES 6

FILLING

700 g (1½ lb) braising or stewing steak

225 g (8 oz) ox kidney

60 ml (4 tbsp) plain flour

salt and pepper

2 small onions

45 ml (3 tbsp) oil

450 ml (¾ pint) beef stock

90 ml (6 tbsp) port

225 g (8 oz) mushrooms

8 canned smoked oysters (optional)

PASTRY

300 g (10 oz) self-raising flour

2.5 ml (½ tsp) salt

150 g (5 oz) suet

PREPARATION TIME
35 minutes
COOKING TIME
About 3½ hours
FREEZING
Not suitable

540 CALS PER SERVING

1. Trim the meat and cut into 2 cm (¾ inch) pieces. Remove the white core from the kidney, then cut into 1 cm (½ inch) chunks. Season the flour with salt and pepper and use to coat the meat.

2. Peel and chop the onions. Heat the oil in a large frying pan and fry the steak in batches until browned on all sides. Transfer to a flameproof casserole or heavy-based saucepan, using a slotted spoon. Brown the kidney in the oil remaining in the frying pan, then transfer to the casserole. Add the onion to the frying pan and fry gently for about 10 minutes until soft, adding a little extra oil if necessary. Add to the meat with the stock, port and seasoning. Bring to the boil, reduce the heat, cover and simmer gently for 1¼ hours.

3. To make the pastry, sift the flour and salt into a bowl and stir in the suet. Add 175 ml (6 fl oz) cold water and mix to a soft dough using a round-bladed knife, adding a little extra water if the pastry is dry.

4. Roll out a scant three quarters of the dough on a lightly floured surface. Use to line a 1.7 litre (3 pint) pudding basin.

5. Halve any large mushrooms and stir the mushrooms into the meat with the oysters if using. Turn into the lined basin.

Brush the top edge of the pastry with water. Roll out the remainder to make a lid and lay over the pudding, pressing the edges together to seal.

6. Cover the basin with a pleated, double thickness layer of greaseproof paper, securing under the rim with string. Cover with foil and place in a steamer or on an upturned saucer in a large saucepan. Pour in enough hot water to come halfway up the sides of the basin. Cover with a lid and steam for 2 hours, checking the water level occasionally.

7. Remove the foil and greaseproof paper and loosen the edges of the pudding. Invert onto a serving plate and serve at once, with vegetables in season.

TECHNIQUE

Use three quarters of the pastry to line the basin, lightly pressing onto the base and around the sides in an even layer.

POULTRY AND GAME

CHICKEN BREASTS WITH PAPRIKA MUSHROOM SAUCE

A rich, warmly spiced mushroom sauce adds excitement to quickly cooked chicken breast fillets. Serve with a green vegetable, such as baby leeks or mangetouts, and sauté potatoes flavoured with garlic.

SERVES 4

15 g (½ oz) dried porcini
   mushrooms (see note)
45 ml (3 tbsp) medium dry
   sherry, preferably
   Amontillado
1 small onion
200 g (7 oz) chestnut or cup
   mushrooms
30 ml (2 tbsp) vegetable oil
50 g (2 oz) butter
4 skinless chicken breast
   fillets
5 ml (1 tsp) chopped fresh
   or dried thyme
125 ml (4 fl oz) crème
   fraîche
about 125 ml (4 fl oz)
   chicken stock
15 ml (1 tbsp) paprika
salt and pepper

PREPARATION TIME
10 minutes
COOKING TIME
20-25 minutes
FREEZING
Not suitable

480 CALS PER SERVING

1. Put the porcini mushrooms in a small bowl. Warm the sherry, pour over the porcini and leave to stand. Peel the onion and chop finely. Slice the fresh mushrooms.

2. Heat the oil and 25 g (1 oz) of the butter in a frying pan. Add the chicken breasts and cook for about 5 minutes each side. Lift out the chicken with a slotted spoon and transfer to a warmed dish; cover and keep warm.

3. Add the onion and thyme to the pan and fry over a gentle heat, stirring frequently, for 5 minutes. Add the remaining butter, then add the fresh mushrooms and cook, stirring, over a moderate heat for 5 minutes.

4. Add the porcini with their soaking liquid and cook for 1 minute, then add the crème fraîche. Stir in sufficient stock to thin the sauce to the desired consistency, and add the paprika. Cook for 2 minutes, then check the seasoning. Pour the sauce over the chicken breasts to serve.

NOTE: If porcini or other dried mushrooms are not available, just use fresh mushrooms, and add the sherry to the sauce after frying them.

VARIATION

Replace the chicken breast fillets with medallions of pork sliced from a tenderloin (fillet).

TECHNIQUE

Stir sufficient stock into the sauce to thin it to the desired consistency.

CHICKEN WITH CASHEWS

Serve this mildly spiced dish with cinnamon-flavoured basmati rice or a mushroom pilaff. For the latter, simply sauté a little chopped onion, a few sliced mushrooms and a little crushed garlic in butter until softened, then add the rice and boiling stock and simmer until tender. Enrich with a knob of butter just before serving.

SERVES 4-6

about 1.4 kg (3 lb) chicken
    pieces, such as thighs and
    drumsticks
2 large onions
3 garlic cloves
2.5 cm (1 inch) piece fresh
    root ginger
50 g (2 oz) cashew nuts
45 ml (3 tbsp) vegetable oil
1 cinnamon stick
15 ml (1 tbsp) coriander
    seeds
10 ml (2 tsp) cumin seeds
4 cardamom pods
150 ml (¼ pint) thick yogurt
45 ml (3 tbsp) chopped fresh
    coriander (optional)
30 ml (2 tbsp) chopped fresh
    mint (optional)
TO SERVE
yogurt
garam masala
chopped coriander and mint
    (optional)

PREPARATION TIME
15 minutes
COOKING TIME
About 50 minutes
FREEZING
Suitable

400-270 CALS PER SERVING

1. Skin the chicken pieces. If there are any large ones, such as breasts, cut into 2 or 3 pieces.

2. Peel and chop the onions. Peel and crush the garlic. Peel the ginger and chop it finely.

3. Put the cashew nuts in a blender or food processor with 150 ml (¼ pint) water and work until smooth.

4. Heat the oil in a large flameproof casserole and add the onions, garlic, ginger and all the spices. Cook over a high heat for 2-3 minutes, stirring all the time. Add the cashew purée and cook for 1-2 minutes. Add the chicken and stir to coat in the spices.

5. Lower the heat, then add the yogurt a spoonful at a time, followed by another 150 ml (¼ pint) water. Season with salt and pepper. Lower the heat, cover and cook gently for about 45 minutes or until the chicken is cooked right through.

6. Add the coriander and mint if using, and check the seasoning. Serve each portion topped with a spoonful of yogurt and sprinkled with garam masala. Scatter with chopped herbs too, if desired.

VARIATIONS

This works equally well with lean tender lamb or raw prawns. The lamb will take a little longer to cook – simply add more water as necessary to prevent it sticking. If using prawns, simmer the sauce for 15 minutes, add the prawns and cook until they look pink and opaque.

TECHNIQUE

Add the chicken pieces to the casserole and turn to coat in the spices and cashew purée.

CHICKEN BAKED WITH SPICES

This is a really easy, tasty supper dish. If you can, set the chicken to marinate the day before to allow plenty of time for it to absorb the flavourings. It will then be ready to pop into the oven when required. Serve with a simple rice pilaff and a crisp green salad.

2 garlic cloves

30 ml (2 tbsp) mild paprika

10 ml (2 tsp) ground coriander

5-10 ml (1-2 tsp) cayenne pepper

finely grated rind and juice of 1 large lemon

30 ml (2 tbsp) chopped fresh mint

30 ml (2 tbsp) chopped fresh coriander

45 ml (3 tbsp) grated fresh coconut (optional)

200 ml (7 fl oz) thick yogurt

salt and pepper

6 chicken suprêmes, or other portions

ghee, butter or vegetable oil, for brushing

TO SERVE

mint and rocket leaves

grated fresh coconut (optional)

lemon or lime wedges

PREPARATION TIME
15 minutes, plus marinating
COOKING TIME
About 25 minutes
FREEZING
Not suitable

260 CALS PER SERVING

1. Crush the garlic and mash with the paprika, coriander, cayenne pepper and lemon rind and juice. Put the herbs, and coconut if using, in a bowl and stir in the yogurt. Beat in the garlic mixture. Add salt and pepper to taste.

2. Skin each chicken suprême or portion and make 2 or 3 deep cuts in the thickest part of the flesh.

3. Drop the chicken portions into the yogurt mixture and turn the portions in the mixture so that they are thoroughly coated on all sides. Make sure that the marinade goes well into the slashes. Leave to marinate in a cool place for at least 30 minutes, or overnight if possible.

4. Preheat the oven to 200°C (400°F) Mark 6. Arrange the chicken in a single layer in a roasting tin and brush with melted butter, ghee or oil. Roast in the oven, basting from time to time, for about 25 minutes until the chicken is cooked right through. To test it, pierce the thickest part with the point of a knife: if the juices run clear, the chicken is cooked; if there is any trace of pink, bake for a further 10 minutes.

5. Serve garnished with mint and rocket leaves, grated coconut if using, and lemon or lime wedges.

VARIATIONS

To simplify the recipe, replace the spices with 30 ml (2 tbsp) ready-made tandoori paste. If fresh herbs are unavailable, use 5 ml (1 tsp) mint concentrate instead.

TECHNIQUE

Make 2 or 3 deep slashes in each chicken suprême to enable the marinade to penetrate.

CHICKEN KORMA

This universally popular chicken dish should be mild, rich and creamy, but not in any way bland. For best results, use a good thick yogurt; rich Greek-style yogurt is ideal. Don't be tempted to use a low-fat yogurt, as this would curdle and make the sauce unappetising. Serve the korma with plenty of rice or Indian bread to mop up the ample sauce.

SERVES 4

3 large onions, peeled
30-45 ml (2-3 tbsp) ghee or
  vegetable oil
2-3 garlic cloves
4 cloves
4 cardamom pods
1 cinnamon stick
10 ml (2 tsp) ground
  coriander
2.5 ml (½ tsp) ground
  turmeric
2.5 ml (½ tsp) ground ginger
2.5 ml (½ tsp) ground cumin
4 chicken breast fillets,
  skinned
squeeze of lemon juice
600 ml (1 pint) thick yogurt
salt
coriander sprigs, to garnish
  (optional)

PREPARATION TIME
15 minutes
COOKING TIME
40 minutes
FREEZING
Not suitable

390 CALS PER SERVING

1. Thinly slice half of the onions. Heat 30 ml (2 tbsp) ghee or oil in a frying pan, add the sliced onions and fry until browned and crisp. Remove with a slotted spoon and drain thoroughly on crumpled kitchen paper; set aside.

2. Finely chop the remaining onion. Peel and crush the garlic. Cook the onion and garlic in the ghee or oil remaining in the pan until softened, adding a little extra if necessary. Add the spices and cook, stirring constantly, for 2 minutes until the onions are lightly browned.

3. Cut each chicken breast fillet into 3 pieces. Add these to the pan with a squeeze of lemon juice and lower the heat. Add the yogurt, a tablespoon at a time, stirring thoroughly after each addition. Gradually stir in 150 ml (¼ pint) water.

4. Half-cover the pan with a lid and simmer gently for about 30 minutes until the chicken is tender and cooked right through. Season with salt to taste.

5. Serve sprinkled with the crisp browned onions, and garnished with coriander if desired.

VARIATION

Replace the chicken with 700 g (1½ lb) shelled large raw prawns or 450 g (1 lb) cooked peeled prawns. Add to the sauce in step 4. Cook for about 4 minutes if using raw prawns, until they turn pink. Cooked prawns only need to be heated through, for about 2 minutes.

TECHNIQUE

Add the chicken pieces to the onion, garlic and spice mixture in the pan, turning to coat them with the flavourings.

ROSYTH ROYAL DOCKYARD

TELEPHONE: 0383 412131

LEMON CHICKEN

Corn-fed chicken pieces are marinated in lemon juice, chilli and garlic, with a touch of honey – to help brown the chicken skin during cooking. Ripe, juicy lemon halves are tucked in and around the joints to impart extra flavour during roasting.

1.6 kg (3½ lb) corn-fed or
   free-range chicken, or
   4 chicken joints
4 really ripe juicy lemons
8 garlic cloves
1-2 small red chillies
15 ml (1 tbsp) honey
60 ml (4 tbsp) chopped fresh
   parsley
salt and pepper

PREPARATION TIME
20 minutes, plus marinating
COOKING TIME
45 minutes
FREEZING
Suitable

190 CALS PER SERVING

1. Using a sharp knife and/or poultry shears, cut the whole chicken, if using, into 8 small or 4 large joints. Place the chicken joints, skin-side down, in a large shallow ovenproof baking dish.

2. Halve the lemons, squeeze the juice and pour into a small bowl; reserve the empty lemon halves.

3. Peel and crush two of the garlic cloves and add to the lemon juice. Halve the chilli(es) lengthwise and remove the seeds. Add to the lemon juice with the honey. Stir well, pour over the chicken and tuck the lemon halves around. Cover and leave to marinate for at least 2 hours, turning once or twice.

4. Preheat the oven to 200°C (400°F) Mark 6. Turn the chicken skin-side up. Halve the rest of the garlic cloves and scatter over the chicken. Roast in the oven for 45 minutes or until golden brown and tender. Stir in the parsley and season with salt and pepper to taste. Serve hot, garnished with the roasted lemon halves.

NOTE: This dish relies on the natural sweetness of really ripe lemons. Do not use under-ripe fruit.

VARIATION

● Spatchcocked poussins may be cooked in the same manner.
● Small oranges or tangerines can be used in place of lemons.

TECHNIQUE

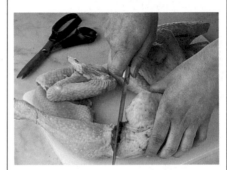

Using a sharp knife and/or poultry shears, cut the whole chicken into 8 small or 4 large joints.

FRENCH ROAST CHICKEN

Roasting the chicken in this way ensures that it is deliciously moist and tender – so it's worth the little extra effort involved. Don't be put off by the amount of garlic – it cooks down to a sweet tasting delicate purée that gives real body to the gravy. This gravy does require giblets which, alas, are missing from most supermarket birds. Instead, search out a good free-range chicken from your butcher or local farm – should you be unsuccessful, make do with chicken or vegetable stock.

SERVES 4

1 roasting chicken, about
  1.4 kg (3 lb), with giblets
1 carrot
1 onion
1 bouquet garni
140 g (4½ oz) butter
2 fresh tarragon sprigs
½ lemon
6 garlic cloves
salt and pepper
10 ml (2 tsp) white flour

PREPARATION TIME
10 minutes
COOKING TIME
About 1¼-1½ hours
FREEZING
Not suitable

470 CALS PER SERVING

1. Preheat the oven to 200°C (400°F) Mark 6. Remove the giblets from the chicken and put them in a saucepan with the carrot, onion, bouquet garni and 600 ml (1 pint) water. Bring to the boil, then cover and simmer for 1 hour while the chicken is cooking.

2. Melt 125 g (4 oz) of the butter. Weigh the chicken and calculate the cooking time, allowing 20 minutes per 450 g (1 lb), plus 20 minutes. Put the tarragon and lemon inside the chicken. Lay the bird on its side in a rack in a roasting tin. Brush the uppermost side with butter. Roast in the oven for 20 minutes of the cooking time.

3. Turn the chicken so that the other side is uppermost, brush with more butter and roast for a further 20 minutes.

4. Turn the chicken again, so that the breast is uppermost. Brush with more butter. Scatter the garlic cloves in the base of the roasting tin. Cook the chicken for the remainder of the cooking time, or until the juices run clear when a thigh is pierced with a skewer.

5. Transfer the chicken to a heated serving dish and leave to rest in a warm place for 10 minutes.

6. To make the gravy, skim off excess fat from the roasting tin. Retrieve the garlic cloves and pop them out of their skins back into the tin; mash with a fork. Strain the giblet stock into the pan and bring to the boil.

7. Beat together the remaining butter and the flour. Whisk this beurre manié, a small piece at a time, into the gravy. Simmer for a few minutes, whisking all the time. Season to taste. Serve the chicken accompanied by the gravy and vegetables of your choice.

VARIATION

Roast whole bulbs of garlic with the chicken, basting occasionally so that they don't burn. Serve as a garnish and encourage guests to scrape out the soft flesh and spread on the chicken.

TECHNIQUE

Pop the tarragon sprigs and lemon half into the cavity of the chicken to impart flavour during roasting.

CHICKEN FAJITAS

Serve this Mexican-style dish with tortillas, guacamole and plenty of soured cream. If you have trouble buying ready-made corn tortillas you could always make your own wheat version (see below).

SERVES 6

3 onions
2-3 hot chillies
2 garlic cloves, crushed
30 ml (2 tbsp) chopped fresh
    coriander
grated rind and juice of 2
    limes
6 chicken breast fillets,
    skinned
8 red, yellow or orange
    peppers (or a mixture)
15-30 ml (1-2 tbsp) olive oil
salt and pepper
TO SERVE
coriander leaves, to garnish
12 tortillas
guacamole (optional)
soured cream

PREPARATION TIME
30 minutes, plus marinating
COOKING TIME
About 15 minutes
FREEZING
Not suitable

335 CALS PER SERVING

1. Peel and halve the onions, leaving most of the root end attached so that they will hold their shape during cooking. Cut each half into wedges, working from the root end to the top. Slice the chillies, discarding the seeds if a milder flavour is preferred.

2. Put the garlic, onions, chillies, chopped coriander, lime rind and juice in a shallow dish and mix thoroughly. Cut the chicken into large pieces and add to the dish. Stir well, cover and leave to marinate in a cool place for at least 1 hour or overnight.

3. Halve the peppers and remove the cores and seeds, then cut into wedges.

4. Heat the oil in a heavy-based frying pan. Remove the chicken and onions from the marinade with a slotted spoon, reserving the marinade. Add the chicken and onions to the pan and cook, turning, over a high heat until thoroughly browned on the outside. Remove the chicken from the pan.

5. Add the peppers to the pan and cook, turning, over a high heat for about 5 minutes until the onions and peppers are softened.

6. Return the chicken to the pan, add the marinade, lower the heat and cook for about 5 minutes, stirring occasionally, or until the chicken is cooked right through.

7. Season with salt and pepper to taste and sprinkle with the coriander leaves. Serve immediately, with the tortillas, guacamole if desired, and plenty of soured cream.

HOMEMADE TORTILLAS

Put 300 g (10 oz) plain white flour in a food processor with 7.5 ml (1½ tsp) salt and 50 g (2 oz) white vegetable fat. Process briefly then, with the machine running, gradually add 150-175 ml (5-6 fl oz) warm water or enough to make a fairly soft dough. Knead briefly on a floured surface, then divide into 12 pieces. Roll out each piece to an 18 cm (7 inch) circle. Cook the tortillas one at a time on an ungreased griddle or frying pan for 1 minute each side.

TECHNIQUE

Add the chicken to the onions, garlic, chillies, coriander and lime. Stir to mix thoroughly.

RICOTTA-FILLED CHICKEN WITH TOMATO AND ORANGE SAUCE

These chicken breasts are filled with a light, fresh mixture of ricotta cheese, herbs and garlic, and served with a delicate sauce of fresh tomatoes simmered with a little orange. Serve them with a mixed leaf salad tossed in a lemon dressing – for a healthy midweek supper.

SERVES 4

175 g (6 oz) ricotta cheese
60 ml (4 tbsp) chopped fresh
 mixed herbs, eg oregano,
 thyme, parsley and chives
2 garlic cloves, crushed
salt and pepper
4 skinless chicken breast
 fillets, each 125-150 g
 (4-5 oz)
4 slices Parma ham
TOMATO AND ORANGE
 SAUCE
350 g (12 oz) plum
 tomatoes
2 shallots
1 orange
1 garlic clove, crushed
15 ml (1 tbsp) orange
 marmalade
TO GARNISH
orange wedges
herb sprigs

PREPARATION TIME
20 minutes
COOKING TIME
35-40 minutes
FREEZING Not suitable

315 CALS PER SERVING

1. Preheat the oven to 200°C (400°F) Mark 6. Place the ricotta cheese in a bowl and break up with a wooden spoon. Stir in the chopped herbs, garlic and seasoning.

2. Cut a 5 cm (2 inch) pocket along one side of each chicken breast. Divide the filling into 4 portions and ease a portion into each pocket. Pull the chicken flesh together to encase the filling.

3. Wrap a slice of Parma ham around each chicken breast: lay the ham over the breast, then fold the ends under to enclose and help seal in the filling.

4. Place the chicken breasts in an oven-proof dish, cover with foil and cook in the oven for 35-40 minutes.

5. Meanwhile, make the sauce. Place the tomatoes in a large bowl, pour over enough boiling water to cover and leave for 1 minute. Lift from the bowl and remove the skins. Roughly chop the tomato flesh.

6. Peel and finely chop the shallots. Grate the orange rind, squeeze the juice and pour 30 ml (2 tbsp) into a large pan.

Stir in the chopped tomatoes, garlic and seasoning, cover and place over a medium heat to sweat for a few minutes. Stir in the marmalade. Bring to the boil, then simmer for about 20 minutes, until the mixture is of a spooning consistency.

7. To serve, place the chicken breasts on warmed serving plates, spoon over the sauce and garnish with orange wedges and herbs. Serve with a mixed green salad.

TECHNIQUE

Cut a 5 cm (2 inch) slit along the thicker side of each chicken breast. Open up to form a pocket and fill with the ricotta mixture.

CINNAMON ROAST POUSSIN WITH COUSCOUS

For this recipe you need spatchcocked poussins. This technique is far easier than it looks, providing you have a good pair of poultry shears. Alternatively, you can buy ready-spatchcocked poussins from some supermarkets and butchers. Depending on the size of your poussins and the appetites of your guests allow ½-1 per person.

SERVES 4

250 g (9 oz) couscous
4 small poussins, each about
    400 g (14 oz)
5 ml (1 tsp) ground
    turmeric
5 ml (1 tsp) ground
    cinnamon
125 g (4 oz) butter
salt and pepper
about 60 ml (4 tbsp) thin
    honey
large pinch of saffron
    strands
2 medium onions
1 garlic clove
50 g (2 oz) pistachio nuts
grated rind and juice of
    1 lemon
TO SERVE
chopped parsley or
    coriander, to garnish
lemon wedges
harissa sauce (see note)

PREPARATION TIME
30 minutes
COOKING TIME
50-55 minutes
FREEZING
Not suitable

720 CALS PER SERVING

1. Preheat the oven to 200°C (400°F) Mark 6. Put the couscous in a bowl and pour over 350 ml (12 fl oz) cold water. Leave to soak for about 15 minutes or until all of the water has been absorbed.

2. Meanwhile, spatchcock the poussins following the instructions on page 7. Place, skin-side uppermost, in two roasting tins.

3. Sprinkle the poussins with the turmeric and cinnamon. Melt 40 g (1½ oz) of the butter and brush over the poussins. Season with salt and pepper. Roast in the preheated oven for 20 minutes. Reduce the temperature to 190°C (375°F) Mark 5 and cook for a further 15 minutes. Brush with a little honey and cook for 15-20 minutes more or until cooked right through.

4. While the poussins are cooking, add the saffron to a little boiling water, then mix with the soaked couscous. Spoon into a large muslin-lined metal sieve and steam over a pan of boiling water for about 35 minutes or until the grains are light and fluffy.

5. Meanwhile peel and slice the onions; peel and chop the garlic.

6. When the poussins are cooked, remove them from the roasting tins;

cover with foil and keep warm. Tip all the juices into one pan, place on the hob and add the onions and garlic. Cook quickly over a high heat until browned and softened. Add the nuts, lemon rind and juice and the remaining butter. Add the couscous and mix carefully with a fork. Season with salt and pepper.

7. Pile the couscous onto a large serving platter. Put the poussins on top and scatter with plenty of chopped fresh parsley or coriander. Serve immediately with lemon wedges, and hot Harissa sauce handed separately.

NOTE: Harissa sauce is available in cans from larger supermarkets and delicatessens.

TECHNIQUE

Sprinkle the poussins with turmeric and ground cinnamon, then brush liberally with melted butter.

THAI CHICKEN CURRY

Serve this exotic curry with a mountain of boiled rice to mop up the delicious juices, and plenty of stir-fried green vegetables. As a main course on its own, rather than part of a meal composed of lots of dishes, it will probably only serve 4. Although that's more than one chicken breast each, the delicious sauce encourages overeating and there's nothing worse than having friends for dinner and feeling that you should have made more!

SERVES 4-6

2 garlic cloves

1 medium onion

1 lemon grass stalk

2.5 cm (1 inch) piece fresh
root ginger

2 small hot chillies

small handful of fresh
coriander

5 ml (1 tsp) ground
coriander

grated rind and juice of
1 lime

2 large tomatoes

6 chicken breast fillets,
skinned

30 ml (2 tbsp) vegetable oil

30 ml (2 tbsp) nam pla (Thai
fish sauce)

900 ml (1½ pints) thick
coconut milk

salt and pepper

TO GARNISH

toasted fresh coconut,
grated

coriander leaves

red chilli slices (optional)

PREPARATION TIME
15 minutes
COOKING TIME
30 minutes
FREEZING
Suitable

775-520 CALS PER SERVING

1. Peel the garlic cloves. Peel and quarter the onion. Halve the lemon grass. Peel the ginger and cut in half. Put these ingredients in a food processor with the chillies, fresh coriander, ground coriander, lime rind and juice. Process until reduced to a chunky paste, adding a couple of spoonful of water if the mixture gets stuck under the blades.

2. Immerse the tomatoes in a bowl of boiling water for 15-30 seconds, then remove, cool slightly and peel away the skins. Roughly chop the tomato flesh. Cut each chicken breast into 3 pieces.

3. Heat the oil in a large heavy-based frying pan or flameproof casserole. Add the spice paste and cook over a fairly high heat for 3-4 minutes, stirring all the time. Add the chicken and cook for about 5 minutes, stirring to coat in the spice mixture.

4. Add the tomatoes, fish sauce and coconut milk. Bring to the boil, then cover and simmer very gently for about 25 minutes or until the chicken is cooked. Season to taste with salt and pepper. Serve garnished with toasted fresh coconut, coriander leaves, and slices of red chilli if desired.

VARIATION

Replace the chicken with 450 g (1 lb) large raw prawns. Peel and devein, then simmer in the sauce for 5-10 minutes only, until they look pink and opaque. Don't overcook or they will be tough.

TECHNIQUE

Process the garlic, onion, lemon grass, ginger, chillies, fresh and ground coriander, lime rind and juice to a chunky paste.

CHICKEN, POTATO AND SPINACH FRITTATA

For this tempting frittata choose waxy potatoes which hold their shape when sautéed. Look for varieties such as Wilja, Belle de Fonteney and Maris Bard. Some supermarkets print information on bags of potatoes or ask your greengrocer if you need advice. Use a good heavy-based frying pan to cook the frittata, or it will stick.

SERVES 4

450 g (1 lb) waxy potatoes
2 onions
225 g (8 oz) cooked chicken
    or turkey
about 60 ml (4 tbsp) olive oil
1 garlic clove, crushed
    (optional)
handful of baby spinach
    leaves or 1 large
    courgette
salt and pepper
freshly grated nutmeg
5 eggs (size 1)

PREPARATION TIME
10 minutes
COOKING TIME
20 minutes
FREEZING
Not suitable

350 CALS PER SERVING

1. Peel the potatoes and cut into 2.5 cm (1 inch) chunks. Peel the onions, cut in half, then slice. Cut the chicken or turkey into bite-sized pieces.

2. Heat half of the oil in a heavy-based, preferably non-stick, frying pan. Add the potatoes, onions and garlic, if using. Cook over a high heat until the vegetables are tinged with brown. Reduce the heat and continue cooking, stirring occasionally, until the potatoes are cooked. If the mixture starts to stick, add a little more oil.

3. When the potatoes are cooked, add the chicken or turkey and cook over a high heat for 5 minutes or until the chicken is heated through. Meanwhile trim the spinach or slice the courgette. Add to the pan and season with salt, pepper and nutmeg. If using courgette, cook for a further 2 minutes to soften.

4. Add a little extra oil to coat the bottom of the pan if necessary. Heat for 1 minute, then add the beaten eggs. Continue cooking over a high heat for about 2 minutes, to set the egg at the bottom, then lower the heat and cook until the egg at the top is just set.

5. Remove the pan from the heat. Using a palette knife, carefully loosen the frittata around the edge. Invert a plate over the pan, then turn the plate and pan over to release the frittata onto the plate. Slide the frittata back into the pan and cook for 1-2 minutes more. Serve immediately, accompanied by a tomato salad and crusty bread.

VARIATION

Add some chopped salami and a handful of olives at stage 3.

TECHNIQUE

Pour the beaten eggs evenly over the ingredients in the pan.

CHICKEN PANINO

A good medium-sized round loaf with a crisp crust is essential for this recipe. The Italian *paglieno* loaf — available from Italian delicatessens, larger supermarkets and specialist bakers — is ideal, but any similar loaf will do. The quantities for the filling ingredients are deliberately vague, as much will depend on the size of your loaf. Do make sure that you pack the filling in well, so that the whole thing holds together when cut. Serve panino as a summer lunch, or as part of a picnic.

SERVES 8

1 large crusty loaf
FILLING
1 large aubergine
salt and pepper
3 large courgettes
chilli, garlic or virgin olive
   oil, for brushing
6 red or orange peppers
2 beef tomatoes, sliced
about 225 g (8 oz) Parma
   ham or thinly sliced
   smoked ham
about 275 g (10 oz) thinly
   sliced cooked chicken
marinated artichokes
   (optional), sliced
few sun-dried tomatoes
   (optional)
few stoned olives (optional)
generous handful of rocket
   or large basil leaves

PREPARATION TIME
40 minutes, plus overnight
chilling
COOKING TIME
10 minutes
FREEZING
Not suitable

300 CALS PER SERVING

1. To prepare the filling, slice the aubergine, sprinkle generously with salt and layer in a colander. Leave for 30 minutes — the salt will draw out the bitter juices and excess water.

2. Meanwhile, thinly slice the courgettes, brush with a little oil and cook under a hot grill for a couple of minutes each side until just tinged with brown and softened but still retaining some bite. Season with salt and pepper and leave to cool.

3. Drain the aubergine slices and rinse thoroughly in cold running water. Pat dry, then brush with a little oil and cook under a hot grill for a few minutes each side until tender. Season with salt and pepper and leave to cool.

4. Cut the peppers in half. Remove the cores and seeds. Arrange cut-side down in a grill pan and cook until the skins are blackened and charred. Cover with a cloth and leave until cool enough to handle, then peel off the skins. Leave to cool completely.

5. Cut a large slice from the rounded top of the bread and set aside. Carefully remove the soft bread from inside the loaf, leaving a 2.5-4 cm (1-1½ inch) shell within the crust. Brush the inside of the loaf with oil.

6. Layer all the filling ingredients into the bread shell, seasoning well and drizzling with a little oil between each layer. Try to arrange the ingredients so as to give a good contrast of colours between the layers.

7. Replace the bread lid. Wrap the whole loaf in foil. Put it in the refrigerator with a weight on top and leave overnight.

8. The next day, unwrap the loaf and cut into wedges, using a serrated knife, to serve.

NOTE: To make your own garlic or chilli oil simply immerse blanched, skinned garlic cloves or whole chillies in good quality oil for at least 2 weeks.

TECHNIQUE

Carefully scoop out the soft bread from inside the loaf, leaving a 2.5-4 cm (1-1½ inch) shell.

DUCK BREASTS WITH RÖSTI AND APPLE

Rosy pink, tender slices of 'roasted' duck breast are served on golden apple and potato cakes and accompanied by sautéed caramelised apple slices. The method used to cook the duck breasts encourages most of the fat to run out and the skin becomes deliciously crisp and brown. If possible buy the large French *magrets* – one of these easily serves two. Otherwise you will need four standard sized duck breasts.

SERVES 4

2 large duck breast fillets,
    each about 350 g (12 oz),
    or 4 medium duck breast
    fillets (at room
    temperature)
salt and pepper
15 ml (1 tbsp) red wine
    vinegar
60 ml (4 tbsp) apple juice
RÖSTI
2 large old potatoes, about
    450 g (1 lb) total weight
1 dessert apple
2 fresh sage leaves
oil, for frying
TO GARNISH
sautéed apple slices
sage sprigs

PREPARATION TIME
30 minutes
COOKING TIME
20-25 minutes
FREEZING
Not suitable

430 CALS PER SERVING

1. Use a sharp knife to score through the skin side of the duck. Rub with salt and pepper. Leave at room temperature for 15 minutes.

2. To make the rösti, peel and finely grate the potatoes and apple. Squeeze out as much moisture as possible and place in a bowl. Chop the sage and mix with the potato and apple. Season well with salt and pepper.

3. Preheat the oven to 150°C (300°F) Mark 2. Heat 15 ml (1 tbsp) oil in a small heavy-based frying pan. Place 2 large tablespoonfuls of the potato mixture in the pan, pressing down hard with a fish slice. Cook for 2 minutes or until golden brown on the underside; turn over and cook until crisp and golden. Remove and drain on kitchen paper. Repeat with the remaining mixture until you have at least 8 rösti. Keep warm in the oven while cooking the duck.

4. Preheat a heavy flameproof casserole. Add the duck breasts skin-side down and cook over a medium heat for 7-10 minutes depending on size, without moving them; the fat that runs out will prevent them sticking. Turn the breasts over and cook for 3-4 minutes, depending on size.

5. Using a slotted spoon, transfer the duck breasts to a warmed serving dish. Cover and leave in the warm oven for 10 minutes to relax and become evenly 'rosy' inside. Meanwhile pour of all the fat from the pan. Add the wine vinegar and apple juice. Bring to the boil and reduce slightly.

6. To serve, place two rösti on each warmed serving plate. Slice the duck thickly and arrange evenly on top of the rösti. Spoon on the sauce and serve immediately, garnished with sautéed apple slices and sage.

TECHNIQUE

Score through the skin of each duck breast on the diagonal, using a sharp knife. This encourages the fat to run out and the skin to crisp on cooking.

FRENCH ROAST PHEASANT WITH GRAPES AND NUTS

Tender moist pheasants are glazed with clementine juice, crushed grapes and Madeira and roasted to perfection. The liquids in the pan stop the pheasant drying out – especially if you baste during cooking. The pan juices are then used to make a rich and luxurious sauce that's Russian in inspiration.

6 clementines

700 g (1½ lb) white or red
   grapes

40 fresh walnuts in shell, or
   225 g (8 oz) walnut halves

15 ml (1 tbsp) green tea
   (Gunpowder or
   Darjeeling)

200 ml (7 fl oz) Madeira or
   sweet sherry

2 young pheasants, plucked,
   drawn and trussed with
   giblets (see note)

softened butter, for basting

salt and pepper

10 ml (2 tsp) balsamic or
   sherry vinegar

15 ml (1 tbsp) dark soy
   sauce

TO GARNISH

extra grapes

pheasant feathers, if
   available

PREPARATION TIME
45 minutes
COOKING TIME
45 minutes
FREEZING
Not suitable

635 CALS PER SERVING

1. Preheat the oven to 200°C (400°F) Mark 6. Grate the rind from 2 clementines and squeeze the juice from all six; place in a bowl. Reserve the ungrated squeezed halves. Whizz the grapes roughly in a food processor and pour into the clementine juice. Shell the fresh walnuts. Pour 300 ml (½ pint) boiling water over the green tea, leave to steep for 5 minutes, then strain and reserve.

2. Pour half the clementine and grape juice into a roasting tin, adding the Madeira and any giblets (except the liver). Place the reserved clementine halves inside the pheasant cavities. Smear the pheasants with butter and season with salt and pepper.

3. Place the birds in the roasting tin on one side, leg uppermost. Roast in the oven for 15 minutes. Turn the birds over on the other side, baste with the pan juices and roast for another 15 minutes. Finally sit the birds upright, baste well and roast for a final 15 minutes or until done. Test by pushing a skewer into the meatiest part of the thigh; the juices should run clear. Transfer the pheasants to a warmed serving platter and keep warm.

4. Pour the reserved clementine and grape juice into the roasting tin. Stir in the tea, balsamic vinegar and soy sauce.

Place over the heat and bring to the boil, scraping up any sediment from the bottom of the pan. Boil for 1-2 minutes, then strain into a saucepan, pressing the juice through the sieve with the back of a wooden spoon. Stir in the walnuts, bring to the boil and reduce to 450 ml (¾ pint). Taste and season well. The sauce should be slightly syrupy; if not, reduce a little more. Spoon the walnuts around the pheasant and pour the sauce into a warmed sauceboat.

5. Dress the pheasant with grapes and cleaned pheasant feathers, if available. Serve with the sauce.

NOTE: If your butcher is preparing the birds, ask him to keep the feathers and giblets. Or use chicken or turkey giblets.

TECHNIQUE

Baste the pheasants with the pan juices as you turn them, to keep them moist.

ROAST STUFFED TURKEY

This roasting method ensures that the bird remains moist and the skin beautifully brown and crisp. Try to use a fresh rather than a thoroughly defrosted frozen turkey – the flavour is much better, and less water emerges during cooking. Free-range bronze turkeys are particularly flavoursome. Stuff the turkey just before roasting.

SERVES 8 (plus leftovers)

4.5-5.5 kg (10-12 lb) turkey
175-225 g (6-8 oz) butter, softened
salt and pepper

LEEK STUFFING

450 g (1 lb) fresh spinach, stalks removed, or 225 g (8 oz) frozen chopped spinach, thawed
450 g (1 lb) leeks
50 g (2 oz) butter
1 garlic clove, crushed
225 g (8 oz) cooked multigrain rice (eg Countrywild)
25 g (1 oz) pine nuts, toasted
45 ml (3 tbsp) chopped mixed fresh herbs
freshly grated nutmeg
1 egg

SAUSAGE STUFFING

350 g (12 oz) spicy Italian pork sausages, skinned
2 onions, peeled
125 g (4 oz) butter
225 g (8 oz) oatmeal
5 ml (1 tsp) chopped thyme

PREPARATION TIME
45 minutes
COOKING TIME
3½-5 hours, plus resting
FREEZING
Suitable: Stuffings only

645 CALS PER SERVING

1. Remove giblets from turkey, discard liver and use the rest to make stock for gravy. Place in a saucepan with flavouring ingredients (1 halved onion, 1 chopped carrot, few parsley sprigs, 1 bay leaf and a few black peppercorns). Cover with at least 600 ml (1 pint) water, bring to the boil, then simmer for 1 hour. Strain.

2. To prepare the stuffings, wash the fresh spinach and cook in a covered pan, with just the water that still clings to the leaves, until just wilted. Drain, squeeze out excess moisture and chop roughly. If using frozen spinach, just squeeze dry. Trim and chop the leeks. Melt the butter in a frying pan, add the leeks and garlic and cook gently until soft. Stir in the spinach, rice, nuts and herbs. Season liberally with nutmeg, salt and pepper. Bind with the egg. Allow to cool.

3. To make the sausage stuffing, break up the sausages in a bowl. Chop the onions and sauté in the butter until soft and golden, then mix in the oatmeal and thyme. Add to the sausagemeat and mix thoroughly. Season well and let cool.

4. Preheat the oven to 180°C (350°F) Mark 4. Wash the bird thoroughly inside and out; dry with kitchen paper. Use one stuffing to stuff the neck flap (cook the other in a separate dish). Spread butter over turkey and season well. Weigh bird and calculate cooking time: allow 20 minutes per 450 g (1 lb), plus 20 minutes extra.

5. Line a large roasting tin with foil, bringing the edges over the rim. Place the turkey in the centre, covering it loosely with another sheet of foil, tucking the edges inside the rim. Roast for the calculated cooking time, removing the covering foil for the last 30 minutes to brown. Test the deepest part of each thigh with a skewer to check that the juices run clear and the bird is cooked through. Transfer to a platter, cover and rest in a warm place for 15 minutes.

6. Skim off the fat from the roasting juices, reserving 45 ml (3 tbsp). Add the juices to the stock. Heat the reserved fat in a saucepan and stir in 15 ml (1 tbsp) flour. Whisk in the stock and bring to the boil. Simmer for 5 minutes, season and strain into a warm sauceboat.

7. Serve the turkey with the gravy and traditional accompaniments.

TECHNIQUE

Stuff the neck of the bird and secure with a skewer or sew up with cotton string.

GUINEA FOWL WITH ROCKET SAUCE AND SPRING VEGETABLES

Rocket or arugula has an unmistakable pungent, peppery flavour and vivid green colour. Buying the quantity needed for this sauce from a supermarket can be expensive as it tends to be sold in small bags at a premium. However, local Greek and Turkish food stores often sell generous bunches of rocket at a fraction of the price.

SERVES 6

75 g (3 oz) butter
30 ml (2 tbsp) olive oil
2 guinea fowl
450 g (1 lb) very small new
　potatoes, scrubbed clean
2 garlic cloves, peeled
300 ml (½ pint) dry white
　wine
8 baby leeks, total weight
　about 125 g (4 oz)
225 g (8 oz) small new
　carrots
125 g (4 oz) broad beans,
　skinned
125 g (4 oz) fresh peas
50 g (2 oz) rocket leaves
150 ml (¼ pint) double
　cream
salt and pepper
chervil, to garnish

PREPARATION TIME
20 minutes
COOKING TIME
1¼-1½ hours
FREEZING
Not suitable

515 CALS PER SERVING

1. Preheat the oven to 200°C (400°F) Mark 6. Heat 50 g (2 oz) of the butter with the oil in a large frying pan and cook the guinea fowl, one at a time, until thoroughly browned on all sides. Arrange the potatoes in the base of a casserole dish and add the garlic. Put the guinea fowl on top. Pour in the wine and 450 ml (¾ pint) water.

2. Cover with a tight-fitting lid and cook in the oven for 45 minutes. Add the leeks, carrots, broad beans and peas. Re-cover the casserole and cook for a further 30-45 minutes or until the guinea fowl are cooked right through and the vegetables are tender.

3. Remove the guinea fowl and vegetables from the casserole and keep warm. Skim off any excess fat from the cooking liquid, then pour into a measuring jug; you should have about 600 ml (1 pint). Make it up to this quantity with wine, stock or water if you haven't got enough.

4. Put the rocket in a food processor with the cooking liquid and cooked garlic cloves and process until smooth. Return the rocket purée to the casserole.

5. Reheat the rocket purée, add the cream and season with salt and pepper to taste. Bring to the boil, then gradually whisk in the remaining butter a little at a time to make a thin, shiny sauce.

6. Carve the guinea fowl and serve each portion with a few vegetables and a little of the sauce poured over.

VARIATIONS

Replace the rocket with sorrel, but halve the quantity. If both sorrel and rocket are unavailable, try making the sauce with watercress. Small chickens could of course, be used instead of guinea fowl.

TECHNIQUE

Gradually whisk the remaining butter into the rocket sauce.

Venison Casserole with Red Wine and Spices

Venison has recently regained popularity, and exceptionally lean steaks are widely stocked in supermarkets throughout the winter. These are ideal for marinating in wine with spices, and then casseroling to a moist tenderness. Rather rich in flavour, venison is best lightened with plenty of vegetables. Creamed potatoes and shredded, sautéed cabbage are suitable accompaniments.

SERVES 6-8

900 g (2 lb) lean venison

1 large onion

2 carrots

3 garlic cloves, peeled

2 bay leaves

4-6 whole cloves

15 ml (1 tbsp) allspice

60 ml (4 tbsp) brandy

300 ml (½ pint) red wine

225 g (8 oz) baby onions

½ small celeriac

125 g (4 oz) rindless streaky bacon

30 ml (2 tbsp) plain flour

salt and pepper

30 ml (2 tbsp) oil

300 ml (½ pint) beef stock

1 cinnamon stick, halved

225 g (8 oz) wild mushrooms

15 ml (1 tbsp) wine vinegar

15 ml (1 tbsp) redcurrant jelly

TO GARNISH

bay leaves

PREPARATION TIME
45 minutes, plus 2-3 days marinating
COOKING TIME
About 2 hours
FREEZING Suitable

420-315 CALS PER SERVING

1. Cut the venison into chunks and place in a large bowl. Peel and quarter the onion. Peel and roughly chop the carrots. Add the vegetables to the bowl with the garlic, bay leaves, cloves, allspice, brandy and wine. Cover and leave to marinate in the refrigerator for 2-3 days, turning daily.

2. Preheat the oven to 160°C (325°F) Mark 3. Peel the baby onions and leave whole. Peel the celeriac and cut into chunks. Dice the bacon. Thoroughly drain the venison and pat dry on kitchen paper, reserving the marinade. Season the flour with salt and pepper and use to coat the meat.

3. Heat the oil in a flameproof casserole. Add the venison and sear on all sides. Remove with a slotted spoon. Add the onions and bacon to the casserole and fry for 3 minutes. Return the venison to the casserole with the celeriac. Strain the marinade juices over the meat, then add the stock and cinnamon stick.

4. Bring just to the boil, reduce the heat and cover with a tight-fitting lid. Cook in the oven for 1 hour. Add the mushrooms, wine vinegar and redcurrant jelly to the casserole and return to the oven for a further 1 hour.

5. Ladle the stew onto warmed serving plates and garnish with bay leaves.

NOTE: This is a good stew for cooking a day in advance and reheating, as it helps to further tenderise the meat.

VARIATION

If wild mushrooms are unobtainable use either chestnut mushrooms or flat mushrooms instead.

TECHNIQUE

Marinate the venison chunks in the brandy and wine, with the vegetables, herbs and spices.

VEGETARIAN MAIN COURSES

MUSHROOM AND PARMESAN RISOTTO

This is a wonderfully warming meal for a cold night. If possible, use the Italian risotto rice – Arborio – which has the capacity to absorb plenty of liquid during cooking without turning mushy. Make sure you pare the lemon rind in one large piece, so it's easy to remove.

SERVES 4

1 medium onion

1 lemon

175 g (6 oz) flat mushrooms

225 g (8 oz) broccoli florets

175 g (6 oz) French beans

salt and pepper

30 ml (2 tbsp) olive oil

350 g (12 oz) Arborio
(risotto) or long-grain
white rice (see note)

pinch of saffron threads
(optional)

60 ml (4 tbsp) dry white
wine

750 ml (1¼ pints) vegetable
stock

TO SERVE

finely pared Parmesan
cheese

PREPARATION TIME
15 minutes
COOKING TIME
20 minutes
FREEZING
Not suitable

420 CALS PER SERVING

1. Peel and finely chop the onion. Finely pare the rind from the lemon, using a vegetable peeler, then squeeze the juice. Wipe the mushrooms clean with a damp cloth, then slice.

2. Break the broccoli into small florets. Top and tail the French beans and cut in half lengthways. Blanch the broccoli and beans together in boiling salted water for 3-4 minutes. Drain and refresh under cold running water.

3. Heat the oil in a heavy-based saucepan or flameproof casserole, and cook the onion gently for about 2-3 minutes until beginning to soften. Stir in the rice and saffron, if using. Season well and pour in the wine. Add the pared lemon rind, 30 ml (2 tbsp) lemon juice and the stock. Bring to the boil, stirring.

4. Cover and simmer the risotto for 5 minutes. Stir in the mushrooms, broccoli and French beans. Re-cover and simmer for a further 5 minutes, or until the rice is tender and most of the liquid is absorbed.

5. Discard the lemon rind and transfer the risotto to warmed serving plates. Top with slivers of Parmesan cheese and serve at once.

NOTE: If you use Arborio rice you may need to add a little more stock and cook the risotto for 1-2 minutes longer.

VARIATION

Replace the broccoli and French beans with 400 g (14 oz) fine asparagus, trimmed and halved.

TECHNIQUE

After 5 minutes, gently stir in the mushrooms, broccoli and French beans.

VEGETABLE COUSCOUS

For this quick tasty version of the famous Moroccan dish, couscous grains are steamed over a nourishing spicy vegetable stew. Use quick-cook couscous – which needs to be moistened before cooking but doesn't require lengthy soaking. Vary the vegetables as you like.

SERVES 4

225 g (8 oz) quick-cook
   couscous
225 g (8 oz) aubergine
175 g (6 oz) courgettes
175 g (6 oz) carrots, peeled
1 large onion, peeled
15 ml (1 tbsp) oil
2 garlic cloves, crushed
10 ml (2 tsp) ground cumin
2.5 ml (½ tsp) mild chilli
   seasoning
2.5 ml (½ tsp) ground ginger
60 ml (4 tbsp) tomato purée
1 bay leaf
175 g (6 oz) canned chick
   peas drained, or frozen
   broad beans
750 ml (1¼ pints) vegetable
   stock
salt and pepper
TO GARNISH
chopped parsley
paprika (optional)

PREPARATION TIME
15 minutes
COOKING TIME
15 minutes
FREEZING
Not suitable

260 CALS PER SERVING

1. Moisten the couscous according to the packet instructions. Cut the aubergine and courgettes into chunks. Chop the carrots. Finely chop the onion. Heat the oil in a saucepan (over which a steamer, metal sieve or colander will fit). Add the onion, carrots, garlic and spices and cook gently for 1 minute, stirring occasionally.

2. Add the tomato purée, bay leaf, aubergine, courgettes and chick peas or broad beans. Stir in the stock. Cover and bring to the boil, then uncover and boil rapidly for 8 minutes.

3. Meanwhile, fork the couscous to break up any lumps and spread in a steamer, metal sieve or colander lined with a double thickness of muslin.

4. Place the couscous container over the cooking vegetables. Cover and cook for 5 minutes or until the vegetables are tender, the sauce is well reduced and the couscous is piping hot. Check the seasoning.

5. Spoon the couscous onto a warmed serving dish and fork through. Pile the vegetables and juices on top. Garnish with plenty of chopped parsley and sprinkle with paprika to serve if desired.

VARIATION

Replace the tomato purée with 350 g (12 oz) fresh tomatoes, skinned and quartered. Include other vegetables, such as cauliflower florets, sliced leeks and diced red pepper.

TECHNIQUE

Moisten the couscous grains with warm water, according to packet instructions.

ROOT VEGETABLE AND LENTIL CASSEROLE

This spicy combination of mixed root vegetables and assorted lentils makes an ideal winter supper dish. Serve it with plenty of warm crusty bread and a side salad or seasonal green vegetable, such as broccoli or spinach.

SERVES 6

5 ml (1 tsp) cumin seeds
15 ml (1 tbsp) coriander seeds
5 ml (1 tsp) mustard seeds
25 g (1 oz) fresh root ginger
3 onions
450 g (1 lb) carrots
350 g (12 oz) leeks
350 g (12 oz) mooli (white radish)
450 g (1 lb) button mushrooms
45 ml (3 tbsp) olive oil
2 garlic cloves, crushed
1.25 ml (¼ tsp) turmeric
175 g (6 oz) split red lentils
50 g (2 oz) brown or green lentils
salt and pepper
30 ml (2 tbsp) chopped coriander leaves (optional)
TO GARNISH
parsley sprigs

PREPARATION TIME
20 minutes
COOKING TIME
About 1 hour
FREEZING
Not suitable

260 CALS PER SERVING

1. Preheat the oven to 180°C (350°F) Mark 4. Crush the cumin, coriander and mustard seeds in a mortar with a pestle (or in a strong bowl with the end of a rolling pin). Peel and grate or finely chop the ginger.

2. Peel and slice the onions and carrots. Clean the leeks thoroughly, then cut into slices. Peel and roughly chop the mooli; halve the mushrooms if large.

3. Heat the oil in a large flameproof casserole. Add the onions, carrots, leeks and mooli, and fry for 2-3 minutes, stirring constantly. Add the mushrooms, garlic, ginger, turmeric and crushed spices, and fry for a further 2-3 minutes, stirring.

4. Rinse the lentils in a colander under cold running water, then drain. Stir the lentils into the casserole with 750 ml (1¼ pints) boiling water. Season with salt and pepper and return to the boil. Cover and cook in the oven for about 45 minutes or until the vegetables and lentils are tender. Stir in the coriander if using, and adjust the seasoning before serving, garnished with parsley.

VARIATION

Replace the mooli (white radish) with parsnips or young turnips.

TECHNIQUE

Use a pestle and mortar to crush the cumin, coriander and mustard seeds.

MIXED ONION CASSEROLE WITH JUNIPER

This delicious casserole is baked slowly in the oven until the onions are partly caramelised and acquire a sweet, mellow flavour. Serve as a tasty accompaniment to a savoury pie or bake. Alternatively, serve with a jacket potato and green beans as a substantial supper dish in its own right.

SERVES 4

6 medium onions
1 bunch of spring onions
6-8 shallots
5 garlic cloves
8 juniper berries
50 g (2 oz) butter
600 ml (1 pint) vegetable
  stock (approximately)
coarse sea salt and pepper
6 slices French bread, 1 cm
  (½ inch) thick
125 g (4 oz) coarsely grated
  vegetarian mature
  Cheddar cheese
TO GARNISH
15 ml (1 tbsp) snipped
  chives

PREPARATION TIME
15 minutes
COOKING TIME
1½ hours
FREEZING
Not suitable

460 CALS PER SERVING

1. Preheat the oven to 180°C (350°F) Mark 4.

2. Peel four of the onions, taking care to trim the minimum from the tops and bases. Cut each one crosswise into quarters, leaving the root end intact to ensure the onions do not fall apart during cooking.

3. Peel, halve and slice the remaining ordinary onions. Trim the spring onions, then slice both the white and green parts. Peel the shallots, leaving them whole. Peel the garlic and slice finely. Crush the juniper berries, using a pestle and mortar.

4. Melt the butter in a saucepan, add the sliced ordinary onions, garlic and juniper berries and fry gently until golden. Add 300 ml (½ pint) of the vegetable stock and bring to the boil. Season with salt and pepper.

5. Stand the quarter-cut onions upright in a 1.2 litre (2 pint) casserole and add the shallots and sliced spring onions. Spoon the sautéed onion and garlic mixture on top. Cook, uncovered, in the oven for 1½ hours. After halfway through cooking check from time to time that the liquid hasn't dried out and top up with more stock as necessary. At the end of the cooking time the liquid should be thick and syrupy.

6. About 15 minutes from the end of the cooking time, butter the slices of French bread and arrange butter-side up on top of the onion mixture. Sprinkle with the grated cheese and return to the oven to crisp and brown. (If by the end of the cooking time the cheese has not browned, flash the dish under a hot grill for 1-2 minutes.) Sprinkle with the snipped chives and serve immediately, directly from the casserole.

NOTE: The temperature isn't crucial for this dish, so if you are cooking a main course at a higher temperature, simply position the casserole lower in the oven. Check that it doesn't dry out and cover with a lid if necessary.

TECHNIQUE

Quarter four of the onions crosswise through the middle, without cutting right through, so they remain intact during cooking.

SUMMER VEGETABLE RISOTTO

For this quick and easy vegetarian risotto, use whatever green vegetables are fresh and in season. Just make sure they are blanched until barely tender before stirring into the rice mixture.

SERVES 4

700 g (1½ lb) mixed French beans, broad beans, mangetouts, peas and asparagus
12 pitted black olives
350 g (12 oz) tomatoes
4 sun-dried tomatoes in oil, drained (optional)
225 g (8 oz) mixed wild and long-grain rice
350 ml (12 fl oz) vegetable stock
15 ml (1 tbsp) oil (from sun-dried tomatoes if using)
1 garlic clove, crushed
salt and pepper

PREPARATION TIME
5 minutes
COOKING TIME
About 25 minutes
FREEZING
Not suitable

350-375 CALS PER SERVING

1. Trim the green vegetables and blanch in boiling water until barely tender. Drain and refresh under cold running water; drain well. Halve the olives. Dice the fresh and sun-dried tomatoes if using.

2. Put the rice and stock in a saucepan. Bring to the boil, lower the heat and simmer, covered, for about 20 minutes or until all the liquid has been absorbed and the rice is tender.

3. Heat the oil in a large non-stick frying pan or wok. Add the garlic and cook, stirring, for 1-2 minutes.

4. Add the tomatoes and rice. Cook, stirring, over a gentle heat for 3-4 minutes. Stir in the blanched vegetables and olives. Increase the heat and cook, stirring, for 1 minute until piping hot. Season with salt and pepper to taste and serve immediately.

NOTE: Packets of mixed wild and long-grain rice are readily available from supermarkets. Refer to the packet instructions for the recommended cooking time. To test if rice is cooked, remove a few grains from the pan and press between finger and thumb. If it squashes easily and there is no hard core the rice is ready.

TECHNIQUE

Stir-fry the rice with the diced fresh and sun-dried tomatoes over a low heat for 3-4 minutes.

ASPARAGUS, BROAD BEAN AND PARMESAN FRITTATA

An Italian omelette which is cooked slowly over a low heat, the filling stirred into the eggs or scattered over the top; sometimes it is finished off under the grill. A frittata is served perfectly set, never folded. This recipe will serve 4 as a snack, or 2 persons as a meal.

SERVES 2-4

175 g (6 oz) small new
    potatoes
225 g (8 oz) asparagus
225 g (8 oz) frozen broad
    beans, thawed
6 eggs
salt and pepper
50 g (2 oz) freshly grated
    Parmesan cheese
45 ml (3 tbsp) chopped
    mixed fresh herbs, such as
    parsley, oregano and
    thyme
50 g (2 oz) butter

PREPARATION TIME
35 minutes
COOKING TIME
15-20 minutes
FREEZING
Not suitable

720-360 CALS PER SERVING

1. Cook the potatoes in boiling salted water for 15-20 minutes until tender. Allow to cool, then slice thickly.

2. Meanwhile, trim the asparagus, removing any woody parts of the stems. Steam for 12 minutes until tender, then plunge into cold water to set the colour and cool completely.

3. Slip the broad beans out of their waxy skins. Drain the asparagus, pat dry, then cut into short lengths. Mix with the broad beans.

4. Put the eggs in a bowl with a good pinch of salt, plenty of pepper and half of the Parmesan cheese. Beat thoroughly until evenly blended, then stir in the asparagus, broad beans and chopped herbs.

5. Melt 40 g (1½ oz) butter in a 25 cm (10 inch) non-stick heavy-based frying pan. When foaming, pour in the egg mixture. Turn down the heat to as low as possible. Cook for about 15 minutes, until the frittata is set and the top is still a little runny.

6. Preheat the grill. Scatter the cooked sliced potato over the frittata and sprinkle with the remaining Parmesan cheese. Dot with the rest of the butter.

7. Place under the hot grill to lightly brown the cheese and just set the top; don't allow it to brown too much or it will dry out. Slide the frittata onto a warmed dish and cut into wedges to serve.

VARIATION

Lay 4 slices of prosciutto over the top of the lightly set frittata and grill for 2-3 minutes until crisp.

TECHNIQUE

Once thawed, frozen broad beans can be removed easily from their skins. Pinch one end of the skin to squeeze out the bean.

SUMMER VEGETABLE FLAN

Young, tender baby vegetables are set in a creamy cheese filling well flavoured with herbs, and baked in a crisp walnut pastry crust. You can use any selection of summer vegetables – just be sure to blanch or sauté them first and keep the total amount to about 700 g (1½ lb).

SERVES 6

WALNUT PASTRY
50 g (2 oz) walnut pieces
175 g (6 oz) plain flour
pinch of salt
125 g (4 oz) vegetable
  margarine or butter
FILLING
1 garlic clove
175 g (6 oz) courgettes
25 g (1 oz) vegetable
  margarine or butter
175 g (6 oz) broccoli florets
  or baby carrots
175 g (6 oz) thin asparagus
50 g (2 oz) peas
125 g (4 oz) tomatoes
50 g (2 oz) sun-dried
  tomatoes in oil, drained
125 g (4 oz) full-fat soft
  cheese
150 ml (¼ pint) single cream
2 whole eggs, plus 1 egg yolk
30 ml (2 tbsp) chopped fresh
  mixed herbs
salt and pepper
40 g (1½ oz) vegetarian
  mature Cheddar cheese

PREPARATION TIME
40 minutes
COOKING TIME
About 1 hour
FREEZING
Suitable: Baked pastry case only

520 CALS PER SERVING

1. To prepare the nut pastry, spread the walnut pieces on a baking sheet and grill until golden, turning frequently. Allow to cool, then grind to a powder in a blender or food processor.

2. Sift the flour and salt into a bowl and stir in the ground walnuts. Rub in the margarine or butter until the mixture resembles fine breadcrumbs. Using a round-bladed knife, mix in sufficient water to bind the pastry; you will need about 45 ml (3 tbsp). Wrap the pastry in greaseproof paper or cling film and chill in the refrigerator for 30 minutes.

3. Roll out the pastry on a lightly floured surface and use to line a 3 cm (1¼ inch) deep, 23 cm (9 inch) loose-based, fluted flan tin. Prick the base of the flan with a fork and chill for 30 minutes.

4. Preheat the oven to 200°C (400°F) Mark 6. Line the flan case with grease-proof paper and baking beans and bake blind in the oven for 20 minutes or until set, removing the paper and beans for the last 5 minutes. Lower the oven temperature to 180°C (350°F) Mark 4.

5. Meanwhile, prepare the filling. Peel and thinly slice the garlic. Thinly slice the courgettes. Heat the margarine or butter in a pan and sauté the courgettes with the garlic until golden.

6. Peel the carrots (if using) and trim

the broccoli and asparagus. Blanch the carrots, asparagus and peas in boiling salted water for 1-2 minutes. Drain thoroughly. Cut the fresh and sun-dried tomatoes into quarters.

7. Put the soft cheese in a bowl and gradually beat in the cream. Add the eggs, egg yolk, herbs and seasoning, mixing well.

8. Pile all the vegetables into the flan case and pour the cream mixture around them; the vegetables should protrude above the sauce. Grate the cheese over the top. Bake in the oven for 35-40 minutes or until just set. Allow to stand for about 15 minutes before serving warm.

TECHNIQUE

Line the pastry case with greaseproof paper and baking beans to bake blind.

BAKED VEGETABLES WITH A SPICY SAUCE

A colourful selection of vegetables are marinated in olive oil flavoured with rosemary, then baked until crisp and browned. Served with a spicy sauce, and some crusty bread for mopping up the juices, they make a tasty main course. Vary the vegetables according to whatever is available.

SERVES 4-6

1 red pepper
1 yellow or orange pepper
6 shallots
1 aubergine
2-3 courgettes
1 fennel bulb
175 g (6 oz) parsnips
125 g (4 oz) baby corn cobs
6-8 cherry tomatoes
225 g (8 oz) mushrooms
   (large closed cup)
2-3 rosemary sprigs
120 ml (4 fl oz) extra-virgin
   olive oil
coarse sea salt and pepper

SPICY SAUCE:
1 small onion
1 garlic clove
1 green chilli
15 ml (1 tbsp) sunflower oil
10 ml (2 tsp) capers
10 ml (2 tsp) soft brown sugar
juice of ½ lemon
175 g (6 oz) passata

PREPARATION TIME
30 minutes, plus standing
COOKING TIME
40 minutes
FREEZING
Not suitable

425-285 CALS PER SERVING

1. First prepare the vegetables. Halve the peppers, then remove the core and seeds. Peel the shallots and leave whole. Cut the aubergine into thin slices. Thickly slice the courgettes on the diagonal. Quarter the fennel bulb lengthwise. Halve or quarter the parsnips. Halve the baby corn lengthwise. Cut a shallow cross on the base of each tomato, but leave them whole. Wipe the mushrooms with a damp cloth and leave whole.

2. Strip the leaves from one of the rosemary sprigs and chop finely to release their fragrance. Pour the olive oil into a large bowl and add the chopped rosemary and whole sprigs with salt and pepper. Add the vegetables and turn carefully with a spoon to coat evenly with the oil. Leave to infuse for 1-2 hours, or longer if time.

3. Preheat the oven to 220°C (425°F) Mark 7.

4. Put all of the vegetables, except the cherry tomatoes, into a large shallow baking tin with the rosemary sprigs and baste with the oil. Cook, turning and basting from time to time, for about 40 minutes until the vegetables are evenly browned and cooked through. Add the cherry tomatoes 10 minutes from the end of the cooking time.

5. To make the sauce, peel and finely slice the onion and garlic. Halve the chilli, remove the seeds and slice finely. Heat the oil in a small pan, add the onion, garlic and chilli and fry gently until tender.

6. Meanwhile put the capers, sugar, lemon juice and passata in a blender or food processor and work until smooth. Season with salt and pepper and add to the chilli mixture. Cover and cook for 5-10 minutes, stirring occasionally, to make a thick sauce. If a thinner sauce is preferred, dilute with a little water. Pour the sauce into a warm serving jug.

7. Transfer the baked vegetables to an oval serving platter and serve at once, accompanied by the sauce.

TECHNIQUE

Toss the vegetables in the rosemary oil and allow to marinate before baking.

LENTIL, BEAN AND VEGETABLE GRATIN

A delicious mixture using the best pulses – Puy lentils and flageolet beans. Both have a good flavour and hold their shape well when cooked. Here Puy lentils are simmered in stock with red wine and herbs, then combined with canned flageolets. The addition of sweet potato makes a nutritious and tasty dish. A crunchy breadcrumb topping – flavoured with goat's cheese, herbs and tomatoes – is the perfect complement.

SERVES 4

1 onion
1 carrot
2 celery stalks
225 g (8 oz) sweet potato
15 ml (1 tbsp) sunflower oil
1 garlic clove, crushed
10 ml (2 tsp) sun-dried
 tomato paste or tomato
 purée
300 ml (½ pint) red wine
125 g (4 oz) Puy lentils
450 ml (¾ pint) vegetable
 stock
1 bay leaf
30 ml (2 tbsp) chopped fresh
 parsley
½ x 300 g (10 oz) can
 flageolet beans, drained
 and rinsed
salt and pepper
TOPPING
125 g (4 oz) goat's cheese
50 g (2 oz) wholemeal
 breadcrumbs
15 ml (1 tbsp) chopped fresh
 parsley
15 ml (1 tbsp) chopped fresh
 thyme
450 g (1 lb) plum tomatoes
 (or other flavourful
 tomatoes)

PREPARATION TIME 15 minutes
COOKING TIME 1-1¼ hours
FREEZING Suitable

410 CALS PER SERVING

1. Peel and finely chop the onion and carrot. Trim and finely chop the celery. Peel the sweet potato and cut into 2.5 cm (1 inch) chunks.

2. Heat the oil in a large pan, add the prepared vegetables and garlic and sauté for a few minutes to soften. Stir in the sun-dried tomato paste or tomato purée and wine. Bring to the boil and cook for 1 minute.

3. Wash the lentils under cold running water. Drain and add to the pan with the stock, bay leaf and parsley. Bring to the boil and simmer for 45 minutes to 1 hour or until the lentils are soft. Add the canned beans and heat through. Taste and adjust the seasoning. Discard the bay leaf.

4. Meanwhile, prepare the topping. Crumble the cheese and stir into the breadcrumbs with the parsley and thyme. Roughly chop the tomatoes.

5. Preheat the grill to medium. Spoon the bean and lentil mixture into an oven-

proof gratin dish. Scatter the chopped tomatoes over the beans, then top with the breadcrumb mixture. Place under the grill for about 10 minutes, until the topping is just crisp. Serve with a watercress and spinach salad and crusty bread.

NOTE: Use the remaining flageolet beans as a vegetable accompaniment to a light main course: toss in a little balsamic vinegar and sprinkle with chopped parsley; or use in a mixed bean salad.

TECHNIQUE

To make the topping, mix the bread-crumbs with the goat's cheese and herbs.

CHEESE SAUSAGE ON APPLE AND WATERCRESS SALAD

Based on a traditional Welsh recipe, these vegetarian sausages fry to a deep golden crust. They are served on a bed of watercress and apple salad, dressed with a walnut vinaigrette. Serve two each as a supper dish: alternatively a single sausage makes a tasty starter.

SERVES 4

125 g (4 oz) Caerphilly
   cheese
200 g (7 oz) fresh white
   breadcrumbs
2.5 ml (½ tsp) dried thyme
30 ml (2 tbsp) finely
   chopped fresh parsley
2 spring onions
salt and pepper
freshly grated nutmeg
2 eggs
a little milk, if necessary
45 ml (3 tbsp) plain white
   flour
10 ml (2 tsp) powdered
   mustard
oil for shallow-frying
SALAD
30 g (¾ oz) walnut halves
10 ml (2 tsp) sherry vinegar
45 ml (3 tbsp) olive oil
15 ml (1 tbsp) walnut oil
1 small red onion
50 g (2 oz) watercress
2 green eating apples

PREPARATION TIME
15 minutes
COOKING TIME
10 minutes
FREEZING
Suitable: Uncooked mixture only

705 CALS PER SERVING

1. Grate the cheese into a bowl and mix with the breadcrumbs, thyme and parsley. Trim and finely chop the spring onions and add to the mixture. Season with a little salt, and generously with pepper and nutmeg. Mix thoroughly.

2. Separate one egg, dropping the white into a shallow dish. In another bowl, beat the whole egg and egg yolk lightly together, then add to the crumb mixture and mix thoroughly. If necessary, moisten with a little milk; the mixture must be soft enough to gather into balls.

3. Prepare the salad dressing. Chop half the walnuts very finely by hand or in a food processor. Beat in the vinegar, olive and walnut oils, and seasoning.

4. Scoop the sausage mixture into 8 balls and shape each one with your hands into a cylindrical sausage. Beat the reserved egg white lightly until frothy. Mix the flour and mustard powder on a plate.

5. Heat the oil for shallow-frying in a frying pan. Brush the sausages lightly all over with egg white then, using 2 forks, roll them in the flour and mustard. Fry the sausages slowly enough to allow them to cook right through, turning frequently to ensure they brown evenly. Drain on kitchen paper.

6. Meanwhile, peel and thinly slice the onion. Trim the watercress. Quarter, core and slice the apples. Toss these ingredients together and arrange on serving plates. Drizzle with the walnut vinaigrette and sprinkle with the remaining walnuts. Serve the cheese sausages piping hot, with the salad.

NOTE: Soft white breadcrumbs are best made in a food processor from day-old bread. The dressing for the salad can be made entirely in a blender or food processor.

VARIATION

Use another sharp white cheese or a strong Cheddar in place of Caerphilly.

TECHNIQUE

Brush the sausages with egg white, then turn each one in the flour and mustard mixture to coat evenly.

CARROT AND CORIANDER ROULADE

This savoury carrot cake makes an interesting and tasty dish. The carrot roulade is rolled around a tasty filling of cream cheese flavoured with garlic, herbs and chopped coriander leaves. Serve it in slices with a mixed leaf and herb salad, and toasted granary or walnut bread.

SERVES 4-6

50 g (2 oz) butter or
    vegetable margarine
450 g (1 lb) carrots, grated
4 eggs (size 2), separated
15 ml (1 tbsp) chopped
    coriander leaves
coarse sea salt and pepper
FILLING
175 g (6 oz) soft cheese
    flavoured with garlic and
    herbs
15 ml (1 tbsp) chopped
    coriander leaves
30-45 ml (2-3 tbsp) crème
    fraîche
TO SERVE
assorted salad leaves
herb sprigs, such as dill and
    chervil or parsley

PREPARATION TIME
30 minutes
COOKING TIME
10-15 minutes
FREEZING
Not suitable

340-230 CALS PER SERVING

1. Preheat the oven to 200°C (400°F) Mark 6. Line a 30 x 20 cm (12 x 8 inch) Swiss roll tin with non-stick baking parchment. Coarsely grate the carrots, using a grating disc in a food processor, or by hand.

2. Melt the butter or margarine in a pan, add the carrots and cook gently, stirring frequently, for 5 minutes or until slightly coloured. Transfer to a bowl, allow to cool slightly, then add the egg yolks and coriander and beat well. Season with salt and pepper.

3. Whisk the egg whites in a bowl until firm peaks form, then stir 30 ml (2 tbsp) into the carrot mixture to lighten it. Carefully fold in the rest of the egg whites.

4. Spread the mixture evenly in the prepared tin and bake in the oven for 10-15 minutes until risen and firm to the touch. Turn out onto a sheet of non-stick baking parchment, cover with a clean, damp cloth and allow to cool.

5. Meanwhile, prepare the filling. Put the soft cheese in a bowl. Using a fork, mix in the chopped coriander and enough crème fraîche to yield a smooth, spreading consistency. Taste and adjust the seasoning if necessary.

6. Remove the cloth from the roulade. Spread evenly with the filling, leaving a 1 cm (½ inch) border all round. Carefully roll up from a short side, using the paper to help.

7. To serve, cut the roulade into slices and arrange on individual plates with the salad leaves and herbs.

VARIATION

Bake the carrot mixture in two 18 cm (7 inch) sandwich tins. Turn out and cool on a wire rack, then sandwich together with the filling.

TECHNIQUE

Lightly fold the whisked egg whites into the roulade mixture, using a large metal spoon.

TOMATO AND GARLIC PIZZA

This thin, crispy pizza has a delicious topping of flavourful fresh tomatoes, black olives, garlic cloves and feta cheese. On baking the garlic loses its pungency and becomes deliciously soft with a mild, nutty flavour.

SERVES 2

1 medium garlic bulb
olive oil, for basting
4 medium tomatoes, about
   400 g (14 oz)
salt and pepper
145 g (5.1 oz) packet pizza-
   base mix
15 ml (1 tbsp) chopped fresh
   rosemary or 10 ml (2 tsp)
   dried
75 g (3 oz) feta cheese
about 8 black olives
about 8 fresh basil leaves

PREPARATION TIME
15 minutes
COOKING TIME
20 minutes
FREEZING
Not suitable

485 CALS PER SERVING

1. Preheat the oven to 220°C (425°F) Mark 7. Divide the garlic into cloves, discarding the outer, papery layers, but leaving the inner skins intact. Toss in a little oil.

2. Meanwhile, roughly chop the tomatoes and place in a bowl with 5 ml (1 tsp) salt. Mix well.

3. Make up the pizza base mix according to the packet instructions. As you are kneading the dough, knead in the rosemary until it is evenly incorporated.

4. Roll out the dough thinly to a 25 cm (10 inch) round on a lightly floured surface. Transfer to a lightly greased and floured baking sheet.

5. Spoon the tomatoes over the pizza base to within 1 cm (½ inch) of the edge and crumble the feta cheese on top. Scatter the olives, garlic cloves and basil over the top. Season with pepper only.

6. Bake in the oven for 20 minutes or until the base is crisp and golden. Serve immediately, mashing down the garlic cloves as you eat.

NOTE: For this recipe the pizza dough is rolled out to a larger round than suggested on the packet instructions to give a thin, crispy result.

VARIATION

Replace the garlic, olives and feta cheese with a 340 g (12 oz) jar of pimientos, drained; 20 ml (4 tsp) capers; and 75 g (3 oz) smoked Vegetarian cheese.

TECHNIQUE

Roll out the pizza dough to a 25 cm (10 inch) round on a lightly floured surface.

Vegetable
accompaniments
and salads

GARLIC POTATOES

Chunky 'chips' of potato are cooked with olive oil, garlic and herbs. Rosemary and thyme impart a wonderful woody aroma to the potatoes as they steam. It is essential to use waxy potatoes for this recipe as floury ones would disintegrate. Use a firm variety, such as Maris Piper, Desirée or Romano.

SERVES 4

575 g (1¼ lb) medium-sized
   waxy potatoes
90 ml (6 tbsp) olive oil
4 unpeeled garlic cloves
few fresh thyme or
   rosemary sprigs
25 g (1 oz) butter
crystal salt, for sprinkling

PREPARATION TIME
15 minutes
COOKING TIME
20 minutes
FREEZING
Not suitable

320 CALS PER SERVING

1. Cut the potatoes lengthwise into quarters, then place in a bowl of cold water. Rinse and pat dry with kitchen paper.

2. Heat the oil in a flameproof casserole or heavy-based pan and, when smoking hot, add the potatoes and garlic. Reduce the heat and fry the potatoes, turning, until browned on all sides. Stir in the herbs, cover tightly and allow the potatoes to cook in their own steam for 15 minutes.

3. Remove the lid and turn the heat up to evaporate any water and crisp the potatoes. Add the butter and toss gently.

4. Scatter with plenty of salt and garnish with thyme or rosemary sprigs to serve.

NOTE: It is important to rinse and dry the potatoes, to help prevent them from sticking during cooking.

VARIATION

Fry 125 g (4 oz) chopped derinded pancetta or unsmoked bacon with the potatoes at stage 2.

TECHNIQUE

Fry the potatoes and whole garlic cloves in the hot oil, turning constantly, until browned on all sides.

POTATO PARSNIP GALETTE

This golden cake of butter-basted potatoes and sweet parsnips with a hint of honey and lemon is a perfect partner to roasts and game dishes. It is really important to clarify the butter – as it lends a wonderful colour to the potatoes and intensifies the flavour.

SERVES 6

900 g (2 lb) firm potatoes,
   such as Desirée, Romano,
   Estima or Wilja
225 g (8 oz) young parsnips
175 g (6 oz) unsalted butter
60 ml (4 tbsp) thin honey
30 ml (2 tbsp) lemon juice
freshly grated nutmeg
salt and pepper

PREPARATION TIME
25 minutes
COOKING TIME
45 minutes
FREEZING
Not suitable

380 CALS PER SERVING

1. Preheat the oven to 200°C (400°F) Mark 6. Peel the potatoes and parsnips. Slice them very thinly either by hand, with a mandoline, or in a food processor. Do not rinse the potatoes to remove the starch as it is needed to help the potato slices stick together. Divide the potatoes into three equal portions. Don't worry if they discolour.

2. To clarify the butter, slowly melt it in a small pan, then skim off any white residue or foam; keep warm. Melt the honey and lemon juice together in a small pan; keep warm.

3. Pour 30 ml (2 tbsp) butter into a heavy 20 cm (8 inch) non-stick frying pan, suitable for oven use (see note). Layer one third of the potatoes over the bottom of the pan in neat overlapping circles, seasoning well.

4. Lay half the sliced parsnips over the potato layer. Brush with honey and lemon juice and season with nutmeg, salt and pepper.

5. Cover with another third of the potato slices, brushing with butter and seasoning well as you go. Layer the remaining parsnips on top. Brush with the remaining honey and lemon juice, and season with nutmeg, salt and pepper. Finish with the remaining potato slices, brushing with butter and seasoning. Pour over any remaining butter.

6. Place the pan over a medium heat and cook carefully for about 5 minutes or until the underside begins to turn golden brown. Test by carefully lifting up the edge with a palette knife.

7. Press the potatoes down firmly and cover with a lid or buttered kitchen foil. Bake for 40-45 minutes or until the potatoes and parsnips are tender when pierced with a sharp knife and the underside is a deep golden brown.

8. Loosen the galette with a palette knife. Place a warmed serving plate over the pan and quickly invert the galette onto the dish. Serve immediately.

NOTE: Ideally you need a non-stick frying pan with an integral metal handle which can therefore be placed in the oven. Alternatively, use a moule á manqué pan instead, buttering it well.

TECHNIQUE

Layer the potato slices over the parsnips in neat, overlapping circles.

ROASTED MIXED WINTER VEGETABLES

Root vegetables roasted together with olive oil make a wonderful partner to any winter meat or poultry dish. The sweet juices from the vegetables caramelise during cooking and give them a beautiful glaze and delicious flavour. Cardamoms add a hint of aroma, without being overpowering.

SERVES 6-8

350 g (12 oz) carrots
350 g (12 oz) parsnips
350 g (12 oz) celeriac
350 g (12 oz) sweet potato
150 ml (¼ pint) olive oil
4 cardamom pods, lightly crushed
15 ml (1 tbsp) soft brown sugar
coarse sea salt and pepper

PREPARATION TIME
20 minutes
COOKING TIME
About 1 hour
FREEZING
Not suitable

355-265 CALS PER SERVING

1. Preheat the oven to 200°C (400°F) Mark 6. Peel all of the vegetables. Quarter the carrots and parsnips lengthwise. Cut the celeriac and sweet potato into chunks.

2. Heat the olive oil in a roasting tin and add the vegetables, turning them to coat well. Roast in the oven for 30 minutes, turning the vegetables twice during cooking.

3. Add the crushed cardamom pods and the brown sugar to the vegetables, turning them to coat evenly. Return to the oven and bake for a further 30 minutes. The vegetables should look very browned and be completely soft, but not disintegrating.

4. Season liberally with coarse salt and pepper and transfer to a warmed serving dish to serve.

VARIATION

For a more distinctive flavour, try replacing the brown sugar with maple syrup or honey. Toss in a handful of raisins 2 minutes before the end of the cooking time, too.

TECHNIQUE

Add the vegetables to the hot olive oil in the roasting tin and turn them to coat thoroughly with the oil.

SWEDE AND CARROTS WITH MUSTARD SEEDS AND GINGER

Swede has often been a much maligned vegetable, yet it has a distinctive flavour which is enhanced by herbs, spices and aromatic ingredients. Swede and carrots go well together, and the addition of mustard seeds and ginger gives the combination a more exciting aspect!

SERVES 4

450 g (1 lb) swede
450 g (1 lb) carrots
2 pieces preserved stem
    ginger in syrup, drained
25 g (1 oz) butter
5 ml (1 tsp) black mustard
    seeds
coarse sea salt and pepper
TO GARNISH
parsley or chervil sprigs

PREPARATION TIME
20 minutes
COOKING TIME
15 minutes
FREEZING
Not suitable

105 CALS PER SERVING

1. Peel the swede and cut into small dice. Peel the carrots and slice thinly. Cook the vegetables separately in boiling salted water until tender.

2. Meanwhile, finely chop the stem ginger. Melt the butter in a small heavy-based saucepan. Add the mustard seeds and heat gently until the seeds begin to pop. Add the chopped ginger and cook for 1 minute over a low heat.

3. Drain the cooked swede and carrots thoroughly, then mash together. Season liberally with freshly ground black pepper and stir in half of the mustard and ginger mixture.

4. Transfer the mashed swede and carrots to a warmed serving dish and drizzle the remaining mustard and ginger mixture over the top. Garnish with parsley or chervil and serve at once.

NOTE: Use a heavy-duty potato masher or a vegetable mill for mashing. Do not use a food processor as this results in an unpleasant glutinous texture.

VARIATION

Make a mustard and ginger cauliflower cheese by tossing cooked cauliflower florets in half of the mustard mixture. Transfer to a gratin dish and spoon on the cheese sauce. Top with the remaining mustard mixture and grated cheese, then brown under the grill.

TECHNIQUE

Mash the carrots and swede together thoroughly, making sure you do not leave any firm lumps.

SHREDDED BRUSSELS SPROUTS WITH BACON

hese buttery shredded sprouts are stir-fried with crispy cubes of bacon. They make an interesting change from traditional boiled or steamed Brussels sprouts and look so attractive. Use lightly smoked bacon, buying it in a piece if possible.

SERVES 4

700 g (1½ lb) Brussels
  sprouts
175 g (6 oz) piece smoked
  bacon
50 g (2 oz) butter
60 ml (4 tbsp) double cream
10 ml (2 tsp) caraway seeds
salt and pepper
freshly grated nutmeg

PREPARATION TIME
10 minutes
COOKING TIME
7 minutes
FREEZING
Not suitable

300 CALS PER SERVING

1. Trim the Brussels sprouts and shred them very finely. Remove the rind from the bacon, then cut into small cubes.

2. Heat a wok or frying pan and add the bacon. Cook over a high heat, stirring all the time, until the fat runs and the bacon is browning and crisp. Stir in the butter.

3. Toss in the Brussels sprouts and stir-fry over a high heat for 2-3 minutes until they begin to wilt. Pour in the cream, add the caraway seeds and stir-fry for 1 minute. Season with salt, pepper and nutmeg. Transfer to a warmed serving dish. Serve immediately.

NOTE: Cubed gammon would be good instead of bacon but you will need to fry it in a little butter rather than dry-fry.

VARIATION

Replace the Brussels sprouts with Savoy cabbage, or white cabbage.

TECHNIQUE

Cut the Brussels sprouts into fine shreds, using a sharp knife.

PARSNIPS IN A LIME GLAZE

The sweet nature of parsnips will complement almost any meal. Here the tang of lime is used to enhance their flavour. If possible, use young tender parsnips. The sharp glaze can be used with any sweet root vegetable to excellent effect – try it with sweet potatoes or carrots, for example.

SERVES 4

675 g (1½ lb) parsnips
1 lime
50 g (2 oz) butter
25 g (1 oz) light muscovado
   sugar
coarse sea salt and pepper
TO GARNISH
thyme sprigs

PREPARATION TIME
5 minutes
COOKING TIME
15 minutes
FREEZING
Not suitable

225 CALS PER SERVING

1. Peel the parsnips and trim off the tops and roots. Cut in half lengthways. (If using older, tougher parsnips cut into quarters and remove the woody core.) Add to a pan of boiling salted water and cook for 5 minutes.

2. Meanwhile, using a canelle knife or a vegetable peeler, carefully pare thin slivers of rind from the lime; set aside for the garnish. Halve the lime and squeeze out the juice.

3. Melt the butter in a large saucepan together with the sugar. Add the lime juice and heat gently, stirring, to dissolve the sugar.

4. Drain the parsnips thoroughly in a colander, then add to the lime mixture in the saucepan. Toss in the buttery lime mixture and cook over a moderate heat, shaking the pan frequently, for approximately 10 minutes until golden brown.

5. Transfer to a warmed serving dish and garnish with the slivers of lime zest and thyme sprigs.

VARIATIONS

Replace 1 parsnip with 3 eddoes. Peel and halve the eddoes and cook with the parsnips. Alternatively use carrots or turnips instead of parsnips. A handful of walnuts tossed in towards the end of the cooking time adds a delicious crunch.

TECHNIQUE

Toss the par-boiled parsnips in the buttery lime mixture.

MIXED VEGETABLES WITH COCONUT

Using fresh coconut is more time-consuming than opting for one of its processed forms but it makes a sauce with a superior texture and flavour. The technique suggested below for cracking a coconut is the quick way – be prepared for the milk to spill out! If you would prefer to catch it, pierce the 'eyes' with a screwdriver and drain the milk before you crack open the coconut.

SERVES 4

1 small or medium coconut
2 medium onions
2 garlic cloves
2.5 cm (1 inch) piece fresh
    root ginger
1 hot green chilli (optional)
5 ml (1 tsp) ground
    turmeric
10 ml (2 tsp) ground
    coriander
10 ml (2 tsp) coriander
    seeds
30 ml (2 tbsp) ghee or oil
2 large green peppers
2 carrots
8 spring onions
125 g (4 oz) green beans
salt and pepper
chopped fresh coriander, to
    garnish (optional)

PREPARATION TIME
30 minutes
COOKING TIME
30 minutes
FREEZING
Not suitable

395 CALS PER SERVING

1. Wrap the coconut in a tea-towel, grip it firmly and crack with a hammer. Remove the coconut flesh and peel off the hard brown skin, using a potato peeler or sharp knife. You will need about 225 g (8 oz) coconut flesh (use the rest for another dish). Roughly chop the flesh then drop it into a blender or food processor and work until very finely chopped. Add 150 ml (¼ pint) cold water and process again. Transfer the mixture from the blender to a bowl and set aside.

2. Peel and quarter the onions. Peel and halve the garlic cloves. Peel and roughly chop the ginger. Chop the chilli, if using, discarding the seeds if a milder flavour is preferred. Add the onions, garlic, ginger, chilli if using, turmeric, ground coriander and coriander seeds to the blender and process until finely chopped. Add a spoonful of water and process again to make a smooth purée.

3. Heat the ghee or oil in a large saucepan, add the onion and spice mixture and cook over a moderate heat, stirring for about 10 minutes until soft and golden brown.

4. Meanwhile, halve, core, deseed and roughly chop the peppers. Peel and slice the carrots. Trim and halve the spring onions. Trim the green beans.

5. Add the prepared vegetables to the pan and stir to coat in the onion and spice mixture. Add the coconut and season with salt and pepper to taste. Bring to the boil, then lower the heat. Cover and simmer very gently for about 20 minutes or until the vegetables are just tender. Check the pan from time to time to make sure that the vegetables are still moist; if they look dry, add a little extra water.

6. Serve sprinkled with chopped coriander if desired.

TECHNIQUE

Peel off the hard brown skin from the coconut flesh, using a vegetable peeler.

AUBERGINE BHAJI

For this recipe it really is advantageous to degorge the aubergines before cooking. These days most aubergines are not bitter, but they do soak up copious amounts of oil during cooking, and degorging can considerably reduce this. An excellent accompaniment to all kinds of Indian dishes, this bhaji is particularly good served as part of a vegetarian meal.

SERVES 4

2 medium aubergines
salt
1 large onion
2 garlic cloves
2.5 cm (1 inch) piece fresh
    root ginger
large handful of fresh
    coriander
about 75 ml (5 tbsp) ghee or
    vegetable oil
15 ml (1 tbsp) coriander
    seeds
15 ml (1 tbsp) mustard
    seeds
15 ml (1 tbsp) poppy seeds
5 ml (1 tsp) cumin seeds
1 tomato, skinned if
    preferred
10 ml (2 tsp) red wine
    vinegar

PREPARATION TIME
15 minutes, plus degorging
COOKING TIME
About 25 minutes
FREEZING
Not suitable

215 CALS PER SERVING

1. Trim the aubergines and cut into fairly thick slices. Halve each slice or cut into thirds. Layer the aubergine in a colander, sprinkling each layer generously with salt. Put a plate on top to weight down and leave to degorge for at least 30 minutes.

2. Peel and quarter the onion. Peel and halve the garlic. Peel and roughly chop the ginger. Trim the coriander and roughly chop.

3. Put the onion, garlic, ginger, coriander and a spoonful of water in a blender and process until smooth.

4. Rinse the aubergines under cold running water to remove all traces of salt. Drain and pat dry thoroughly with kitchen paper.

5. Heat the ghee or oil in a large frying pan or wok. Add the onion mixture and cook, stirring, for 5 minutes, until golden brown. Add the spices and cook for 2 minutes, stirring all the time.

6. Add the aubergines and turn to coat in the spice mixture (see note). Cook over a high heat, turning frequently, until they are just tinged with brown and coated in the spice mixture.

7. Chop the tomato and add to the pan with 30 ml (2 tbsp) water. Lower the heat and simmer for about 15 minutes or until the aubergines are just tender but still retain their shape. Add the vinegar and salt and pepper to taste. Serve immediately.

NOTE: Unless your wok or frying pan is very large, you will need to fry the aubergines in 2 or 3 batches, adding a little more ghee or oil to the pan as necessary. Once browned, return them all to the pan.

VARIATION

Enrich the sauce with 60 ml (4 tbsp) thick yogurt. Stir in, a tablespoon at a time, after adding the tomato. Omit the water and vinegar.

TECHNIQUE

Stack a few aubergine slices on top of one another, then cut down to slice each round into three.

OKRA WITH ONION AND TOMATO

This makes a tasty side dish to serve with plain grilled fish or meat. The quantity of masala spice mix is more than you need for this recipe, but it can be stored in an airtight jar and used as required. If you're short of time you could omit the spice mix and simply serve the okra sprinkled with the crisp onions.

SERVES 4

2 medium onions
45 ml (3 tbsp) ghee or
    vegetable oil
2 garlic cloves
2.5 cm (1 inch) piece fresh
    root ginger
1 hot chilli (optional)
3 tomatoes
450 g (1 lb) okra
10 ml (2 tsp) ground
    coriander
2.5 ml (½ tsp) turmeric
2.5 ml (½ tsp) ground
    cinnamon
salt and pepper
30 ml (2 tbsp) thick yogurt
30 ml (2 tbsp) chopped fresh
    coriander

MASALA SPICE MIX
15 ml (1 tbsp) coriander
    seeds
15 ml (1 tbsp) cumin seeds
10 ml (2 tsp) black
    peppercorns
3 dried red chillies

PREPARATION TIME
20 minutes
COOKING TIME
25 minutes
FREEZING Not suitable

175 CALS PER SERVING

1. First make the masala spice mix. Dry-fry the spices in a small frying pan for about 3 minutes until they begin to pop and release their aroma; stir frequently to ensure that they don't burn. Let cool slightly, then grind using a pestle and mortar. Store in an airtight jar until required.

2. Peel the onions. Halve and thinly slice one onion; quarter the other. Heat the ghee or oil in a frying pan, add the sliced onion and cook over a medium heat for about 10 minutes until dark golden brown and crisp. Drain on kitchen paper and set aside. Reserve the oil in the pan.

3. Peel and roughly chop the garlic and ginger. Slice the chilli, discarding the seeds if a milder flavour is preferred. Skin the tomatoes if preferred, then chop the flesh. Trim the okra.

4. Put the quartered onion, garlic and ginger in a blender with 15 ml (1 tbsp) water and process until smooth. Add the spices and process again.

5. Reheat the ghee or oil remaining in the frying pan, add the onion paste and cook over a high heat for 2 minutes, stirring all the time. Lower the heat and cook for 5 minutes or until the onion paste is golden brown and softened.

6. Add the chopped tomatoes with the chilli if using. Season with salt and pepper to taste. Cook for 5 minutes until the tomato has reduced down, then add the okra and stir to coat in the mixture. Cover and simmer gently for about 5 minutes until the okra is just tender.

7. Stir in the yogurt, a spoonful at a time, then add the coriander and heat through gently. Transfer to a serving dish and sprinkle with the crisp onions and a little of the masala spice mix to serve.

TECHNIQUE

Trim the okra, removing a small piece from each end. Do not cut into the flesh, or the dish will acquire an unpleasant glutinous texture during cooking.

STEAMED BASIL AND MUSTARD SEED RICE

Wonderfully fragrant, this rice is a little sticky, but great for mopping up juices. It goes equally well with fish, meat or game. Black mustard seeds impart a nutty flavour to the rice without being too hot. You can, however, use yellow mustard seeds as an alternative – for a hotter flavour.

SERVES 4

225 g (8 oz) basmati rice
12 large basil leaves
30 ml (2 tbsp) sunflower oil
30 ml (2 tbsp) black
  mustard seeds
5 ml (1 tsp) salt
TO GARNISH
basil leaves

PREPARATION TIME
10 minutes
COOKING TIME
25 minutes
FREEZING
Not suitable

270 CALS PER SERVING

1. Wash the rice in several changes of cold water or in a sieve under cold running water until the water runs clear. Drain well. Shred the basil leaves or tear into pieces.

2. Heat the oil in a medium non-stick saucepan and add the mustard seeds. Cook for a few minutes until the seeds start to pop.

3. Stir in the rice, salt and 300 ml (½ pint) water. Bring to the boil, stir, then boil rapidly until the water has evaporated and there are steam holes all over the surface.

4. Stir in all but 15 ml (1 tbsp) of the basil and cover very tightly, so no steam can escape. Set on a simmering mat (see note) over a very low heat for 15 minutes for the rice to swell. Fluff up with a fork, adding the reserved basil. Serve immediately, garnished with basil leaves.

NOTE: A simmering mat is used here to ensure the heat is *very* low and evenly distributed. You can obtain one of these mats from a cookshop or hardware store. If you do not have one make sure the heat is kept to a minimum and add a little more water if necessary to prevent the rice sticking.

VARIATION

Use multi-grain rice, but allow longer to cook: fast boil with 450 ml (¾ pint) water until evaporated, then continue as above.

TECHNIQUE

Wash the basmati rice thoroughly, running the grains through your fingers, to remove excess starch.

SUGAR SNAP PEAS IN A MINTED LEMON DRESSING

Sugar snap peas are available all year round and make an excellent accompaniment. Here they are served in a light crème fraîche dressing, flavoured with fresh mint and lemon. Fresh peas are equally good served this way — it's well worth seeking them out during their short season or, better still, grow some yourself . . . the flavour of homegrown peas is incomparable.

SERVES 4

400-450 g (14 oz-1 lb) sugar
  snap peas
SAUCE
60 ml (4 tbsp) crème fraîche
15 ml (1 tbsp) finely
  shredded or chopped
  fresh mint
finely pared or grated rind
  and juice of ½ lemon
90 ml (3 fl oz) yogurt
coarse sea salt and pepper
TO GARNISH
mint sprigs

PREPARATION TIME
10 minutes
COOKING TIME
5-10 minutes
FREEZING
Not suitable

105 CALS PER SERVING

1. Top and tail the sugar snap peas, then steam or cook them in boiling water until just tender.

2. Meanwhile gently heat the crème fraîche in a small saucepan, then add the finely chopped mint, lemon rind and juice, stirring gently. When the sauce is warmed through, add the yogurt; do not overheat at this stage otherwise the sauce may curdle. Season with salt and pepper to taste.

3. Drain the sugar snap peas and transfer to a warmed serving dish. Pour over the minted lemon sauce. Garnish with mint sprigs and serve at once.

VARIATIONS

Instead of sugar snap peas, use mangetouts or fresh peas. You will need 675 g (1½ lb) fresh peas in pods to give the correct shelled weight. Steam or cook in boiling water for 5-10 minutes until tender; continue as above.

  Young broad beans are also delicious steamed and served with this sauce.

TECHNIQUE

Add the mint, lemon rind and juice to the sauce, stirring over a low heat.

ROASTED ASPARAGUS SALAD

Roasting is a great way to cook asparagus. There is no water added so the true flavour of the vegetable is not 'diluted'. The cooking time applies to stalks of medium thickness and should be increased if you are using fatter asparagus stems.

1. Preheat the oven to 200°C (400°F) Mark 6. Trim the asparagus spears and use a potato peeler to peel the bottom 5 cm (2 inches) of each stalk. Arrange the asparagus in a shallow roasting tin.

2. Spoon 60 ml (4 tbsp) of the olive oil over the asparagus and shake lightly to mix. Roast in the oven for about 20 minutes until just tender, turning the asparagus spears once during cooking. Allow to cool.

3. To serve, spoon the remaining olive oil over the asparagus and sprinkle with the lemon juice. Season with coarse sea salt and freshly ground black pepper and toss lightly. Serve with rocket leaves and lemon wedges. Sprinkle with finely pared shavings of Parmesan, if liked.

TECHNIQUE

Peel the base of each asparagus stalk, using a swivel potato peeler.

ROASTED SQUASH AND PEPPER BAKE

This is a really colourful bake, ideal for serving to vegetarians. Squash has a wonderful sweetness and dense texture which makes it a good base for a bake. Yellow and red peppers add colour and flavour. The tomato sauce has a touch of spiciness balanced with a little marmalade for sweetness.

SERVES 4

2 butternut squash, about
  1 kg (2 lb) total weight
30 ml (2 tbsp) orange juice
30 ml (2 tbsp) chopped
  fresh coriander
1 red onion
1 yellow pepper
1 red pepper
25 g (1 oz) freshly grated
  Parmesan cheese
25 g (1 oz) pine nuts
TOMATO SAUCE
450 g (1 lb) tomatoes
2 shallots
1 red chilli
30 ml (2 tbsp) olive oil
2 garlic cloves, crushed
15 ml (1 tbsp) orange
  marmalade
pinch of paprika
salt and pepper

PREPARATION TIME
20 minutes
COOKING TIME
45-55 minutes
FREEZING
Not suitable

300 CALS PER SERVING

1. First, prepare the tomato sauce. Immerse the tomatoes in a large bowl of boiling water for 1 minute. Drain and refresh under cold running water, then peel away the skins. Roughly chop the flesh. Peel and finely chop the shallots. Halve, deseed and finely chop the chilli. (Wear rubber gloves to do this to avoid skin irritation.)

2. Heat the olive oil in a large pan. Stir in the shallots, garlic and chilli and fry gently for a few minutes until soft. Stir in the prepared tomatoes, add the marmalade, and season with paprika, salt and pepper to taste. Cover and simmer for 20 minutes.

3. Meanwhile, preheat the oven to 200°C (400°F) Mark 6 and prepare the squash. Cut in half, scoop out the seeds and discard. Remove the skin with a sharp knife or vegetable peeler and cut the flesh into small pieces; the skin is quite tough, so you may find it easier to cut the squash into small pieces first and then remove the skin. Place in a large ovenproof dish. Add the orange juice and coriander; toss well.

4. Peel and slice the onion into strips. Cut the peppers in half, remove the core and seeds, then cut into small cubes. Add to the squash and season with salt

and pepper. Spoon over the hot tomato sauce, then sprinkle with the Parmesan and pine nuts. Bake in the oven for 45-55 minutes until the top is golden.

5. Serve immediately, as a vegetable accompaniment with roast lamb, or with a green vegetable as a vegetarian main course.

VARIATION

Replace the squash with sweet potatoes. For speed, instead of making a tomato sauce slice the tomatoes, chop the shallots and crush the garlic and arrange in the dish in layers with the squash and peppers. Mix the olive oil with 60 ml (4 tbsp) pesto sauce and pour over the top. Bake as above.

TECHNIQUE

Cut the butternut squash in half, scoop out and discard the seeds.

BAKED FENNEL WITH LEMON AND OLIVES

Florence fennel bulbs are braised to tender sweetness with smoky black olives and lemon juice. Fennel has a slightly aniseed flavour which goes well with fish dishes and cuts the richness of stews and braised meat dishes. Celery can be cooked in the same way. This dish is equally delicious hot or cold.

SERVES 4

3 large fennel bulbs, or
   4 medium ones
90 ml (6 tbsp) olive oil
grated rind and juice of
   1 lemon
salt and pepper
12 black or green olives
30 ml (2 tbsp) chopped fresh
   parsley

PREPARATION TIME
15 minutes
COOKING TIME
45 minutes
FREEZING
Not suitable

225 CALS PER SERVING

1. Preheat the oven to 200°C (400°F) Mark 6. Trim the fennel and cut away any bruised parts. Cut off the fibrous tops, halve the bulbs lengthways and cut out the core. Cut larger bulbs into quarters.

2. Place the fennel halves or quarters cut-side up, in a baking dish. Mix the lemon rind and juice with the olive oil, salt and pepper.

3. Pour the lemon mixture over the fennel, scatter over the olives and bake in the oven for 15 minutes. Turn the fennel and bake for a further 15 minutes. Turn once more and bake for a final 15 minutes until tender. Serve sprinkled with the parsley.

NOTE: For a softer texture, blanch the fennel quarters in boiling water for 2 minutes and drain well before baking.

VARIATION

Use 2 fennel bulbs and 3 heads of chicory. Quarter the fennel and halve the chicory bulbs, removing the bitter core. Continue from stage 2, mixing the fennel and chicory together.

TECHNIQUE

Halve or quarter the fennel bulbs and cut out the core.

GRILLED CHICORY AND RADICCHIO WITH ORANGE

Grilling the chicory and radicchio transforms them by caramelising the juices – and the addition of creamy, fresh British goat's cheese gives this recipe true dinner-party status! Any other cheese will do, but the goat's cheese seems to have a special affinity with bitter leaves like chicory and radicchio. Serve this accompaniment with roast or grilled meats or poultry.

SERVES 4

2 plump heads of chicory
1 large firm head of
   radicchio
1 orange
olive oil, for basting
125 g (4 oz) fresh goat's
   cheese
a little chopped fresh or
   dried thyme
pepper
30 ml (2 tbsp) pine nuts

PREPARATION TIME
15 minutes
COOKING TIME
About 10 minutes
FREEZING
Not suitable

230 CALS PER SERVING

1. Cut the chicory in half lengthways. Cut the radicchio into quarters. Over a bowl to catch the juice, peel the orange of all pith and cut into segments, discarding the membrane.

2. Preheat the grill to high. Place the chicory and radicchio in a grill pan, cut side up, and brush liberally with olive oil. Cook under the grill, as near to the heat as possible, for about 3-4 minutes until just beginning to char and soften. Turn, baste with more olive oil and cook for a further 2-3 minutes.

3. Carefully turn the chicory and radicchio again. Arrange the orange segments on top and sprinkle with the reserved orange juice. Crumble the goat's cheese on top. Brush with oil, sprinkle with thyme and season with pepper. Grill until the cheese bubbles and begins to brown. The chicory will be very soft, so carefully transfer it to warmed plates. Alternatively, transfer to a flameproof serving dish before adding the cheese, then grill in the dish.

4. Meanwhile toast the pine nuts in a dry pan over moderate heat, shaking the pan constantly, until evenly golden. Sprinkle the toasted nuts over the grilled chicory and radicchio, to serve.

NOTE: The chicory and radicchio will change colour, but don't worry – they will taste delicious – as long as you use olive oil for basting.

VARIATION

Omit the goat's cheese and top with orange slices instead of segments.

TECHNIQUE

Peel the orange (as you would an apple) over a bowl to catch the juice, making sure you remove all of the white pith.

CAESAR SALAD

A true classic, this is possibly one of the most famous of all salads. It is traditionally made with cos lettuce, but this version uses the sweet tender little gem lettuces instead.

4 little gem lettuces,
   trimmed
75 g (3 oz) day-old bread
30 ml (2 tbsp) olive oil
5 ml (1 tsp) paprika
pinch of cayenne pepper
25 g (1 oz) Parmesan cheese
DRESSING
75 ml (5 tbsp) light olive oil
4 garlic cloves, peeled
2 anchovy fillets in oil,
   drained and chopped
15 ml (1 tbsp) balsamic
   vinegar
22 ml (1½ tbsp) Dijon
   mustard
salt and pepper
1 egg

PREPARATION TIME
15 minutes
COOKING TIME
12 minutes

1. Discard any tough outer leaves from the lettuce, then separate the leaves. Wash briefly and shake off excess water. Transfer to a plastic bag, seal and refrigerate for 30 minutes. Remove and allow to return to room temperature.

2. Preheat the oven to 220°C (425°F) Mark 7. Cut the bread into cubes. Combine the oil, paprika and cayenne in a bowl, add the bread and toss until thoroughly coated. Spread the bread cubes out on a baking sheet and roast in the oven for 6-8 minutes until crisp and golden. Set aside.

3. To prepare the dressing, place the oil in a small saucepan, add the garlic and anchovies and heat gently for 5-6 minutes until soft and golden. Set aside until cold, then strain and reserve the oil.

4. Mash the garlic cloves and anchovies together in a bowl to a paste, then place in a bowl with the vinegar, mustard and seasoning. Gradually whisk in the strained oil in a steady stream until thickened.

5. Cook the egg in boiling water for 2 minutes only, cool under running water, then shell and whisk directly into the dressing until combined.

6. Place the lettuce leaves in a large bowl, and scatter over the croûtons.

Finely pare the Parmesan cheese over the top. Pour over the dressing and toss well until the leaves and croûtons are well coated. Serve immediately.

NOTE: If preferred, thin the dressing with a little boiling water.

VARIATION

Prepare Parmesan-flavoured croûtons and omit the Parmesan from the salad. Toss the croûtons in the oil, then in 25 g (1 oz) freshly grated Parmesan cheese to coat evenly. Cook as above until golden.

TECHNIQUE

For the dressing, slowly add the oil to the anchovy mixture, whisking all the time.

CARROT SALAD

This pretty salad is a good accompaniment to spicy meat and fish dishes. You could replace the orange slices with mango or papaya, or use blood oranges when they are in season. A few black olives scattered on top of the salad just before serving provide a striking contrast to the vivid shades of orange.

SERVES 4-6

450 g (1 lb) carrots
2 small thin-skinned oranges
few fresh chives, snipped
few small fresh mint leaves
DRESSING
1-2 garlic cloves
1 green chilli
1 red chilli
60 ml (4 tbsp) vegetable oil
5 ml (1 tsp) black mustard
    seeds
5 ml (1 tsp) cumin seeds
15 ml (1 tbsp) orange juice
15 ml (1 tbsp) lemon juice
salt and pepper
few drops of orange flower
    water

PREPARATION TIME
20 minutes
COOKING TIME
About 5 minutes
FREEZING
Not suitable

190-125 CALS PER SERVING

1. Grate the carrots, using the coarse side of a grater. (Do not use a food processor as it tends to make them very wet.) Pat dry with kitchen paper.

2. Peel the oranges, removing all the bitter white pith. Do this over a bowl to catch the juice (use for the dressing). Cut the oranges into very thin slices. Arrange the orange slices and carrots on a large serving plate and scatter with the chives and mint leaves.

3. To make the dressing, peel and thinly slice the garlic. Slice the chillies, removing the seeds for a milder flavour.

4. Heat half of the oil in a small pan, add the garlic and cook for 1-2 minutes until just golden brown. Add the mustard and cumin seeds and cook over a high heat for 1 minute, stirring all the time. Remove from the heat and add the remaining oil. Leave to cool.

5. Add the orange and lemon juices to the dressing with the chillies and salt and pepper to taste. Pour the dressing over the salad and turn the carrots and orange slices to ensure that they are evenly coated.

6. Leave the salad to stand at room temperature for at least 30 minutes to allow the flavours to develop. Sprinkle with a few drops of orange flower water just before serving, if liked.

NOTE: If using orange flower water, apply sparingly as the flavour can be overpowering.

VARIATIONS

Soak a handful of sultanas or raisins in a little orange juice until plump. Scatter over the salad before serving. For a more substantial salad, add a handful of cooked chick peas too.

TECHNIQUE

Peel the oranges as you would an apple, making sure you remove all the bitter white pith.

Mixed leaf salad with croûtons

A crisp, colourful salad featuring peppery rocket, watercress and radishes. Crunchy grilled croûtons are the perfect complement – heart-shaped ones look particularly attractive, but you can of course use any cutter or simply cut the bread into squares. Vary the salad leaves according to availability.

SERVES 6-8

1 head of radicchio
1 bunch of watercress
½ head of fine frisée
50 g (2 oz) baby spinach
   leaves
50 g (2 oz) rocket
250 g (9 oz) radishes
5 thin slices of bread
FRENCH DRESSING
30 ml (2 tbsp) olive oil
30 ml (2 tbsp) vegetable oil
22 ml (1½ tsp) white wine
   vinegar
pinch of sugar
1 small garlic clove, crushed
salt and pepper

PREPARATION TIME
10 minutes
COOKING TIME
3-4 minutes
FREEZING
Not suitable

140 CALS PER SERVING

1. Tear the radicchio into bite-sized pieces; cut the stalks off the watercress; discard any tough outer leaves from the frisée. Wash all the salad leaves in cold water. Drain and pat dry. Halve or quarter the radishes. Put the salad leaves and radishes in a large polythene bag and refrigerate until needed.

2. Preheat the grill. Using a heart-shaped cutter, stamp out shapes from the bread. Grill until golden on both sides.

3. For the French dressing, put all the ingredients in a screw-topped jar and shake vigorously to combine.

4. To serve, transfer the salad leaves and radishes to a serving bowl. Pour on the dressing and toss lightly. Scatter the warm croûtons over the salad and serve at once.

NOTE: French dressing is a hidden source of calories. Just 15 ml (1 tbsp) contains 105 calories. Slimmers may prefer to use a low-calorie version.

VARIATION

Replace the rocket with lamb's lettuce (mâche). Use oakleaf lettuce instead of the frisée.

TECHNIQUE

For the croûtons, use a heart-shaped cutter to stamp out hearts from the bread.

CRUNCHY-TOPPED ASPARAGUS AND COURGETTES

This is a really quick and simple way of serving seasonal vegetables. The crunchy breadcrumb and Parmesan topping provides an excellent contrast to the melting texture of the asparagus and courgettes. Try it with other vegetables too, such as broccoli or cauliflower.

SERVES 4-6

225 g (8 oz) thin asparagus
225 g (8 oz) baby courgettes
salt and pepper
125 g (4 oz) butter
175 g (6 oz) fresh white
   breadcrumbs
50 g (2 oz) freshly grated
   Parmesan cheese

PREPARATION TIME
15 minutes
COOKING TIME
5-6 minutes
FREEZING
Not suitable

445-300 CALS PER SERVING

1. Trim the asparagus and cut into 5 cm (2 inch) lengths. Cut the courgettes into quarters lengthways. Bring a pan of salted water to the boil. Drop in the asparagus and courgettes, return to the boil and cook for 3 minutes. Drain and refresh immediately in cold water to stop the cooking. Remove and drain on kitchen paper.

2. Heat the butter in a frying pan and fry the breadcrumbs until lightly golden and crisp. Stir in the Parmesan cheese.

3. Preheat the grill. Place the asparagus and courgettes in a warmed shallow flameproof dish. Cover thickly with the crumbs and place under the grill for 2-3 minutes or until the topping is golden and the vegetables are heated through. Serve immediately.

VARIATION

Replace the asparagus and/or courgettes with any other green vegetable – try broccoli florets, cauliflower, French beans, or even carrots, but be sure to half-cook them before adding the topping.

TECHNIQUE

To quickly stop the vegetables cooking, remove from the boiling water and briefly immerse in a bowl of cold water. The easiest way to do this is to contain the vegetables in a blanching basket during cooking.

POTATO SALAD WITH CELERY, WALNUTS AND BLUE CHEESE

In this warm, tasty salad, the earthy flavour of potato is perfectly complemented by celery, walnuts and blue cheese. The warmth of the cooked potatoes marries the flavours together and melts the blue cheese slightly. It is important to serve the salad immediately, in a warmed dish.

450 g (1 lb) new potatoes
2 garlic cloves (see note)
coarse sea salt and pepper
60 ml (4 tbsp) walnut oil
125 g (4 oz) walnuts
1 celery heart
125 g (4 oz) vegetarian blue
  Stilton cheese
TO GARNISH
thyme sprigs
celery leaves (optional)

PREPARATION TIME
10 minutes
COOKING TIME
15-20 minutes
FREEZING
Not suitable

560-370 CALS PER SERVING

1. Scrub the potatoes clean; cut any larger ones in half. Cook in boiling salted water for 15-20 minutes depending on size, until tender.

2. Meanwhile, peel the garlic and crush with a little salt, using a pestle and mortar. Add the walnut oil and half of the walnuts and work to a thick sauce. Alternatively put the garlic, salt, oil and half of the walnuts in a food processor or blender and whizz to combine.

3. Roughly chop the remaining walnuts. Crumble the cheese into small pieces. Thinly slice the celery, reserving some leaves for garnish if available.

4. When the potatoes are cooked, drain thoroughly and turn into a warmed serving bowl. Immediately add the dressing, celery, remaining walnuts and crumbled cheese and toss lightly. Garnish with thyme, and celery leaves if available, and serve immediately, while the potatoes are still warm and the cheese is melting slightly.

NOTE: If smoked garlic is available, use it for this salad — it will impart a delicious smoky flavour.

VARIATION

Substitute roasted hazelnuts and hazelnut oil for the walnuts and walnut oil.

TECHNIQUE

Use a pestle and mortar to mix the garlic, salt, walnut oil and half of the walnuts to a thick sauce.

APRICOT AND CASHEW NUT SALAD

This is a quick and easy salad to prepare. Dried apricots are soaked in white wine, then tossed with a selection of bitter leaves, carrot and pepper julienne, and chopped coriander. Roasted salted cashews add a delicious crunch. You can of course use any combination of leaves.

SERVES 4-6

125 g (4 oz) dried apricots
150 ml (¼ pint) dry white
   wine, such as Chardonnay
1 head of chicory
50 g (2 oz) watercress
25 g (1 oz) rocket leaves
handful of young spinach
   leaves
1 small carrot
½ medium green pepper
50-75 g (2-3 oz) roasted
   salted cashew nuts
15 ml (1 tbsp) chopped fresh
   coriander

DRESSING
reserved wine from soaking
   apricots
60 ml (4 tbsp) extra-virgin
   olive oil
30 ml (2 tbsp) orange juice
   (freshly squeezed)
5 ml (1 tsp) clear honey
coarse sea salt and pepper

PREPARATION TIME
10-15 minutes, plus soaking
COOKING TIME
Nil
FREEZING
Not suitable

345-230 CALS PER SERVING

1. Cut the apricots into slices, using a sharp knife or scissors. Place in a bowl and pour over the wine. Leave to soak for 2 hours.

2. Meanwhile prepare the salad. Separate the chicory leaves. Wash all the salad leaves and carefully pat dry with kitchen paper. Peel the carrot and cut into julienne strips. Remove the core and seeds from the green pepper and slice thinly. Pick over the watercress, removing any discoloured leaves or tough stalks. Combine all of the salad leaves and vegetables in a salad bowl.

3. To make the dressing, drain the wine from the apricots into a screw-topped jar. Add the olive oil, orange juice, honey and seasoning. Shake well to combine.

4. Add the apricots, cashew nuts and chopped coriander to the salad and toss lightly. Drizzle over some of the dressing; serve the remainder separately.

VARIATION

Replace the apricots with dried pears, and the cashew nuts with pecans. Add 1.25 ml (¼ tsp) French mustard to the dressing.

TECHNIQUE

Wash the salad leaves in a colander under cold running water.

RED CABBAGE SLAW

Nothing tastes quite as good as homemade coleslaw and this recipe is particularly rich and creamy. As the flavours develop on standing, the salad is best prepared in advance. It is good served as part of a selection of salads, and is an ideal side dish to accompany barbecued foods.

1. Coarsely grate or shred the cabbage, carrots and beetroot, using a food processor fitted with a coarse grater if possible. Finely slice the onion. Quarter, core and grate the apples.

2. Roughly chop the pecan nuts and place in a large bowl with all the prepared vegetables, apples and garlic.

3. To make the dressing, in a bowl beat together the mayonnaise, yogurt, orange juice, vinegar and seasoning. Stir in the chives.

4. Spoon the dressing over the vegetables and nuts and stir well until thoroughly blended. Cover and set aside for 30 minutes to allow the flavours to develop. Toss the salad before serving.

NOTE: Use bought mayonnaise if you haven't time to make your own or if you are unhappy about using raw egg yolks. You will need 150 ml (5 fl oz).

TECHNIQUE

Using a food processor fitted with a medium grating disc, grate the cabbage, carrots and beetroot.

Warm Salad Niçoise

There are many variations of this wonderful Provençal salad and this one is a little different still, as all the ingredients are combined and eaten while still warm. As it is rich, this dish is best served as a starter, or with plenty of crusty bread as a lunch.

SERVES 4

225 g (8 oz) small new potatoes, or halved if larger

125 g (4 oz) French beans, trimmed

2 eggs

225 g (8 oz) fresh tuna steak (see note)

90 ml (6 tbsp) extra-virgin olive oil

4 ripe tomatoes

1 garlic clove, crushed

25 g (1 oz) anchovies in oil, drained

25 g (1 oz) small French capers, drained and washed (see note on page 60)

15 ml (1 tbsp) red wine vinegar

30 ml (2 tbsp) chopped fresh basil

15 ml (1 tbsp) chopped fresh parsley

50 g (2 oz) olives (preferably Niçoise)

salt and pepper

TO GARNISH

lemon wedges

parsley sprigs

PREPARATION TIME
10 minutes
COOKING TIME
15 minutes

425 CALS PER SERVING

1. Cook the potatoes in lightly salted boiling water for 7-9 minutes, add the beans and cook for a further 3-4 minutes, until just tender. Drain and place in a large bowl.

2. Place the eggs in cold water, bring to the boil and simmer for 7-9 minutes, according to taste. Immediately plunge the eggs into cold water, peel and immerse in fresh cold water until required.

3. Wash and dry the tuna and cut into 2.5 cm (1 inch) cubes. Heat half of the oil in a frying pan, add the tuna and fry over a high heat for 1-2 minutes until browned on all sides. Add to the potatoes and beans.

4. Roughly chop the tomatoes and add to the pan with the garlic, anchovies and capers. Stir-fry for 1 minute, then add the remaining oil, vinegar and herbs. Add to the potato and tuna mixture and toss well.

5. Divide the salad between individual plates. Cut the eggs into quarters and add to the salad with the olives. Garnish with lemon wedges and parsley and serve at once.

NOTE: If fresh tuna is unobtainable, use a 200 g (7 oz) can of tuna in olive oil instead. Drain, flake and add to the pan with the tomatoes.

TECHNIQUE

Fry the tuna over a high heat for 1-2 minutes, turning constantly, until browned on all sides.

ITALIAN SEAFOOD SALAD

This is a fairly typical Italian seafood salad, and one which is always a great favourite at dinner parties. Vary the fish and shellfish according to availability and preference.

SERVES 4-6

48 mussels in shells (see
  note)
20 large raw Mediterranean
  prawns, about 350 g
  (12 oz)
225 g (8 oz) small squid
225 g (8 oz) monkfish fillet,
  skinned
90 ml (6 tbsp) extra-virgin
  olive oil
30 ml (2 tbsp) lemon juice
1 garlic clove, crushed
salt and pepper
125 g (4 oz) French beans,
  trimmed
2 shallots, peeled
2 celery sticks
25 g (1 oz) anchovy fillets
  marinated in oil, drained
30 ml (2 tbsp) chopped fresh
  parsley
15 ml (1 tbsp) chopped fresh
  basil
15 ml (1 tbsp) chopped fresh
  chervil
50 g (2 oz) Italian olives
chervil sprigs, to garnish

PREPARATION TIME
30 minutes, plus chilling
COOKING TIME
15 minutes

460-305 CALS PER SERVING

1. Prepare the seafood. Scrub the mussels and pull away any beards that are still attached. Peel the prawns and remove the dark vein from the back of each one. Prepare the squid (according to the instructions on page 34). Cut the monkfish into 5 mm (¼ inch) slices.

2. Place the mussels in a saucepan with about 100 ml (3½ fl oz) water. Cover with a tight-fitting lid and cook over a high heat for 4-5 minutes until the shells have steamed open. Discard any that remain closed. Immediately refresh the mussels under cold water, reserving the cooking liquid. Remove the mussels from their shells if preferred and place in a large bowl.

3. Return the poaching liquid to the pan and bring to the boil, adding a little extra water if necessary. Add the prawns and cook for 4 minutes, then add the monkfish and cook for 1 minute. Finally add the squid and cook for a further 1 minute. Strain and reserve 30 ml (2 tbsp) of the liquid. Plunge the seafood into cold water, then drain, pat dry and add to the mussels.

4. In a small bowl, whisk the olive oil, lemon juice, garlic and reserved poaching liquid together, seasoning with a little salt and pepper. Pour over the seafood, toss well and leave to marinate in the refrigerator for 1 hour.

5. Just before serving, blanch the beans in lightly salted boiling water for 3 minutes; drain and refresh under cold water. Thinly slice the shallots and celery; roughly chop the anchovies.

6. Add these ingredients to the seafood along with the herbs and olives. Toss to mix and serve at once, garnished with chervil. Accompany with a leafy salad if wished, and plenty of crusty bread.

NOTE: Alternatively buy cooked, shelled mussels, in which case you will need 225 g (8 oz).

TECHNIQUE

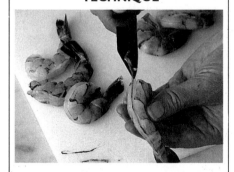

Make a shallow slit along the back of each prawn and remove the dark intestinal vein.

PASTA
AND NOODLES

RIGATONI BAKED WITH SPICY SAUSAGE

You can use any good quality spicy sausages for this recipe, but – if at all possible – buy Italian-style uncooked sausages 'loose' from a good butcher or delicatessen, rather than prepacked ones. Prepare the sauce in advance if you wish, but don't toss with the pasta until ready for the oven, otherwise the pasta will become soggy.

SERVES 4-6

45 ml (3 tbsp) extra-virgin
   olive oil
350 g (12 oz) uncooked
   spicy sausage
1 onion
2 garlic cloves
12 black olives
5 sun-dried tomatoes
90 ml (3 fl oz) dry white wine
30 ml (2 tbsp) chopped fresh
   oregano
15 ml (1 tbsp) chopped fresh
   parsley
Two 397 g (14 oz) cans plum
   tomatoes
salt and pepper
400 g (14 oz) dried rigatoni
15 g (½ oz) butter
175 g (6 oz) mozzarella
   cheese (preferably
   smoked), diced
50 g (2 oz) Parmesan
   cheese, in one piece
oregano sprigs, to garnish

PREPARATION TIME
15-20 minutes
COOKING TIME
30-35 minutes
FREEZING
Not suitable

1000-670 CALS PER SERVING

1. Heat 15 ml (1 tbsp) of the oil in a large frying pan, then add the sausage, cut into lengths to fit the pan, if necessary. Fry on a medium high heat for 4-5 minutes, turning frequently, until lightly browned. Transfer to a plate and cut into slices. Set aside.

2. Peel and chop the onion and garlic. Slice the olives from their stones; dice the sun-dried tomatoes. Add the remaining oil to the frying pan. Stir in the onion and garlic and cook over a medium heat for 5 minutes, until softened but not browned. Return the sliced sausage to the pan and add the wine and herbs. Increase the heat and cook for 3-4 minutes until about two thirds of the wine has evaporated.

3. Stir in the canned tomatoes and their juice, breaking them up with a wooden spoon. Add the sun-dried tomatoes and olives. Cook, uncovered, over a medium heat for 15-20 minutes until the tomatoes are pulp-like; do not reduce the sauce too much. Season to taste.

4. Meanwhile, preheat the oven to 200°C (400°F) Mark 6. Cook the rigatoni in a large pan of boiling salted water until almost 'al dente', or for about 2 minutes less time than packet instructions. Drain thoroughly.

5. Butter a baking dish large enough to hold the pasta and sauce. Transfer the pasta to the dish and toss with the sauce. Scatter the mozzarella over the rigatoni. Using a potato peeler 'shave' the Parmesan cheese over the top. Bake near the top of the oven for about 15 minutes, until piping hot. Serve at once, garnished with oregano sprigs.

VARIATION

Use cooked sausages, such as chorizo, instead of raw ones. Omit stage 1. Simply slice the sausages and add at stage 2.

TECHNIQUE

Toss the rigatoni with the sauce just before baking. The pasta will finish cooking in the sauce.

SPAGHETTI ALLA CARBONARA

This classic Italian pasta dish – with its rich smoky flavour and light, soft scrambled egg texture – is cooked as it should be, with the heat of the spaghetti setting the eggs to give a creamy sauce. If pecorino cheese is unobtainable, simply double the quantity of Parmesan.

SERVES 4-6

125-150 g (4-5 oz) smoked pancetta, in slices (see note)

1 garlic clove, peeled

30 ml (2 tbsp) extra-virgin olive oil

25 g (1 oz) butter

3 eggs

30 ml (2 tbsp) chopped fresh parsley

30 ml (2 tbsp) dry white wine

40 g (1½ oz) Parmesan cheese, grated

40 g (1½ oz) pecorino cheese, grated

salt and pepper

400 g (14 oz) spaghetti

PREPARATION TIME
About 15 minutes
COOKING TIME
About 7 minutes
FREEZING
Not suitable

675- 450 CALS PER SERVING

1. Remove the rind from the pancetta, then cut into tiny strips. Halve the garlic. Heat the oil and butter in a heavy-based pan. Add the pancetta and garlic and cook over a medium heat for 3-4 minutes until the pancetta begins to crisp. Turn off the heat; discard the garlic.

2. Meanwhile, in a mixing bowl large enough to hold the cooked spaghetti later, beat the eggs with the parsley, wine and half of each of the cheeses. Season with salt and pepper.

3. Cook the spaghetti in a large pan of boiling salted water until 'al dente', or according to packet instructions.

4. When the spaghetti is almost cooked, gently reheat the pancetta in the pan. Drain the spaghetti thoroughly, then immediately add to the egg mixture in the bowl with the pancetta. Toss well to cook the eggs until they are creamy. Add the remaining cheeses, toss lightly and serve at once.

NOTE: Smoked pancetta is obtainable from Italian delicatessens. If it is not available use smoked bacon but you will need to increase the quantity to 175-225 g (6-8 oz) to give sufficient flavour.

VARIATION

Spaghetti with smoked salmon and scrambled eggs is prepared in a similar way. Omit the pancetta and garlic. Instead, add 125 g (4 oz) smoked salmon strips to the egg mixture at stage 2. Heat the butter and oil and add with the pasta at stage 4. Finish as above, adding the remaining cheese and tossing in the same way.

TECHNIQUE

Toss the hot pasta and pancetta with the egg mixture. The heat from the pasta will cook the eggs.

SPAGHETTI WITH MUSSELS

This simple dish, spiced with chilli and garlic, relies heavily on the quality of the tomatoes used. The plump mussels and fragrant basil marry well with the intense flavour of the reduced wine and tomato sauce. There is not a lot of sauce – any more would overpower the mussels.

SERVES 4

900 g (2 lb) fresh mussels in shells
900 g (2 lb) really ripe fresh tomatoes
I onion
4 garlic cloves, peeled
6 basil leaves
150 ml (¼ pint) white wine
2 red chillies
30 ml (2 tbsp) olive oil
salt and pepper
450 g (I lb) dried spaghetti
small basil leaves, to garnish

PREPARATION TIME
20 minutes
COOKING TIME
35 minutes
FREEZING
Not suitable

575 CALS PER SERVING

1. Scrub the mussels thoroughly under cold running water and pull off the hairy 'beard' that protrudes from the shell. Discard any mussels with cracked or broken shells, and those that do not close when sharply tapped with the back of a knife.

2. Put the mussels into a large pan with a cupful of water. Cover with a tight-fitting lid and quickly bring to the boil. Cook for about 5 minutes, shaking the pan occasionally, until the mussels have opened. Transfer them to a bowl with a slotted spoon, discarding any unopened ones; set aside.

3. Strain the cooking juices through a muslin-lined sieve to remove any sand or grit; reserve.

4. Quarter the tomatoes and place them in a shallow saucepan. Peel and chop the onion; crush two of the garlic cloves. Add the onion and crushed garlic to the tomatoes with the basil. Bring to the boil and simmer for about 20 minutes until the tomatoes are beginning to disintegrate.

5. Press the tomato sauce through a nylon sieve or mouli to remove the seeds and skins. Return to the rinsed-out pan and pour in the reserved mussel liquid and wine. Bring to the boil and boil rapidly for 5 minutes or until reduced by about half.

6. Chop the other 2 garlic cloves; halve, deseed and chop the chillies. Heat the oil in another pan, add the garlic and chillies and cook until golden. Stir in the tomato sauce and mussels. Cover and simmer for 2-3 minutes until well heated through. Season with salt and pepper to taste.

7. Bring a large pan of salted water to the boil and add the spaghetti. Cook at a fast boil until *al dente*, tender but firm to the bite. Drain, holding back 30 ml (2 tbsp) cooking liquid – this will help the sauce to cling to the pasta. Stir in the mussel sauce. Pile into a large warmed serving dish and sprinkle with basil leaves. Serve immediately.

NOTE: If you prefer not to have the shells in the dish, remove the cooked mussels from their shells in stage 2, when they are cool enough to handle.

TECHNIQUE

Strain the mussel cooking liquor through a muslin-lined sieve to remove any sand or grit.

SPINACH TAGLIATELLE WITH BLUE CHEESE

This tasty main course can be prepared and cooked in a matter of minutes. If you happen to have a local Italian delicatessen which sells freshly made pasta, do use it for this recipe, otherwise dried pasta is fine. Serve as soon as it is ready, accompanied by a mixed salad.

SERVES 4

4-6 spring onions
400 g (14 oz) fresh or dried spinach tagliatelle
150 g (5 oz) ricotta cheese
150 g (5 oz) vegetarian blue Stilton cheese
150 g (5 oz) crème fraîche
15 ml (1 tbsp) chopped fresh coriander leaves
coarse sea salt and pepper
TO GARNISH
coriander sprigs

PREPARATION TIME
5 minutes
COOKING TIME
2-12 minutes
FREEZING
Not suitable

695 CALS PER SERVING

1. Trim the spring onions and finely chop them.

2. Cook the tagliatelle in a large pan of boiling salted water, until *al dente*, tender but still firm to the bite. The worst thing you can do to pasta is to overcook it, so be careful! Fresh pasta will only take 2-3 minutes to cook; for dried pasta, refer to the packet instructions.

3. While the pasta is cooking, crumble the ricotta and Stilton cheeses together into a bowl. Add the crème fraîche and stir to mix well.

4. Drain the pasta thoroughly in a colander and turn into a heated serving dish. Immediately add the crumbled cheese mixture, spring onions and chopped coriander leaves. Using two forks, lift the tagliatelle to coat with the sauce. Garnish with sprigs of coriander and serve immediately.

VARIATION

Replace the spring onions with 225 g (8 oz) leeks. Clean the leeks thoroughly then slice. Sauté in a little olive oil until softened. Add to the pasta with the crumbled cheese mixture and toss well.

TECHNIQUE

Drain the pasta thoroughly in a colander as soon as it is cooked.

PASTA WITH COURGETTES AND BALSAMIC VINEGAR

Courgettes are cooked until meltingly soft and their sweet flavour is enlivened with the addition of balsamic vinegar. Small to medium courgettes work best in this dish and, for the pasta, choose either large ribbons, such as tagliatelle or pappardelle, or shapes such as tubes or twists.

450 g (1 lb) courgettes
1 small onion
2 garlic cloves
75 ml (5 tbsp) extra-virgin olive oil
45 ml (3 tbsp) pine nuts
45 ml (3 tbsp) chopped fresh parsley
salt and pepper
400 g (14 oz) tagliatelle, pappardelle or pasta shapes
15-30 ml (1-2 tbsp) balsamic vinegar
90 ml (6 tbsp) freshly grated Parmesan or pecorino cheese

PREPARATION TIME
10 minutes
COOKING TIME
25 minutes
FREEZING
Not suitable

725-480 CALS PER SERVING

1. Cut the courgettes into thin slices. Peel and finely chop the onion and garlic.

2. Heat 30 ml (2 tbsp) olive oil in a large frying pan. Add the pine nuts and cook, stirring, over a medium high heat for 2-3 minutes until lightly browned. Transfer to a small bowl and set aside.

3. Add the remaining 45 ml (3 tbsp) oil to the pan. Stir in the onion and garlic and cook over a gentle heat for 2 minutes to soften. Add the courgettes and increase the heat. Cook, stirring, for about 4 minutes until just beginning to brown.

4. Add the parsley, seasoning and 30 ml (2 tbsp) water to the pan. Cover, lower the heat and cook gently for 15 minutes, stirring twice.

5. Meanwhile, cook the pasta in a large pan of boiling salted water until 'al dente', or according to packet instructions. (Fresh pasta ribbons will need only 2-3 minutes cooking time.)

6. Uncover the courgettes and cook for a moment or two over a high heat, stirring gently, until any excess liquid has evaporated. Remove from the heat and sprinkle with the balsamic vinegar and pine nuts.

7. Drain the pasta thoroughly and add to the courgettes with two thirds of the grated cheese. Toss to mix. Serve at once, sprinkled with the remaining grated Parmesan or pecorino.

NOTE: Balsamic vinegar can be bought at reasonable prices in many supermarkets. If you are buying it from a specialist shop you may find prices vary, depending on the maturity of the vinegar. The longer the vinegar has been matured the more concentrated the flavour, so – although more expensive – you won't need to use as much.

TECHNIQUE

Cook the courgette slices with the onion and garlic over a high heat, stirring constantly, until they are beginning to brown.

FETTUCINE WITH GORGONZOLA AND SPINACH

The rich and creamy flavour of this pasta sauce belies its few simple ingredients. Use small young, tender spinach leaves if possible. Larger spinach leaves can be used, but they will need to have their stalks removed and will require shredding or rough chopping before cooking. Serve this pasta dish accompanied by some flavoured bread and, perhaps, a crisp colourful salad.

SERVES 4-6

350 g (12 oz) young leaf
  spinach
225 g (8 oz) gorgonzola
  cheese
75 ml (3 fl oz) milk
25 g (1 oz) butter
salt and pepper
400 g (14 oz) fettucine,
  tagliatelle or long fusilli
TO SERVE
freshly grated nutmeg

PREPARATION TIME
About 15 minutes
COOKING TIME
10 minutes
FREEZING
Not suitable

630-420 CALS PER SERVING

1. Wash the spinach thoroughly and remove any large stalks. Place in a clean saucepan and cook, stirring, over a medium high heat for 2-3 minutes until wilted. There is no need to add extra water – the small amount clinging to the leaves after washing provides sufficient moisture. Drain well in a colander or sieve, pressing out any excess liquid.

2. Cut the gorgonzola into small pieces. Place in a clean pan with the milk and butter. Heat gently, stirring, until melted to a creamy sauce. Stir in the drained spinach. Season to taste with pepper; salt may not be necessary because the gorgonzola is quite salty.

3. Just before serving, cook the pasta in a large pan of boiling salted water until 'al dente' or according to packet instructions. (Fresh pasta will require only 2-3 minutes cooking time.)

4. Drain the pasta thoroughly and add to the sauce. Toss well to mix. Serve at once, sprinkled with a little freshly grated nutmeg.

VARIATIONS

Add 125 g (4 oz) cooked smoked ham, cut into small dice or fine strips, to the sauce with the wilted spinach.

As an alternative to gorgonzola, make this dish with dolcelatte cheese, which will provide a milder, sweeter flavour.

TECHNIQUE

Drain the cooked spinach thoroughly, pressing it with the back of a wooden spoon to remove as much liquid as possible.

PASTA WITH CHORIZO

Chorizo is a spicy Spanish sausage, liberally flavoured and coloured with paprika. It is available both raw by the piece, and cured ready to slice and eat. If you are unable to buy it raw in one piece, use cured chorizo – sold pre-packed in supermarkets – and cook in the sauce for 5 minutes only. A robust red wine is the ideal accompaniment to this rustic dish.

SERVES 4-6

1 onion
2 garlic cloves
30 ml (2 tbsp) olive oil
30 ml (2 tbsp) tomato purée
30 ml (2 tbsp) mild paprika
1 dried chilli
2 bay leaves
2 fresh thyme sprigs
2 fresh rosemary sprigs
150 ml (¼ pint) dry red
   wine
425 g (15 oz) can chopped
   tomatoes
salt and pepper
450 g (1 lb) raw chorizo
   sausage, in one piece
400-450 g (14 oz-1 lb) fresh
   or dried pasta
chopped parsley, to garnish

PREPARATION TIME
10 minutes
COOKING TIME
About 50 minutes
FREEZING
Suitable

950-630 CALS PER SERVING

1. Peel and finely chop the onion. Crush the garlic. Heat the oil in a heavy-based saucepan, add the onion and garlic and sauté for about 5 minutes or until softened. Add the tomato purée and paprika and cook for 2 minutes, stirring all the time.

2. Crumble in the chilli, then add the bay leaves, thyme and rosemary. Pour in the wine and bring to the boil. Cook for 2 minutes, stirring. Add the tomatoes with their juice and bring to the boil again. Lower the heat and simmer gently for 30 minutes. Season generously with salt and pepper.

3. Cut the chorizo sausage into thick slices and add to the sauce. Cook for 15 minutes.

4. Meanwhile bring a large pan of boiling salted water to the boil. Add the pasta, bring back to the boil and stir once. Cook until *al dente*, tender but firm to the bite. Dried pasta will take about 10-12 minutes; fresh pasta 1-5 minutes.

5. Drain the pasta in a colander, shaking it vigorously to remove all water. Divide between warmed individual serving bowls or turn into a large warmed serving bowl. Spoon the sauce on top of the pasta, sprinkle with plenty of chopped parsley and serve immediately.

TECHNIQUE

Add the pasta to the boiling water and stir once to ensure it doesn't stick together.

PASTA AND COURGETTES IN TOMATO CREAM

A beautiful pink and creamy dish, combining ribbon pasta with pretty green-edged ribbons of courgettes in a creamy tomato sauce. Serve as a vegetarian starter or supper dish, accompanied by a salad if you like. Alternatively, it makes an excellent accompaniment to grilled fish, chicken or lamb.

1. Using a swivel vegetable peeler, pare strips lengthways from the courgettes to make ribbons, discarding the outside skin pieces; set aside. Immerse the tomatoes in a bowl of boiling water for 30 seconds, then drain and peel away the skins. Roughly chop the tomato flesh.

2. Cook the pasta in a large pan of boiling salted water until *al dente* (tender but still firm to the bite).

3. Meanwhile, melt the butter in a pan, add the chopped tomatoes and cook gently until softened. Add the cream and season with salt and pepper. Gently stir in the courgette ribbons and simmer for about 2 minutes, until they are just soft.

4. Drain the pasta and transfer to a warmed serving bowl. Pour the sauce over the pasta and sprinkle on half of the Parmesan. Toss very gently to mix. Scatter with the remaining Parmesan and basil leaves and serve immediately.

VARIATION

Use leeks, cut in long thin strips, instead of the courgettes. Rather than cook them in the sauce, add them to the pasta for the last 2 minutes of its cooking. Drain together with the pasta and toss in the tomato cream sauce.

TECHNIQUE

Using a swivel vegetable peeler and pressing firmly, shave long strips from the courgettes to make ribbons.

PASTA WITH ROASTED VEGETABLES

Pappardelle is a wide ribbon pasta which always looks attractive served with vegetables. Here it is tossed in a light, fresh-flavoured sauce and topped with roasted Mediterranean vegetables, to make a wonderful wholesome dish with an intense flavour.

SERVES 4

1 fennel bulb
2 yellow peppers
1 red onion
2 garlic cloves, peeled
15 ml (1 tbsp) olive oil
150 ml (¼ pint) low-fat bio yogurt
125 g (4 oz) ricotta or other curd cheese
30 ml (2 tbsp) semi-skimmed milk
30 ml (2 tbsp) chopped fresh basil
30 ml (2 tbsp) chopped fresh parsley
salt and pepper
350 g (12 oz) fresh pappardelle or tagliatelle
30 ml (2 tbsp) freshly grated Parmesan cheese
30 ml (2 tbsp) black olives
30 ml (2 tbsp) capers
TO GARNISH
flat-leaf parsley

PREPARATION TIME
20 minutes
COOKING TIME
20-25 minutes
FREEZING
Not suitable

485 CALS PER SERVING

1. Preheat the oven to 220°C (425°F) Mark 7. Trim the fennel and cut lengthwise into slices, about 2.5 cm (1 inch) thick; reserve a few fronds for garnish. Cut the peppers in half, remove the seeds and core and cut into broad 2.5 cm (1 inch) long strips. Peel and slice the onion. Place the vegetables, including the whole garlic cloves, on a baking sheet. Brush lightly with the oil and bake in the oven for 20-25 minutes, until browning along the edges.

2. Meanwhile, place the yogurt, cheese and milk in a bowl. Add the basil and parsley, season liberally with black pepper and mix to form a pale green sauce. Transfer the sauce to a pan and heat through gently.

3. Cook the pasta in a large pan of boiling salted water for 4-5 minutes, until *al dente* (tender but firm to the bite); drain thoroughly. Add to the sauce with the Parmesan and toss well. Transfer to a warmed serving dish.

4. Remove the vegetables from the oven, mix in the olives and capers and serve on top of the pasta. Garnish with flat-leaf parsley and the reserved fennel fronds. Serve at once.

VARIATION

For a roasted ratatouille sauce, replace the fennel with 1 small aubergine; a few tomatoes and 1-2 courgettes. Roast as above. Omit the capers.

TECHNIQUE

Place the prepared vegetables on a baking sheet and brush lightly with oil before roasting.

PASTA WITH CHICKEN AND NIÇOISE SAUCE

Although this isn't a traditional Provençale recipe, it has many of the flavours associated with that fertile area – thyme, olives, tomatoes, courgettes and, of course, garlic. If you're making this during the summer and you come across some ripe, red squashy tomatoes use them, rather than opening a can. Flavourless tomatoes simply will not do!

SERVES 4

2 shallots or 1 onion

2 garlic cloves

1 hot red chilli

2 chicken breast fillets, skinned

45 ml (3 tbsp) virgin olive oil

2 fresh thyme sprigs

425 g (15 oz) can chopped tomatoes

generous splash of red wine

2 small courgettes (optional)

about 450-700 g (1-1½ lb) dried pasta ribbons, such as pappardelle or tagliatelle

handful of black and green olives

15 ml (1 tbsp) capers (optional)

salt and pepper

chopped fresh parsley, to garnish

PREPARATION TIME
10 minutes
COOKING TIME
About 20 minutes
FREEZING
Suitable: Sauce only

640 CALS PER SERVING

1. Peel and finely chop the shallots or onion and the garlic. Chop the chilli. Cut the chicken into bite-sized pieces.

2. Heat the olive oil in a large saucepan. Add the chicken and cook over a high heat until browned all over. Remove from the pan and set aside. Add the shallots or onion, garlic and chilli and cook for a few minutes until softened.

3. Return the chicken to the pan and add the thyme, tomatoes and wine. Bring to the boil, lower the heat and simmer for about 15 minutes or until the chicken is cooked right through.

4. Meanwhile, trim and roughly chop the courgettes, if using. Add the pasta to a large pan of boiling salted water and cook, according to the packet instructions, until *al dente* (cooked but still firm to the bite).

5. Add the courgettes and olives to the sauce, with the capers if using. Season with salt and pepper to taste. Simmer for 5 minutes or until the courgettes are just softened but still retain some bite.

6. Drain the pasta thoroughly in a colander. Serve topped with the sauce and garnished with plenty of chopped parsley.

VARIATION

Halve 2 peppers and grill, cut-side down, until the skins are charred. Cover with a cloth and leave to cool slightly, then peel away the skins. Discard the cores and seeds, and cut the flesh into strips. Add to the sauce with the courgettes.

TECHNIQUE

Fry the bite-sized chicken pieces in the hot oil, turning constantly, until evenly browned.

VEGETARIAN LASAGNE

This vegetarian lasagne has a rich Mediterranean vegetable filling complemented by a set custard-like topping made from goat's cheese, eggs and cream. Use the mild soft young goat's cheese – Chèvre Frais – which is usually sold in tubs for this. Alternatively you can use cream cheese or curd cheese instead.

SERVES 6

4 red, orange or yellow
   peppers
2 medium aubergines
2 onions, peeled
4 garlic cloves, peeled
75 ml (5 tbsp) extra-virgin
   olive oil
45 ml (3 tbsp) chopped fresh
   oregano
75 ml (5 tbsp) red wine or
   water
90 ml (6 tbsp) sun-dried
   tomato paste
salt and pepper
12 sheets dried lasagne
TOPPING
350 g (12 oz) fresh soft
   goat's cheese
2 eggs
150 ml (¼ pint) single
   cream
45 ml (3 tbsp) dry white
   breadcrumbs
30 ml (2 tbsp) freshly grated
   Parmesan cheese

PREPARATION TIME
About 1 hour
COOKING TIME
40 minutes, to bake
FREEZING
Suitable: Before baking

685 CALS PER SERVING

1. Preheat the grill to hot. Grill the whole peppers, turning from time to time, until the skins are blackened and blistered all over. This will take about 20 minutes. Allow to cool slightly, then over a bowl to catch the juices, remove the skins. Chop the flesh, discarding the seeds, and set aside with the juices.

2. Meanwhile, cut the aubergines into 1 cm (½ inch) dice. Place in a colander, rinse, then sprinkle liberally with salt. Leave for 20 minutes, to extract the bitter juices. Rinse again, then blanch in boiling water for 1 minute; drain well.

3. Chop the onions; thinly slice the garlic. Heat the oil in a large saucepan. Add the onions and cook, stirring frequently, for about 8 minutes until soft and golden. Add the garlic and cook for a further 2 minutes. Add the wine and allow to bubble for 1 minute, then stir in the aubergine, oregano and sun-dried tomato paste. Cover and cook over a medium heat for 15-20 minutes, stirring frequently. Remove from the heat and stir in the grilled peppers and seasoning.

4. Preheat the oven to 190°C (375°F) Mark 5. Cook the lasagne in a large pan of boiling salted water until 'al dente' or according to packet instructions. Drain, then drop into a bowl of cold water with 30 ml (2 tbsp) oil added to prevent the sheets from sticking. Drain again and lay on a clean tea towel.

5. Oil a baking dish, measuring about 25 x 18 x 8 cm (10 x 7 x 3½ inches). Spread one third of the filling in the base and then cover with a layer of pasta, trimming to fit the dish as necessary. Add another third of the filling and cover with pasta as before. Cover with the last of the filling and arrange the remaining pasta sheets over the top.

6. To make the topping, place the goats' cheese in a bowl, add the eggs and beat well. Stir in the cream and seasoning. Pour over the lasagne and spread evenly. Sprinkle with the breadcrumbs and Parmesan, then bake for about 35-40 minutes, until heated through and lightly browned on top.

VARIATION

Replace the goat's cheese topping with 350 g (12 oz) mozzarella, cut into slices.

TECHNIQUE

Layer the filling and pasta sheets in the baking dish, trimming to fit as necessary.

GARLIC AND HONEY PORK WITH VEGETABLE NOODLES

Lean, thin cuts of tender meat, pork tenderloins can be quickly cooked in a hot oven. The savoury liquid that flavours the meat during cooking then dresses the vegetables and noodles that accompany it.

1. Preheat the oven to 220°C (425°F) Mark 7. Trim any fat and membrane from the pork tenderloins and prick them all over with a fork. Arrange them side by side but not touching in a roasting tin.

2. Peel and grate the ginger. Mix the garlic, ginger, honey, soy sauce, sherry and oil together in a bowl, then pour over the pork tenderloins, turning them to coat all over.

3. Roast in the oven for 25 minutes, turning the pork, basting and sprinkling with the sesame seeds after 15 minutes.

4. Meanwhile, prepare the 'vegetable noodles'. Halve the pepper lengthways. Remove the core and seeds, then shred finely. Trim the spring onions and slice diagonally. Remove the coarse outer leaves from the lemon grass, then shred the stalks very thinly. Rinse and drain the beansprouts in a large colander. Mix the lemon rind and juice with the sesame oil.

5. When the meat is ready, leave to stand in the switched-off oven. Put the noodles in a heatproof bowl, pour on boiling water to cover and stir to separate the noodles.

6. Heat the oil in a wok or sauté pan, add the yellow pepper, spring onions and lemon grass and stir-fry for 1 minute. Drain the noodles through the beansprouts in the colander, shake well and add to the stir-fry.

7. Transfer the pork tenderloins to a carving board. Pour the liquid from the roasting tin over the noodle mixture. Add the lemon and sesame oil mixture and stir-fry briefly. Carve the meat into slices, about 5 mm (¼ inch) thick, and serve with the vegetable noodles.

TECHNIQUE

Cut the yellow pepper into long fine slices. Slice the spring onions on the diagonal.

THAI STIR-FRIED NOODLES WITH TOFU

This recipe is based on the classic Thai noodle dish called *phat thai* which is basically a combination of rice noodles, dried shrimp, tofu, eggs and vegetables coated in a tangy peanut sauce. This dish, or a variation of it, is typical of the noodle dishes sold as snacks from street stalls throughout Thailand.

SERVES 4

125 g (4 oz) tofu
8 shallots, peeled
1 garlic clove, peeled
2.5 cm (1 inch) piece fresh
   root ginger, peeled
30 ml (2 tbsp) sweet soy
   sauce
5 ml (1 tsp) rice vinegar
225 g (8 oz) rice noodles
30 ml (2 tbsp) sunflower oil
15 g (½ oz) dried shrimp
   (optional)
1 egg, beaten
25 g (1 oz) bean sprouts
25 g (1 oz) raw peanuts,
   chopped and toasted
SAUCE
1 dried red chilli, seeded
30 ml (2 tbsp) lemon juice
15 ml (1 tbsp) Thai fish sauce
15 ml (1 tbsp) caster sugar
30 ml (2 tbsp) smooth
   peanut butter
TO GARNISH
basil leaves

PREPARATION TIME
25 minutes
COOKING TIME 35 minutes
FREEZING Not suitable

400 CALS PER SERVING

1. Preheat the oven to 200°C (400°F) Mark 6. Drain the tofu and cut into 2.5 cm (1 inch) cubes. Halve the shallots and place in a small roasting pan with the tofu.

2. Crush the garlic and ginger and blend with the sweet soy sauce, vinegar and 30 ml (2 tbsp) water. Pour over the tofu and shallots and toss well. Roast near the top of the oven for 30 minutes until the tofu and shallots are golden.

3. Meanwhile soak the noodles according to the packet instructions. Drain, refresh under cold running water and set aside.

4. Make the sauce. Finely chop the chilli and place in a small pan with the remaining ingredients. Stir over a gentle heat until the sugar is dissolved. Keep warm.

5. Heat the oil in a wok and stir-fry the dried shrimp, if using, for 1 minute. Add the noodles and egg to the wok and stir over a medium heat for 3 minutes. Add the tofu and shallots, together with any pan juices. Stir well, then remove from the heat.

6. Stir in the bean sprouts and sauce and divide between warmed serving plates. Sprinkle with the toasted peanuts and serve at once, garnished with basil.

VARIATION

Replace the tofu with 125 g (4 oz) minced pork. Quickly stir-fry the pork, shallots, garlic and ginger in a little oil until browned. Stir in the noodles and eggs and stir-fry for 2 minutes, then add the remaining ingredients, cover the pan and heat through.

TECHNIQUE

Drain the noodles, then refresh under cold running water.

CRISPY NOODLES WITH VEGETABLES

Crisp deep-fried transparent noodles are tossed with stir-fried vegetables and topped with coriander omelette shreds. If preferred, flavour the omelette with 15 ml (1 tbsp) soy sauce instead of coriander.

SERVES 4

125 g (4 oz) thin,
    transparent rice noodles
    or rice sticks
vegetable oil, for deep-frying
2.5 cm (1 inch) piece fresh
    root ginger
175 g (6 oz) shiitake or
    button mushrooms
few Chinese leaves
1 red chilli
15 ml (1 tbsp) peanut or
    vegetable oil
125 g (4 oz) mangetouts
75 g (3 oz) beansprouts
30 ml (2 tbsp) soy sauce
30 ml (2 tbsp) dry sherry
5 ml (1 tsp) sugar
CORIANDER OMELETTE
2 eggs
30 ml (2 tbsp) milk
45 ml (3 tbsp) chopped fresh
    coriander
salt and pepper
a little vegetable oil or
    butter, for frying

PREPARATION TIME
20 minutes
COOKING TIME
About 10 minutes
FREEZING
Not suitable

390 CALS PER SERVING

1. To make the omelette, put the eggs, milk, coriander and seasoning in a jug and whisk together, using a fork.

2. Heat a little oil or butter in an omelette pan or small frying pan. Pour in the egg mixture and cook over a high heat until it begins to set. As it sets around the edge, use a palette knife to pull the set mixture towards the middle, letting the uncooked mixture run underneath. Cook until the egg is set all over.

3. Turn the omelette out onto a sheet of non-stick baking parchment and leave to cool. When cool, roll up and cut into thin slices.

4. Break the noodles into lengths, about 7.5 cm (3 inches) long. Heat the oil in a deep-fat fryer to 175°C (345°F). Test the temperature by dropping in a cube of bread – it should sizzle and become golden brown in 1 minute. Cook the noodles in batches. Deep-fry a small handful at a time for about 30 seconds until they swell and puff up. Remove from the pan with a slotted spoon and drain on crumpled kitchen paper. Don't cook too many at a time as they expand on cooking.

5. Peel and shred the ginger. Thickly slice the mushrooms. Coarsely shred the Chinese leaves. Slice the chilli, removing the seeds if a milder flavour is preferred.

6. Heat the peanut oil in a wok. Add the mushrooms and ginger and stir-fry over a high heat for 2 minutes. Add the chilli, mangetouts, beansprouts and shredded leaves and stir-fry for 1 minute. Add the soy sauce, sherry and sugar and cook for 1 minute to heat through. Add the noodles to the pan and toss to mix, being careful not to crush them. (Don't worry if they won't mix properly.)

7. Turn the vegetables and noodles into a warmed serving bowl and top with the omelette shreds. Serve immediately.

VARIATIONS

Stir-fry 50 g (2 oz) cashew nuts or almonds with the vegetables.

TECHNIQUE

When cold roll up the omelette, like a Swiss roll, and cut into thin slices.

DESSERTS

TIRAMISU

Tiramisu literally means 'whip me up' and this explains how easy it is to prepare this popular velvety smooth Italian dessert. It is the rich mascarpone and coffee liqueur which makes it a totally indulgent experience. If preferred, you can use savoiadi (sponge fingers) instead of cake.

SERVES 6-8

250 ml (8 fl oz) hot strong coffee
10 ml (2 tsp) brown sugar
125 ml (4 fl oz) coffee liqueur, such as Tia Maria or Kahlua
3 eggs, separated
75 g (3 oz) caster sugar
350 g (12 oz) mascarpone cheese
125 ml (4 fl oz) Marsala
225 g (8 oz) Madeira cake or plain sponge
50-75 g (2-3 oz) plain chocolate, grated
TO FINISH
30 ml (2 tbsp) cocoa powder
chocolate curls (optional)

PREPARATION TIME
25 minutes, plus chilling
COOKING TIME
Nil
FREEZING
Not suitable

670-500 CALS PER SERVING

1. Sweeten the coffee with the brown sugar and allow to cool, then stir in the coffee liqueur.

2. Put the egg yolks and sugar in a large bowl and beat until the mixture is pale and thick, then gradually beat in the mascarpone. Stir in the Marsala.

3. In a separate bowl, whisk the egg whites until they stand in stiff peaks. Carefully fold into the mascarpone mixture.

4. Cut the sponge cake into 2 cm (¾ inch) thick slices. Arrange in a layer over the base of a 1.2 litre (2 pint) glass serving bowl. Pour the cooled coffee mixture evenly over the cake and leave for a few minutes until absorbed.

5. Spoon two thirds of the cheese mixture over the sponge and scatter with half of the grated chocolate. Cover with the rest of the cheese mixture and top with the remaining chocolate. Chill in the refrigerator for at least 1 hour.

6. To serve, dust with a little sifted cocoa and decorate with chocolate curls if desired.

CHOCOLATE CURLS: Spread melted plain chocolate on a marble slab to a depth of 5 mm (¼ inch). When just set, draw a fine-bladed knife across the surface of the chocolate at a 45° angle to shave off curls.

VARIATION

As an alternative to mascarpone, you could use a blend of cream cheese and thick cream. Although not quite so rich the result is still pretty good.

TECHNIQUE

Carefully fold the whisked egg whites into the mascarpone mixture until evenly blended.

TARTE TATIN

This classic French pudding is cooked upside down. Apples are cooked first in a buttery caramel, then covered with a layer of pastry. After baking the tart is turned over so the fruit layer is on top and the buttery, caramel juices ooze into the crisp puffy crust. Serve it warm with a scoop of vanilla ice cream.

SERVES 6

225 g (8 oz) ready-made puff pastry (see note)
FILLING
75 g (3 oz) caster sugar
4-5 eating apples
50 g (2 oz) unsalted butter, in pieces

PREPARATION TIME
25 minutes
COOKING TIME
25-30 minutes
FREEZING
Not suitable

310 CALS PER SERVING

1. First make the filling. Put the sugar in a saucepan with 45 ml (3 tbsp) water. Dissolve over a low heat, stirring occasionally, then increase the heat and without stirring, cook the syrup to a rich brown caramel. Carefully pour into a shallow heavy-based 20 cm (8 inch) cake tin or ovenproof frying pan and swirl round to coat the base of the tin evenly with caramel.

2. Preheat the oven to 220°C (425°F) Mark 7. Cut the apples in half, then peel them and scoop out the cores, using a teaspoon.

3. Dot the caramel with half of the butter. Arrange the apple halves curved side down on top, packing them as tightly as possible. Fill any gaps with smaller wedges of apple. Dot the remaining butter on top. Place the tin or pan over a medium heat and cook for about 5 minutes to par-cook and lightly brown the apples. Watch carefully to ensure the apples do not burn.

4. Roll out the puff pastry on a lightly floured surface to a round, slightly larger than the diameter of the tin or pan. Prick all over with a fork. Carefully lift the pastry round and place on top of the apples. Pat down gently, tucking the edges of the pastry down the side of the tin. Bake in the oven for 20-25 minutes until the pastry is well risen, crisp and golden brown.

5. Allow to cool for 10 minutes. To remove from the tin, cover with a large serving plate, carefully tip out any cooking juices into a bowl, then turn the tin and plate over. Give the base of the tin a few sharp taps with a rolling pin, then carefully lift off. Drizzle over the buttery juices and serve at once, cut into wedges, with a dollop or two of vanilla ice cream.

NOTE: If you have time, make your own puff pastry according to the step-by-step recipe on page 6. You will need approximately one third of the quantity.

VARIATION

Replace the apple with 3 large ripe, richly scented mangoes. Peel, then cut the flesh from the stone into large wedges. If the mangoes are very ripe and soft, omit the cooking on the hob.

TECHNIQUE

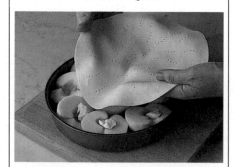

Lift the pastry round over the apples, making sure they are completely covered.

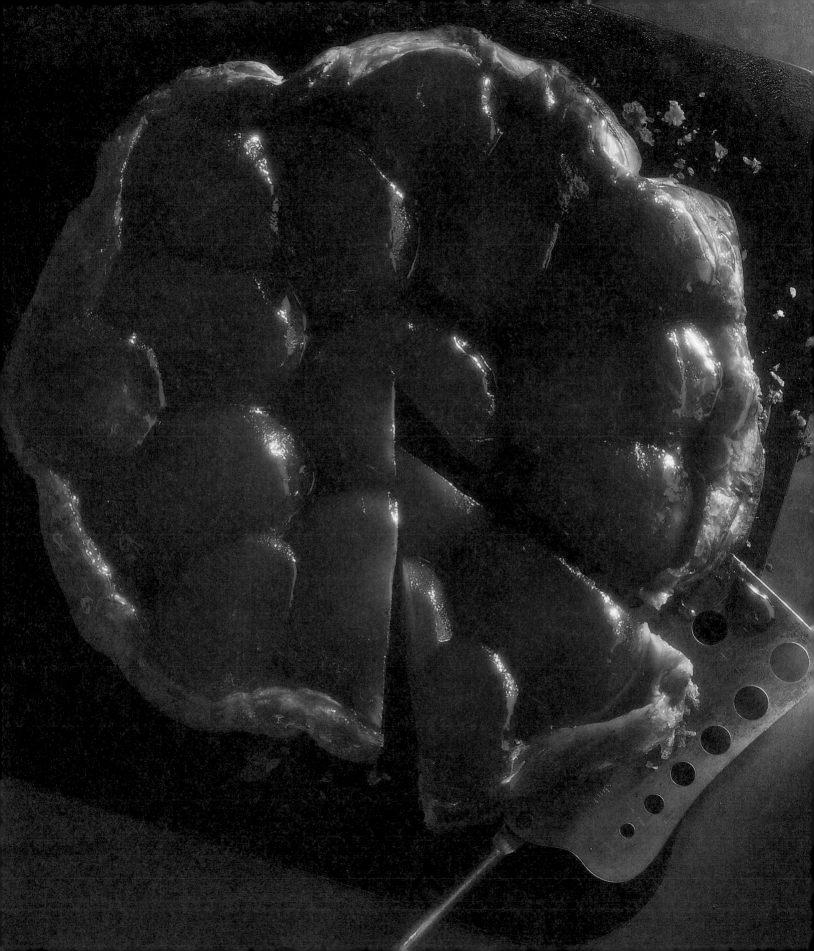

ALMOND AND AMARETTI CHEESECAKE

A light, creamy cheesecake mixture is encased in a crumbly, crunchy almond case and topped with crushed amaretti biscuits. Make the cheesecake a day before you need it – the texture improves on keeping. Serve a fruity accompaniment – nectarines poached in sweetened red or white wine are perfect.

SERVES 8

BASE
75 g (3 oz) butter
125 g (4 oz) digestive
  biscuits
25 g (1 oz) blanched
  almonds
FILLING
125 g (4 oz) mascarpone
  cheese
125 g (4 oz) ricotta cheese
50 g (2 oz) caster sugar
2 eggs, separated
2.5 ml (½ tsp) vanilla
  essence
15 ml (1 tbsp) cornflour
100 ml (3½ fl oz) crème
  fraîche
TOPPING
50 g (2 oz) amaretti biscuits
NECTARINE COMPOTE
4 ripe nectarines
150 ml (¼ pint) wine
75 g (3 oz) caster sugar
1 vanilla pod

PREPARATION TIME
35 minutes
COOKING TIME
1½ hours
FREEZING
Not suitable

445 CALS PER SERVING

1. Preheat the oven to 150°C (300°F) Mark 2. Grease and line a 20 cm (8 inch) loose-based or springform cake tin. Melt the butter in a small pan. Meanwhile, whizz the biscuits and almonds in a food processor, or crush the biscuits using a rolling pin and chop the almonds finely, then mix into the butter.

2. Spread the biscuit mixture over the base and about 1 cm (½ inch) up the side of the tin, pressing it firmly with the back of a spoon. Set aside.

3. Place the mascarpone and ricotta cheeses in a large bowl and beat together well. Add the sugar, egg yolks, vanilla essence and cornflour and beat again, then fold in the crème fraîche. Whisk the egg whites until holding soft peaks. Stir one third of the egg whites into the cheesecake mixture, then carefully fold in the rest.

4. Pour the mixture into the prepared tin. Crumble the amaretti biscuit into chunky crumbs and scatter over the top. Bake in the oven, just below the middle, for 1½ hours until just firm to the touch. Turn off the heat and leave the cheesecake to cool in the oven.

5. Meanwhile, make the nectarine compote. Halve the nectarines, remove the stones, then cut into quarters and place in a saucepan with the wine, sugar, vanilla pod and 150 ml (¼ pint) water. Bring slowly to the boil, then reduce the heat, cover and simmer very gently for about 5 minutes until the nectarines are just tender. Allow to cool, then discard the vanilla pod and chill in the refrigerator for several hours.

6. Serve the cheesecake, cut into wedges, with the compote.

NOTE: If mascarpone and/or ricotta are not available, substitute cream cheese and curd cheese respectively.

TECHNIQUE

Press the biscuit mixture evenly over the base and about 1 cm (½ inch) up the side of the tin, using the back of a spoon.

RASPBERRY MOUSSE GÂTEAU

Moist hazelnut sponge rounds are layered with softly whipped cream, tangy raspberry mousse and fresh raspberries. The gâteau is topped with a crown of cream quenelles, toasted nuts and more raspberries.

HAZELNUT CAKE

175 g (6 oz) shelled
   hazelnuts

4 eggs

125 g (4 oz) light muscovado
   sugar

125 g (4 oz) plain flour

2.5 ml (½ tsp) baking
   powder

25 g (1 oz) butter, melted
   and cooled

FILLING AND TOPPING

450 g (1 lb) raspberries

1 egg, separated

25 g (1 oz) caster sugar

7.5 ml (1½ tsp) powdered
   gelatine

450 ml (¾ pint) double
   cream

150 ml (¼ pint) Greek-style
   yogurt

PREPARATION TIME
1½ hours
COOKING TIME
30-35 minutes
FREEZING
Suitable

1. Preheat the oven to 180°C (350°F) Mark 4. Grease and base line a 20 cm (8 inch) round cake tin. Spread out the hazelnuts on a baking sheet and bake for 15-20 minutes until browned. Leave to cool, then roughly chop 25 g (1 oz) and set aside. Whizz the rest in a food processor or blender until finely ground.

2. Whisk the eggs and sugar in a large bowl over a pan of barely simmering water until the mixture is thick and pale and will hold a trail. Remove bowl from heat and whisk for a further 3 minutes. Sift flour and baking powder together and fold into the mixture alternately with the ground hazelnuts and melted butter.

3. Spread the mixture in the prepared tin and bake for 30-35 minutes until risen and firm to the touch. Turn out, remove paper and cool on a wire rack.

4. To make the mousse filling, rub half the raspberries through a sieve. Whisk the egg yolk, sugar and raspberry purée in a large bowl over a pan of barely simmering water until the mixture is thick and foamy and will hold a trail. Remove bowl from heat and continue whisking until the mixture is cold.

5. Sprinkle the gelatine over 30 ml (2 tbsp) water in a small heatproof bowl and leave to swell, then stand the bowl in a pan of hot water until the gelatine is dissolved. Meanwhile, whip 50 ml (2 fl oz) cream and fold into the raspberry mixture. Gently stir in the gelatine. Whisk the egg white until holding soft peaks, then fold into the mixture.

6. Line a 20 cm (8 inch) spring-release cake tin with cling film. Cut the hazelnut cake into 3 rounds and trim to a 20 cm (8 inch) diameter. Place one sponge round in the base of the tin. Whip 150 ml (¼ pint) cream and fold in the yogurt, then spread over the cake. Scatter over one third of the reserved raspberries and cover with a second sponge round. Spoon on the mousse, scatter over another third of the raspberries and cover with the remaining sponge. Press down gently, then chill for 2 hours or until the mousse is set.

7. To serve, carefully transfer to a serving plate. Whip the remaining cream and spoon oval mounds around the edge of the cake. Scatter the reserved raspberries and chopped nuts in the middle.

TECHNIQUE

Spoon the raspberry mousse evenly over the second sponge round in the lined tin.

CHOCOLATE CUPS WITH COFFEE SYLLABUB

Circles of melted milk chocolate, loosely draped and set over moulds, make pretty containers for chocolate mousses, custards and other creamy desserts. Here the filling is a whipped syllabub flavoured with espresso coffee and liqueur. Piped chocolate decorations add a professional finishing touch.

CASES
150 g (5 oz) milk chocolate
15 g (½ oz) unsalted butter
SYLLABUB
90 ml (3 fl oz) strong black
   coffee
60 ml (4 tbsp) Tia Maria
300 ml (½ pint) double
   cream
15 ml (1 tbsp) icing sugar
grated rind of 1 lemon
TO FINISH
piped chocolate decorations
   (see page 10)
cocoa powder, for dusting
   (optional)

PREPARATION TIME
25 minutes, plus setting and
piped decorations
COOKING TIME
Nil
FREEZING
Not suitable

430 CALS PER SERVING

1. For the cases, break up the chocolate and place in a heatproof bowl set over a pan of simmering water. Add the butter and leave until melted. Draw six 12 cm (5 inch) circles on greaseproof paper. Cut out each one, 1 cm (½ inch) outside the drawn circles.

2. Place 6 narrow tumblers, upturned, on a large baking sheet. Spoon half the melted chocolate mixture onto three of the greaseproof paper circles. Using the back of a teaspoon, swirl the chocolate over the circles, making attractive fluted edges which just meet the 12 cm (5 inch) markings.

3. Lift each chocolate-covered circle over a tumbler so that it falls softly around the side. Repeat with the remaining three circles. Chill for at least 1 hour until set firm, then carefully peel away the greaseproof paper. Chill the cases while making the filling.

4. For the syllabub, mix together the coffee and liqueur. Put the cream, icing sugar and lemon rind in a bowl and beat using an electric whisk, until peaking. Gradually blend in the coffee mixture until softly peaking.

5. Spoon the syllabub into the prepared cases, peaking each serving in the centre.

Decorate with piped chocolate decorations and serve at once, dusted with cocoa powder if preferred.

NOTE: Avoid over-whisking the syllabub otherwise it will gradually lose its smooth texture and eventually curdle.

VARIATIONS

Scatter soft fruits or broken walnuts around the syllabub to serve.

TECHNIQUE

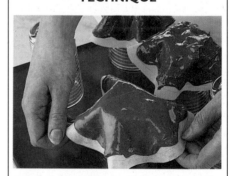

Lift each chocolate-covered greaseproof paper circle over a tumbler so that it flutes softly around the side.

PINEAPPLE AND FIG TART WITH COCONUT PASTRY

This is a fruit tart with the taste of the tropics to conjure up thoughts of warm seas, blue skies and deserted white sandy beaches! A fresh pineapple and fig filling in coconut pastry is hidden by a delicious almond topping. Serve warm, with pouring cream or Greek-style yogurt.

SERVES 6

PASTRY
50 g (2 oz) creamed coconut
175 g (6 oz) plain flour
pinch of salt
100 g (3½ oz) butter or
**   vegetable margarine**
25 g (1 oz) icing sugar
a little freshly squeezed lime
**   juice, to bind**
FILLING
1 small pineapple
3 figs
TOPPING
125 g (4 oz) butter or
**   vegetable margarine**
125 g (4 oz) caster sugar
2 eggs
125 g (4 oz) ground almonds
TO FINISH
icing sugar, for dusting

PREPARATION TIME
30 minutes, plus chilling
COOKING TIME
50-55 minutes
FREEZING
Suitable

730 CALS PER SERVING

1. To make the pastry, dissolve the creamed coconut in 30 ml (2 tbsp) boiling water in a small bowl. Mix to a smooth paste and allow to cool.

2. Sift the flour and salt into a bowl. Cut the butter into pieces and rub into the flour, using your fingertips. Stir in the icing sugar. Using a round-bladed knife, mix in the creamed coconut paste together with the lime juice to form a soft dough. Knead gently in the bowl until smooth. Wrap in cling film and chill in the refrigerator for about 20 minutes.

3. Preheat the oven to 200°C (400°F) Mark 6. Lightly butter a 3 cm (1¼ inch) deep, 23 cm (9 inch) fluted flan tin.

4. Roll out the pastry on a lightly floured surface and use to line the prepared flan tin. Chill again for 20 minutes. Line the pastry case with greaseproof paper or foil and baking beans and bake 'blind' for 10-15 minutes. Remove the paper and beans and return to the oven for 5 minutes to cook the base. Reduce the oven temperature to 180°C (350°F) Mark 4.

5. Meanwhile, cut off the top and bottom of the pineapple and stand it on a board. Cut away the skin, then remove the brown 'eyes' with the tip of a small knife. Quarter the pineapple and cut away the woody core. Cut the flesh into 2 cm (¾ inch) pieces. Halve the figs and scrape out the flesh into a bowl.

6. To make the topping, cream the butter or margarine and sugar together in a bowl using an electric beater or wooden spoon. Beat in the eggs, then stir in the ground almonds. Spread the fig flesh over the base of the pastry case and arrange the pineapple pieces on top. Spread the almond mixture evenly over the filling. Bake in the centre of the oven for 35-40 minutes or until the topping is set. Check after 30 minutes and, if necessary, cover with foil to prevent over-browning.

7. Serve warm, dusted liberally with icing sugar and accompanied by pouring cream or Greek-style yogurt.

TECHNIQUE

Stand the pineapple on a board, then cut away the skin in vertical strips.

STICKY DATE AND ORANGE PUDDING

Wallow in glorious indulgence with this steaming hot, wintery dessert. Distinctly flavoured with oranges, dates and flecks of white chocolate, the light-textured spongy pudding is served topped with a delicious toffee sauce. Serve with custard or pouring cream.

SERVES 6

175 g (6 oz) stoned dates
150 ml (¼ pint) fresh orange
  juice
50 g (2 oz) white chocolate
75 g (3 oz) unsalted butter,
  softened
150 g (5 oz) light muscovado
  sugar
2 eggs
150 g (5 oz) self-raising
  white flour
25 g (1 oz) cocoa powder
2.5 ml (½ tsp) bicarbonate
  of soda
grated rind of 1 orange
SAUCE
125 g (4 oz) light muscovado
  sugar
75 g (3 oz) unsalted butter
60 ml (4 tbsp) double cream
15 ml (1 tbsp) lemon juice
TO SERVE
pouring cream or custard

PREPARATION TIME
20 minutes
COOKING TIME
2 hours
FREEZING
Not suitable

625 CALS PER SERVING

1. Butter a 1.4 litre (2½ pint) pudding basin and line the base with a circle of greaseproof paper. Roughly chop the dates and place in a saucepan with the orange juice. Bring to the boil, reduce the heat and simmer gently for 5 minutes. Leave to cool while preparing the pudding.

2. Roughly chop the white chocolate. Put the butter, sugar and eggs in a large bowl. Sift the flour, cocoa powder and bicarbonate of soda into the bowl and beat well until evenly combined.

3. Remove one third of the date pieces from the saucepan, using a slotted spoon; set aside. Add the remaining dates and orange juice to the pudding mixture with the orange rind and chopped chocolate. Stir well, then turn into the prepared basin.

4. Cover the basin with a double thickness of greaseproof paper and sheet of foil. Secure under the rim with string. Place in a steamer and add boiling water. Cover and steam for 2 hours. Top up with more boiling water as necessary during cooking.

5. Meanwhile, make the sauce. Put the sugar, butter and cream in a small pan. Heat gently until the sugar dissolves, then stir in the reserved dates and lemon juice. Boil for 1 minute.

6. Remove the pudding from steamer and invert onto a serving plate. Pour toffee sauce over the pudding to coat evenly. Hand any remaining sauce separately. Serve with pouring cream or custard.

NOTE: If you don't have a steamer, rest the pudding basin on an upturned old saucer in a large saucepan. Pour sufficient boiling water into the pan to come halfway up the sides of the basin.

VARIATIONS

Use chopped prunes, figs or pears in place of the dates.

TECHNIQUE

Cover the pudding basin with greased greaseproof paper, then a layer of foil. Secure under the rim with string.

SQUIDGY CINNAMON MERINGUE CAKE

Really a Pavlova in disguise, this meringue – with its marshmallowy middle – is flavoured with cinnamon and baked in rectangles, then sandwiched together with cream and fromage frais tossed with chunks of fresh strawberries. It is better assembled an hour or two in advance and allowed to soften slightly. Serve in slices in a pool of cassis-flavoured strawberry sauce.

SERVES 8

MERINGUE
3 egg whites
175 g (6 oz) caster sugar
5 ml (1 tsp) cornflour
2.5 ml (½ tsp) ground cinnamon
5 ml (1 tsp) lemon juice
FILLING
200 ml (7 fl oz) double cream
75 g (3 oz) fromage frais
20 ml (4 tsp) vanilla sugar (see note on page 12)
350 g (12 oz) strawberries
STRAWBERRY SAUCE
450 g (1 lb) strawberries
60 ml (4 tbsp) caster sugar
60 ml (4 tbsp) crème de cassis liqueur (optional)
TO FINISH
a little ground cinnamon, for dusting

PREPARATION TIME
30 minutes
COOKING TIME
50 minutes
FREEZING
Suitable

300 CALS PER SERVING

1. Preheat the oven to 150°C (300°F) Mark 2. Line two baking sheets with non-stick baking parchment. Draw three 11 x 23 cm (4½ x 9 inch) rectangles on the paper then turn the paper over so the pencil marks are underneath.

2. Place the egg whites in a large bowl and whisk with an electric beater or large balloon whisk until very stiff. Whisk in the sugar 30 ml (2 tbsp) at a time, whisking well after each addition until the meringue is stiff and shiny. When all the sugar is incorporated, whisk in the cornflour, cinnamon and lemon juice.

3. Pipe or spoon the meringue mixture on to the rectangles on the prepared baking sheets and spread out to fill them evenly. Place in the oven, reduce the temperature to 140°C (275°F) Mark 1 and bake for 50 minutes. Turn off the oven and leave the meringues in the oven until cold.

4. To make the strawberry sauce, either whizz the strawberries in a food processor or blender, then sieve to remove the pips; or simply push them through a fine sieve. Stir in the sugar and liqueur (if using) and chill in the refrigerator until ready to serve.

5. To finish, remove the meringues from the baking sheets, carefully peeling off the paper. For the filling, whip the cream until holding soft peaks and fold into the fromage frais with the vanilla sugar. Chop the strawberries and fold gently into the cream mixture. Sandwich the meringues together with the strawberry mixture, then dust the top with a little cinnamon. Serve, cut into slices, on a pool of the strawberry sauce.

NOTE: If you have a fan-assisted oven, the meringues should bake quite evenly. However in a conventional oven you should switch the baking sheets around halfway through cooking to ensure the meringues cook evenly.

TECHNIQUE

Sandwich the meringue rectangles together with the strawberry cream mixture.

PEACH CROUSTADE

For this hot summer pie, fresh peaches are cooked in a buttery caramel sauce, then encased in delicate filo pastry. The pie is dusted liberally with caster sugar and baked until the crumbled pastry top is dark golden brown, very crisp and caramelised. The recipe is based on a traditional French pie.

SERVES 6

6 large, ripe peaches
100 g (3½ oz) unsalted
   butter
45 ml (3 tbsp) armagnac (or
   other brandy)
175 g (6 oz) caster sugar
1 packet filo pastry, about
   225 g (8 oz) (see note)

PREPARATION TIME
40 minutes
COOKING TIME
35-40 minutes
FREEZING
Not suitable

385 CALS PER SERVING

1. Immerse the peaches in a large bowl of boiling water for 30 seconds, then lift out with a slotted spoon and slip off the skins. Halve and stone the peaches, then cut into thick slices.

2. Melt half of the butter in a frying pan, add the peach slices and sprinkle with the armagnac and half of the sugar. Cook over a medium heat for 3-5 minutes until just tender, then leave to cool.

3. Preheat the oven to 200°C (400°F) Mark 6. Melt the remaining butter in a small pan and use a little to butter a 23 cm (9 inch) flan tin. Sprinkle 15 ml (1 tbsp) of the remaining sugar over the base of the tin.

4. Lay one sheet of filo pastry in the flan tin, allowing the corners to overlap the edge of the tin. Brush with a little of the butter, then repeat with two more sheets of filo.

5. Spoon the peaches and buttery juices into the flan tin. Flip the corners of the filo into the flan tin, then, one at a time, brush the remaining sheets of filo with butter. Crumple them and arrange on top of the peaches, covering the fruit completely. Tuck in the edges neatly down the side of the tin.

6. Sprinkle the remaining butter and sugar over the top, then bake for 20 minutes. Reduce the oven temperature to 180°C (350°F) Mark 4 and bake for a further 15-20 minutes until the pastry is crisp and golden and the sugar has caramelised. Serve warm with cream.

NOTE: Filo pastry sheets come in a variety of shapes and sizes, but the shape isn't too crucial in this recipe. Make sure though that, when you arrange the first three sheets, the corners are staggered so the tin is lined evenly.

TECHNIQUE

Immersing the peaches in boiling water loosens the skins, so they can then be peeled away quite easily.

BANANAS GRILLED WITH CARDAMOM BUTTER

Cooking magically intensifies the flavour of bananas and transforms their flesh to a melting softness. Here the flavour is further enhanced with the most exotic of spices, and a crisply caramelised crust contrasts the soft texture. Ice cream is the perfect complement.

SERVES 4

4 large bananas, rinsed

2-3 cardamom pods

50 g (2 oz) soft dark brown sugar

50 g (2 oz) butter, at room temperature

TO SERVE

vanilla, coffee or chocolate ice cream (optional)

PREPARATION TIME
10 minutes
COOKING TIME
5-8 minutes, depending on size and ripeness of bananas
FREEZING
Not suitable

280 CALS PER SERVING

1. Line the grill pan with foil, then replace the grill rack. Preheat the grill. Slit each banana skin along its length and cut the skin back a little at each end so that you can open it out slightly.

2. Break open the cardamom pods and empty the seeds into a mortar. Crush them with a pestle, adding half of the sugar in the latter stages of crushing.

3. Beat the butter and cardamom-flavoured sugar together in a bowl, then push some of the mixture along the slit in each banana.

4. Place the bananas open-side up on the grill rack and grill for 3-5 minutes until the butter melts into them and the flesh begins to soften. Sprinkle the remaining sugar on top and flash back under the grill until the bananas are softened and the topping is caramelised.

5. Serve the bananas hot in their skins, with ice cream if you like.

NOTE: The buttery syrup which exudes during cooking can be spooned from the lined grill pan back over the bananas when you serve them.

VARIATIONS

Other spices, such as cinnamon or ginger, can ring the changes on cardamom, or you could use vanilla sugar.

TECHNIQUE

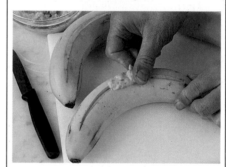

Insert the spiced butter into the slit bananas.

Two-Chocolate Lace Pancakes

Dark, chocolate-flavoured lacy pancakes are filled with a rich white chocolate mousse, then served dusted with cocoa and icing sugar on a lake of single cream. You will find that a little of the filling goes a long way. Try rolling and folding the pancakes in different ways.

SERVES 6

PANCAKES
125 g (4 oz) plain white
flour, less 30 ml (2 tbsp)
30 ml (2 tbsp) cocoa powder
15 ml (1 tbsp) icing sugar
pinch of salt
1 egg, plus 1 egg yolk
300 ml (½ pint) milk
15 ml (1 tbsp) sunflower oil
a little extra oil, for cooking
CHOCOLATE MOUSSE
250 g (9 oz) quality white
chocolate (see note)
30 ml (2 tbsp) Grand
Marnier or other orange-
flavoured liqueur
350 ml (12 fl oz) double
cream
TO SERVE
150 ml (¼ pint) single
cream
cocoa powder, for dusting
icing sugar, for dusting

PREPARATION TIME
45 minutes, plus chilling
COOKING TIME
2 minutes per pancake
FREEZING
Suitable: Pancakes only
(interleaved with greaseproof)

715 CALS PER SERVING

1. Place all the ingredients for the pancakes in a blender or food processor and work until smooth. Pour into a jug and leave to rest in a cool place for at least 30 minutes.

2. Heat a 15 cm (6 inch) crêpe pan until very hot and wipe with a little oil. (The hotter the pan the lacier your crêpes will be). Pour in about 30 ml (2 tbsp) batter, quickly swirling it around the pan. Don't worry if there are small holes in the pancake – they will look good in the final version! As soon as it sets, turn over and cook the other side. Transfer to a warmed plate and continue until all the batter is used up, heating the pan well each time and interleaving the cooked pancakes with greaseproof paper to prevent them sticking. You should have sufficient batter for 12 pancakes.

3. To make the mousse, chop the chocolate into tiny pieces and place in a heatproof bowl with the liqueur and 45 ml (3 tbsp) water. Stand over a pan of hot water and stir constantly until the chocolate is melted and smooth. Allow to cool until tepid.

4. Whisk the cream until it forms soft peaks and fold into the chocolate mixture. Working quickly – as the mousse sets fast – place 30 ml (2 tbsp) on each

pancake and roll or fold carefully to enclose the filling. Place on a tray as you go. Chill for at least 1 hour.

5. To serve, pour a little single cream onto each serving plate and place two pancakes on top. Dust liberally with cocoa powder, then icing sugar. Serve immediately.

NOTE: Use only white chocolate that has been made with pure cocoa butter for optimum flavour and texture. Lindt and Tobler are both suitable brands. The pancakes should look delicate when filled – don't make them too large!

TECHNIQUE

Fold each lacy pancake around 30 ml (2 tbsp) of the mousse filling, working as quickly as possible.

CHRISTMAS PUDDING

A rich and sticky figgy pudding packed with dried fruits plumped up with brandy and porter. The pudding is kept moist with butter instead of suet and is lightened with fresh breadcrumbs. It can be steamed in any heatproof bowl or mould – old jelly moulds make lovely shapes.

MAKES 2 PUDDINGS
EACH SERVES 8-10

two 225 g (8 oz) packets
  dried mixed fruit salad
125 g (4 oz) dried dates
225 g (8 oz) sultanas
225 g (8 oz) seedless raisins
150 ml (¼ pint) porter
60 ml (4 tbsp) brandy, dark
  rum or armagnac
1 lemon
1 orange
125 g (4 oz) ready-to-eat figs
125 g (4 oz) preserved stem
  or crystallised ginger
225 g (8 oz) whole
  unblanched almonds
225 g (8 oz) fresh brown
  breadcrumbs
225 g (8 oz) dark
  muscovado sugar
5 ml (1 tsp) grated nutmeg
5 ml (1 tsp) ground cinnamon
5 ml (1 tsp) ground ginger
175 g (6 oz) butter, chilled
4 eggs (size 2)
TO SERVE
90 ml (6 tbsp) brandy

PREPARATION TIME
30 minutes, plus overnight soaking
COOKING TIME
6 hours, plus 2 hours reheating
FREEZING
Suitable: Stage 5

465-370 CALS PER SERVING

1. Place the dried fruit salad, dried dates, sultanas and raisins in a shallow bowl and pour over the porter or stout and brandy. Grate the rind from the lemon and orange and reserve; squeeze the juice and add to the dried fruits. Stir well, cover and leave to soak overnight, stirring occasionally.

2. The next day, drain the soaked fruit, reserving any juices; discard any stones. Roughly chop the fruit, figs and ginger; place in a large mixing bowl.

3. Stir in the almonds, breadcrumbs, sugar and spices. Grate the butter and fold into the mixture. Beat the eggs with any liquid remaining from the soaked fruit and stir into the mixture with the reserved orange and lemon rind.

4. Butter two 1.2 litre (2 pint) pudding basins (or decorative metal or porcelain jelly moulds). Divide the mixture equally between the two, smoothing the surface. Cover with pleated double greaseproof paper (this allows the pudding to expand whilst cooking), and top with a pleated sheet of foil. Secure with string and make a handle to help lift the puddings out of the pan(s).

5. Place the puddings in one or two large saucepans and pour in enough boiling water to come halfway up the sides of the basins. Cover and steam for 6 hours, checking the water level and topping up

with *boiling* water as necessary. *Do not let the pans boil dry.* Cool completely, then wrap in fresh greaseproof paper and foil and store in a cool place until needed.

6. To serve, steam each pudding as before for 2 hours. Remove the papers and turn out onto a warmed serving dish. Heat the brandy in a small pan and pour over the pudding. Ignite with a match or taper and tip the plate from time to time to burn off all the alcohol. Serve with brandy or rum butter, or a thin real custard.

NOTE: If porter is unobtainable, use sweet stout instead.

TECHNIQUE

Tie securely with a piece of string and make a handle to help lift the pudding out of the pan once it is cooked.

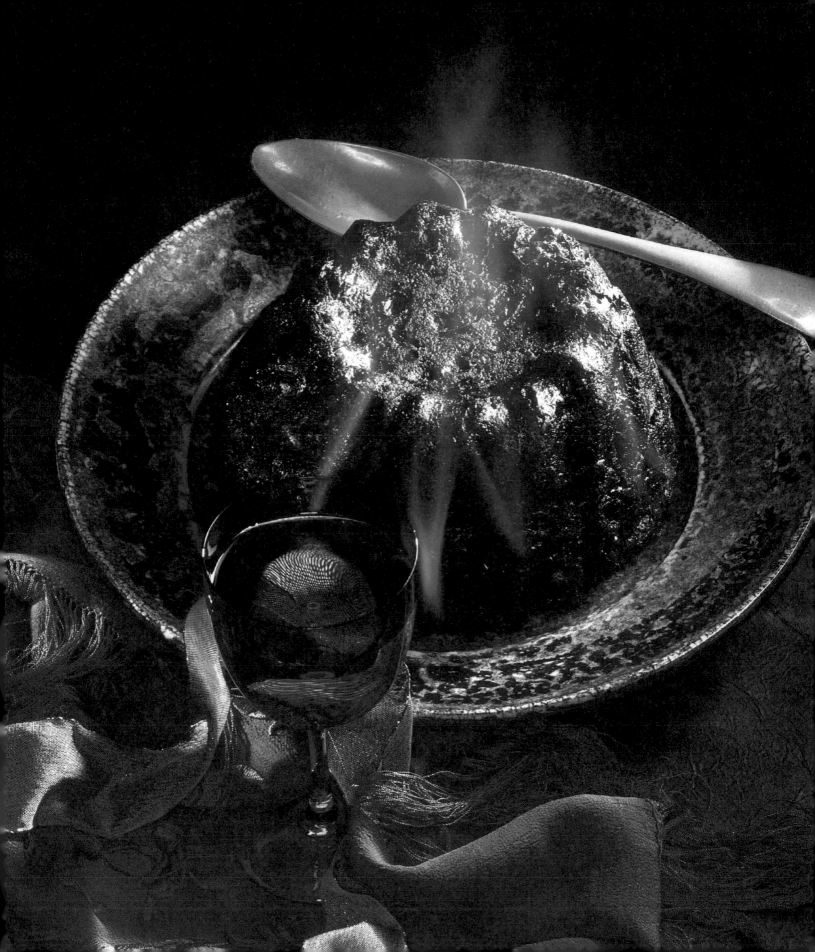

MINCEMEAT FLAN

A rich crumbly orange and almond pastry case is filled with homemade mincemeat and banana, then topped with a border of honey-glazed grilled star fruit. The mincemeat needs to be prepared at least 2 weeks ahead to allow time to mature. Alternatively you could buy some 'luxury mincemeat' instead.

1. To make the mincemeat, core and grate the apple; roughly chop the cherries and nuts. Place in a large bowl. Work the currants and sultanas in a food processor for 30 seconds, just to break them up, then stir into the apple mixture, together with all the remaining ingredients. Mix well. Cover and leave to macerate for 2 days in a cool place. Pack into sterilised jars and seal.

2. For the pastry, toast the almonds until evenly golden; do not let burn. Allow to cool *completely*, then grind finely in a food processor or electric grinder.

3. Sift the flour and pinch of salt into a bowl and stir in the almonds, orange rind and sugar. Rub in the butter until mixture resembles fine breadcrumbs. Beat the egg yolk with 30 ml (2 tbsp) orange juice and stir into the pastry until it begins to hold together; add more juice if necessary to bind the pastry. Gather the dough into a ball and knead lightly on a clean work surface until smooth. Wrap and chill for at least 1 hour. (The pastry is quite fragile and crumbly).

4. Allow the pastry to come to room temperature. Peel the bananas, cut into cubes and toss in lemon juice. Mix with two thirds of the mincemeat; set aside.

5. Roll out the pastry and use to line a 2.5 cm (1 inch) deep, 23 cm (9 inch) fluted flan tin. Chill for 15 minutes.

6. Preheat the oven to 190°C (375°F) Mark 5. Spoon the mincemeat and banana mixture evenly into the flan. Bake for 35-40 minutes until the pastry is golden brown.

7. Meanwhile, preheat the grill to high. Cut the star fruit into 5 mm (¼ inch) slices and place on a foil-lined grill pan. Brush with a little warmed honey and brown under the grill for 3-5 minutes; watch them closely! Allow to cool.

8. Decorate the flan with the star fruit and serve warm.

NOTE: The basic mincemeat recipe makes about 1.4 kg (3 lb), which is more than you will need for this flan. Use the rest to make individual festive mince pies.

TECHNIQUE

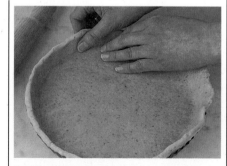

Lift the pastry into the flan tin and press well into the fluted edge. If it breaks, simply patch it up – imperfections won't show!

BREAD AND BUTTER PUDDING

Traditional puds, like this one, are enjoying something of a renaissance. Here, light and flaky croissants replace the usual bread. The baking dish is set in a bain-marie, so the custard cooks to a quite blissful consistency – only just softly set and wonderfully creamy. Soak the sultanas in a little brandy to plump them up, if you like. Serve the pudding just warm, with double or clotted cream.

SERVES 6

4 large croissants (see note)
75 g (3 oz) unsalted butter
   (at room temperature)
50 g (2 oz) sultanas
CUSTARD
300 ml (½ pint) milk
   (at room temperature)
300 ml (½ pint) double
   cream (at room
   temperature)
1 vanilla pod, split
6 egg yolks
125 g (4 oz) caster sugar
TO FINISH
15 ml (1 tbsp) icing sugar,
   for dusting

PREPARATION TIME
15 minutes
COOKING TIME
45-50 minutes
FREEZING
Suitable: Before baking

645 CALS PER SERVING

1. Preheat the oven to 180°C (350°F) Mark 4. Butter a 1.7 litre (3 pint) shallow baking dish.

2. Slice the croissants thickly, then spread with the butter. Arrange the croissant slices, butter-side up and over-lapping, in the prepared dish, scattering in the sultanas as you do so.

3. To make the custard, pour the milk and cream into a saucepan. Add the vanilla pod and place over a very low heat for about 5 minutes until the mixture is almost boiling and well flavoured with vanilla.

4. Meanwhile, in a large bowl, whisk together the egg yolks and caster sugar until light and foamy. Strain the flavoured milk on to the egg mixture, whisking all the time.

5. Pour the egg mixture evenly over the croissants. Place the dish in a bain-marie or large roasting tin and pour in enough boiling water to come half-way up the sides of the dish. Bake in the oven for 45-50 minutes until the custard is softly set and the top is crisp and golden.

6. Remove from the oven and leave the pudding in the bain-marie until just warm. Sprinkle with the icing sugar and serve with cream.

NOTE: The croissants are better used when slightly stale. Leave them in a cool place for a day or two, to dry and firm up before slicing.

VARIATION

Replace the croissants with 4-6 individual brioche (depending on size) and substitute roughly chopped, ready-to-eat dried apricots for the sultanas. When preparing the custard, flavour with the pared rind of 1 orange instead of the vanilla pod.

TECHNIQUE

Cut the croissants into thick slices, then spread with butter.

CHOCOLATE BREAD AND BUTTER PUDDING

This irresistible recipe has all the comforting qualities of a traditional bread and butter pudding – it's sweet, eggy, soft-textured and so difficult to resist. The bonus here is the generous pockets of dark, gooey chocolate sauce, melting into the spiced vanilla custard to create a perfect balance of flavours.

SERVES 6

200 g (7 oz) plain chocolate
75 g (3 oz) unsalted butter
225 g (8 oz) fruited bun loaf
  or light teabread
5 ml (1 tsp) vanilla essence
2.5 ml (½ tsp) ground
  cinnamon
3 eggs
25 g (1 oz) caster sugar
600 ml (1 pint) milk
cocoa powder and icing
  sugar, for dusting

PREPARATION TIME
15 minutes, plus standing
COOKING TIME
45-55 minutes
FREEZING
Not suitable

500 CALS PER SERVING

1. Lightly grease the sides of a 1.7 litre (3 pint) ovenproof dish. Break up the chocolate and put into a heatproof bowl set over a pan of simmering water. Add 25 g (1 oz) of the butter and leave until melted. Stir lightly.

2. Cut the fruited bread into thin slices and arrange a third of the slices, overlapping, in the prepared dish. Spread with half the chocolate sauce. Arrange half the remaining bread in the dish and spread with the remaining sauce. Finally arrange the last of the bread slices in the dish.

3. Melt the remaining butter. Remove from the heat and stir in the vanilla essence, cinnamon, eggs, sugar and milk. Beat thoroughly, then pour over the bread. Leave to stand for 1 hour until the bread has softened. Preheat the oven to 180°C (350°F) Mark 4.

4. Bake the pudding in the oven for 45-55 minutes until the custard has set and the bread is deep golden brown. Leave to stand for 5 minutes. Dust with cocoa powder and icing sugar before serving.

NOTE: Use a teabread that's lightly dotted with fruits, otherwise the pudding will be too heavy. Allow to stand for a full 1 hour before baking to ensure a really good texture.

VARIATION

Substitute the fruited bread with brioche or ordinary unsliced bread. Lightly scatter with raisins when layering the bread in the dish.

TECHNIQUE

Spoon half the chocolate sauce over the first layer of bread slices in the dish.

BRAMBLE AND APPLE CRUMBLE WITH LEMON ICE

It's fashionable to serve hot puddings with ice cream – and here, the combination of hot, autumn fruits and crisp crumble with lemon yogurt ice is scrummy! The ice cream takes 3-4 hours to freeze, so either make it to serve as soon as it is firm; or freeze ahead and allow to soften in the refrigerator for 20 minutes before serving.

CRUMBLE TOPPING

50 g (2 oz) plain flour

25 g (1 oz) plain wholemeal flour

75 g (3 oz) muscovado sugar

50 g (2 oz) ground almonds

50 g (2 oz) unsalted butter

FILLING

575 g (1¼ lb) eating apples

50 g (2 oz) unsalted butter

50 g (2 oz) caster sugar

30 ml (2 tbsp) Calvados (apple brandy) (optional)

225 g (8 oz) blackberries

LEMON YOGURT ICE

3-4 large lemons

2 eggs

2 egg yolks

200 g (7 oz) caster sugar

75 g (3 oz) unsalted butter, in pieces

500 g (1 lb 2 oz) Greek strained yogurt

PREPARATION TIME
45 minutes, plus freezing
COOKING TIME
25 minutes
FREEZING
Suitable: Ice cream and crumble topping only (stage 4).

1. First make the lemon yogurt ice. Finely grate the rind from the lemons and place in a heatproof bowl. Beat together the whole eggs and egg yolks, then strain on to the lemon rind. Add the sugar and butter. Squeeze the juice from the lemons and add 175 ml (6 fl oz) to the bowl.

2. Place bowl over a pan of simmering water and stir for about 20 minutes, until the sugar dissolves and the mixture thickens. Remove the bowl from the pan and leave to cool, stirring occasionally.

3. When the lemon mixture is cold, fold it into the yogurt until evenly blended, then pour into a freezerproof container. Freeze for about 3-4 hours until firm.

4. To make the crumble topping, sift the flours into a bowl, then tip in any bran from the sieve. Stir in the sugar and ground almonds, then work in the butter using your fingertips to make a very crumbly mixture. Set aside.

5. Preheat the oven to 190°C (375°F) Mark 5. Butter a 1.7 litre (3 pint) ovenproof dish.

6. Quarter the apples, then peel, core and cut into 2.5 cm (1 inch) chunks. Melt the butter in a large frying pan. Add the apples, with the sugar, and cook, stirring, over a high heat for 3-5 minutes until golden brown and tender.

7. In a small pan, warm the Calvados, if using. Ignite it and pour over the apples, then spread in the ovenproof dish. Scatter the blackberries on top. Spoon over the crumble topping and bake in the oven for 25 minutes until the topping is golden brown. Serve warm, with a spoonful or two of the ice cream.

Replace the brambles with 225 g (8 oz) mixed summer fruits, such as red and blackcurrants, raspberries and stoned cherries. In the winter, use frozen fruits.

TECHNIQUE

To make the crumble topping, lightly rub the butter into the flour, sugar and ground almond mixture – using your fingertips.

SUMMER PUDDING

This quintessential British pudding needs nothing more than a dollop of cream. It uses the most basic of ingredients – white bread – to enclose gleaming red fresh summer fruits, and turns out to be something quite sublime. It's extremely easy to make – and like all great dinner party puddings – is made the night before, ready to turn out and serve when required.

SERVES 6-8

450 g (1 lb) raspberries
225 g (8 oz) redcurrants
225 g (8 oz) blackcurrants
75 g (3 oz) caster sugar
8 large slices white bread,
   5 mm (¼ inch) thick
   (see note)
TO DECORATE
sprigs of redcurrants
lemon balm or mint leaves

PREPARATION TIME
35 minutes, plus chilling
COOKING TIME
5 minutes
FREEZING
Suitable

180-135 CALS PER SERVING

1. Place the raspberries in a saucepan, with the red and black currants, sugar and 45 ml (3 tbsp) water. Bring to a gentle simmer over a low heat, then cook gently for 3-4 minutes until the juices begin to run. Remove from the heat and set aside.

2. Remove the crusts from the bread slices, then cut a round of bread from one slice to fit the base of a 1.5 litre (2½ pint) pudding basin. Cut the remaining slices in half lengthways.

3. Arrange the bread slices around the side of the pudding basin, overlapping them slightly at the bottom, so they fit neatly and tightly together. Position the round of bread to cover the hole in the middle.

4. Spoon about 100 ml (3½ fl oz) of the fruit juice into a jug and set aside. Spoon the remaining fruit and its juice into the bread-lined pudding basin. Cover completely with the remaining bread slices, trimming them to fit as necessary.

5. Cover the pudding with a saucer, that fits just inside the top of the pudding basin, then set a 2 kg (4 lb) weight on the saucer. Chill the pudding in the refrigerator overnight.

6. To serve the pudding, remove the weight and saucer and invert the serving plate over the pudding basin. Hold the two firmly together and turn them over. Give them a firm, shake (up and down, rather than side to side), then lift off the pudding basin.

7. Spoon the reserved juice over the pudding and decorate with redcurrant sprigs and lemon balm or mint sprigs. Serve, cut into wedges, with cream.

NOTE: Choose a good quality close-textured large white loaf, preferably one-day old.

VARIATION

Vary the fruits according to availability. Blackberries, blueberries, cherries and plums are all suitable. Just ensure that the total weight of fruit is 900 g (2 lb).

TECHNIQUE

Line the side of the pudding basin with bread, overlapping the slices slightly at the bottom, to ensure that there are no gaps.

INDIVIDUAL SUMMER PUDDINGS

An old favourite, individual summer puddings are ideal to serve as part of a healthy diet, especially if you use wholemeal bread. Fruit of any description is good to use as part of a healthy diet – full of vitamins, fruit sugars and fibre, but with very little fat. Summer puddings can be made into autumn puddings by using apples, pears and plums (see variation).

SERVES 6

10-12 large slices of
  wholemeal bread
300 g (10 oz) blackberries
400 g (14 oz) raspberries
125 g (4 oz) gooseberries
175 g (6 oz) redcurrants
150 ml (¼ pint) red grape
  juice
30 ml (2 tbsp) chopped mint
artificial sweetener or sugar,
  to taste
lemon balm or apple mint
  sprigs, to decorate

PREPARATION TIME
30 minutes
COOKING TIME
10-12 minutes
FREEZING
Suitable

160 CALS PER SERVING

1. Line six 150 ml (¼ pint) dariole moulds or individual pudding basins with cling film. Remove the crusts from the bread. Cut a 5 cm (2 inch) circle of bread to fit the base of each mould. Cut six 7.5 cm (3 inch) circles of bread and set aside. Cut the remaining bread into strips and use to line the sides of the moulds completely.

2. Hull the blackberries and raspberries, and top and tail the gooseberries. Strip the redcurrants off their stalks. Place the gooseberries in a saucepan with the grape juice, cover and cook for 5 minutes. Add the remaining fruit and cook gently until the currants start to burst and the juice runs; this will take 5-7 minutes. Stir the mint into the fruit and add artificial sweetener or sugar to taste.

3. While the fruit is still warm, spoon into the lined moulds, using a slotted spoon, and pour on sufficient fruit juice to moisten. Reserve the rest of the fruit juice. Cover with the reserved bread rounds. Top with a saucer or plate and press down with a heavy weight. Place in the refrigerator for several hours or overnight.

4. Turn out the puddings onto serving plates and pour on the reserved juice to cover them. Decorate with lemon balm or apple mint sprigs.

VARIATION

For an autumnal pudding, use cox's apples, pears and plums. Slice the fruit, removing the stones, cores and peel as necessary. Gently poach with apple mint for 10-15 minutes, until tender.

TECHNIQUE

Fill the lined moulds with the warm fruit, using a slotted spoon.

HOT MANGO AND BANANA SALAD

This is a fruit salad with a difference: it's served hot! The delicious combination of tropical tastes, spiked with a little rum, won't ruin your diet – as it provides less than 200 calories per portion. Quick to prepare, it makes an ideal midweek dessert that's something of a treat.

SERVES 4

2 large oranges

2 firm but ripe mangoes, about 700 g (1½ lb) total weight

4 small bananas

25 g (1 oz) very low-fat spread

5 ml (1 tsp) light soft brown sugar

30 ml (2 tbsp) Malibu or rum

30 ml (2 tbsp) lemon or lime juice

PREPARATION TIME
10 minutes
COOKING TIME
5 minutes
FREEZING
Not suitable

200 CALS PER SERVING

1. Thinly pare the rind from one orange and squeeze the juice. Cut the pared rind into very thin strips and blanch in boiling water for 1 minute, to soften. Set the rind and juice aside. Peel the other orange with a serrated knife and slice the flesh crosswise into rounds.

2. Peel the mangoes with a vegetable peeler. Slice the flesh either side of the central stone, then remove any flesh from around the stone. Cut all the flesh into bite-sized pieces. Peel and thickly slice the bananas.

3. Melt the low-fat spread in a large non-stick frying pan. Add the sugar, mango and banana and sauté for 2-3 minutes or until just beginning to soften.

4. Pour in the Malibu or rum, lemon or lime juice and reserved orange juice. Add the orange slices. Bring to the boil, then serve immediately, decorated with the reserved orange rind.

NOTE: Mangoes are ripe when they yield to gentle pressure in your hand.

VARIATION

Guavas and pineapple also combine well with banana and mango and could be used instead of the orange slices, or in addition to make a larger salad. If you like a hint of spice, add 2.5 ml (1 tsp) ground cinnamon.

TECHNIQUE

Slice the mango flesh either side of the central stone.

PEARS WITH A HOT FUDGE SAUCE

A rich, gooey fudge sauce is the perfect foil for delicate slices of juicy dessert pear. For maximum contrast, chill the sliced pears before pouring on the hot sauce. Serve with a spoonful of good quality vanilla ice cream.

SERVES 4

4 large, ripe dessert pears,
  such as Comice or
  William
juice of 1 lemon
SAUCE
75 g (3 oz) butter
15 ml (1 tbsp) golden syrup
75 g (3 oz) soft brown sugar
pinch of salt
60 ml (4 tbsp) evaporated
  milk
TO SERVE
vanilla ice cream

PREPARATION TIME
10 minutes
COOKING TIME
7-8 minutes
FREEZING
Not suitable

325 CALS PER SERVING

1. Peel, halve and core the pears, then cut each half into slices. Arrange on individual serving plates and sprinkle all over with lemon juice to prevent discoloration. Chill in the refrigerator until required.

2. When you are ready to serve the dessert, put the butter, syrup, brown sugar, salt and evaporated milk in a heavy-based pan over a low heat. Stir until the sugar dissolves, then bring to the boil without further stirring.

3. Pour the hot fudge sauce over the chilled pear slices and serve immediately, with ice cream.

NOTE: Allow the sauce to cool a little before serving, especially to children.

VARIATION

The fudge sauce also makes a good topping for plain, nut or praline ice cream.

TECHNIQUE

Stir the ingredients for the hot fudge sauce in a heavy-based pan over a low heat until the sugar dissolves, then bring to the boil without further stirring.

RED FRUIT TERRINE

An unusual way to serve the best of summer's soft fruits. Redcurrants, strawberries and raspberries are layered in a loaf tin to make an attractive fruit terrine. A special dinner party dessert that will be good for your guests – low in fat and high in fibre.

SERVES 6

65 g (2½ oz) caster sugar

275 ml (9 fl oz) medium-dry
white wine

45 ml (3 tbsp) lemon juice

20 ml (4 tsp) powdered
gelatine

225 g (8 oz) redcurrants

225 g (8 oz) medium ripe
strawberries

225 g (8 oz) raspberries

TO DECORATE

mint sprigs

few strawberry slices

small redcurrant sprigs

PREPARATION TIME
55 minutes, plus chilling
COOKING TIME
Nil
FREEZING
Not suitable

100 CALS PER SERVING

1. Put the sugar in a pan with 250 ml (9 fl oz) water. Heat gently until the sugar dissolves, then bring to the boil and simmer for 1 minute. Pour into a bowl, cool, then stir in the wine and lemon juice.

2. Spoon 60 ml (4 tbsp) water into a small bowl and sprinkle over the gelatine. Soak for about 10 minutes or until sponge-like. Stand the bowl over a pan of gently simmering water for 2-3 minutes until it clears and liquefies. Pour into the wine syrup and leave to cool.

3. Strip the redcurrants off their stalks. Hull the strawberries, then slice into 5 mm (¼ inch) thick pieces.

4. Place a 1.1 litre (2 pint) non-stick loaf tin in a roasting pan. Surround the loaf tin with ice cubes and pour in enough cold water to come halfway up the sides of the tin. Arrange a thin layer of redcurrants over the base of the tin and gently spoon over enough liquid jelly to cover. Leave to set.

5. Cover with sliced strawberries, then a layer of raspberries. Repeat the layers, then carefully spoon over the remaining jelly to fill.

6. Leave the mould in the roasting pan until the jelly is just set, then transfer to the refrigerator for at least 3 hours or preferably overnight, to set completely.

7. To serve, fill a large bowl with hot water. Dip the loaf tin in the water for 3-4 seconds, then immediately invert onto a flat platter, gently shaking the tin to release the jelly. Decorate with mint sprigs, strawberry slices and redcurrants. Slice and serve with single cream or yogurt.

TECHNIQUE

Arrange the fruit in layers in the tin, then spoon over the jelly to fill.

SHERRY TRIFLE WITH SOFT FRUIT

Unlike many hastily assembled trifles, a 'real' trifle, based on a homemade sponge and proper custard, is a heavenly treat. For convenience, you can prepare this trifle a day in advance. Keep refrigerated, but remove from the fridge about an hour before serving for optimum flavour.

SERVES 10

SPONGE
125 g (4 oz) self-raising flour
1.25 ml (¼ tsp) baking powder
75 g (3 oz) unsalted butter, softened
75 g (3 oz) caster sugar
2 eggs
grated rind of 1 orange or lemon

CUSTARD
4 egg yolks
15 ml (1 tbsp) cornflour
5 ml (1 tsp) vanilla essence
125g (4 oz) caster sugar
600 ml (1 pint) milk

TO FINISH
60 ml (4 tbsp) raspberry conserve
700 g (1½ lb) mixed soft fruits (eg raspberries, redcurrants, blackberries)
100 ml (3½ fl oz) sherry
90 ml (3 fl oz) freshly squeezed orange juice
750 ml (1¼ pints) double cream
15 ml (1 tbsp) icing sugar
30 ml (2 tbsp) brandy
finely grated rind of 1 orange
soft fruits and mint sprigs, to decorate

PREPARATION TIME
45 minutes, plus cooling
COOKING TIME
40 minutes
FREEZING
Not suitable

660 CALS PER SERVING

1. To make the sponge, grease and line an 18 cm (7 inch) cake tin with greaseproof paper. Preheat the oven to 180°C (350°F) Mark 4. Sift the flour and baking powder into a bowl. Add the butter, sugar, eggs and orange or lemon rind and beat using an electric whisk until pale and creamy. Turn into the prepared tin and bake for about 40 minutes until risen and just firm to the touch. Leave to cool.

2. For the custard, in a bowl whisk the egg yolks, cornflour, vanilla and caster sugar with a little of the milk. Bring the remaining milk to the boil in a saucepan, then pour over the egg mixture, whisking constantly. Return to the saucepan and cook gently, stirring, until thickened enough to coat the back of the spoon; do not boil.

3. Turn the custard into a bowl and cover the surface with greaseproof paper to prevent a skin forming. Leave to cool completely.

4. Split the sponge and sandwich with the raspberry conserve. Cut into pieces and scatter into a glass serving dish. Scatter the fruit over the sponge.

5. Mix together the sherry and orange juice and pour over the fruits and sponge. Cover with the custard.

6. Whip the cream in a bowl with the icing sugar, brandy and orange rind until just peaking. Spread over the custard.

7. Serve decorated with soft fruits and mint or lemon balm.

NOTE: If you haven't time to make your own sponge, use 350 g (12 oz) bought Madeira cake instead.

TECHNIQUE

Cook the custard, without boiling, until it is thick enough to coat the back of the wooden spoon.

Warm Salad of Summer Fruits

This is a lovely way to use up any leftover summer fruits after making a summer pudding perhaps, or at the end of the berry season. The fruits are warmed through in a red wine and port syrup – just long enough to soften them slightly. A spoonful of crème fraîche is the perfect complement.

SERVES 4

250 g (8 oz) strawberries
250 g (8 oz) cherries
2 firm ripe nectarines or
  peaches
175 g (6 oz) raspberries
175 g (6 oz) blueberries
125 g (4 oz) blackberries
50 g (2 oz) granulated sugar
75 ml (3 fl oz) fruity red
  wine
30 ml (2 tbsp) ruby port or
  brandy
15 ml (1 tbsp) balsamic
  vinegar
juice of 1 orange
pinch of ground mixed spice
TO DECORATE
strawberry leaves or herb
  sprigs

PREPARATION TIME
10 minutes
COOKING TIME
5-6 minutes

170 CALS PER SERVING

1. Prepare the fruits. Hull the strawberries and halve, if large. Stone the cherries if wished. Halve and stone the nectarines or peaches, then cut into thin wedges. Combine all of the fruits together in a bowl.

2. Place the sugar in a heavy-based frying pan over a low heat until melted, then increase the heat and cook without stirring, to a golden caramel: do not let it burn.

3. Meanwhile, in a jug mix together the wine, port, vinegar and orange juice. Stir in the mixed spice. Pour this mixture into the pan, taking care as the caramel will immediately spit and splatter. Stir over a low heat for 1-2 minutes until the syrup is smooth and thickened slightly.

4. Add all of the fruits to the pan. Toss in the hot syrup for 1 minute until they start to soften, then remove from the heat and leave to cool slightly. Decorate with strawberry leaves or herb sprigs and serve with crème fraîche or soured cream.

VARIATION

For a winter version, put 675 g (1½ lb) mixed dried fruits in a bowl, pour on boiling tea to cover and leave to soak overnight. Drain and reserve 75 ml (3 fl oz) of the tea. Continue from step 2, replacing the wine and port with reserved tea and 30 ml (2 tbsp) brandy.

TECHNIQUE

Protecting your hand with an oven glove, carefully pour the wine mixture onto the caramel. The caramelised sugar may set on impact, but it will melt into the liquid on heating.

THREE CLASSIC SORBETS

This book would not be complete without three of the most refreshing sorbets imaginable! The Sicilian orange sorbet is delicately flavoured with exotic orange flower water and orange juice; strawberry sorbet has a hint of rich balsamic vinegar which is almost imperceptible but brings out the flavour of the strawberries; while melon sorbet is just a taste of sunshine!

EACH SORBET SERVES 4-6

MELON SORBET
about 900 g (2 lb) very ripe
    cantaloupe or other
    orange-fleshed melon
225 g (8 oz) caster sugar
juice of 1 lemon or 2 limes
1 egg white
ORANGE SORBET
200 g (7 oz) caster sugar
10 juicy oranges
30 ml (2 tbsp) orange flower
    water
1 egg white
STRAWBERRY SORBET
450 g (1 lb) fresh sweet
    strawberries
250 g (9 oz) caster sugar
15 ml (1 tbsp) balsamic
    vinegar
1 egg white

PREPARATION TIME
20 minutes per sorbet, plus
chilling
COOKING TIME
Nil
FREEZING TIME
3-4 hours

165-280 CALS PER SERVING

1. To make the melon sorbet, halve and deseed the melon, cutting out any bad parts. Scoop out the melon flesh into a blender or food processor. Process until smooth, then press through a sieve into a bowl. Cover and chill for 2-3 hours.

2. Pour 300 ml (½ pint) water into a saucepan, add the sugar and heat gently to dissolve. Boil for 1 minute. Cool, then chill.

3. Stir the syrup into the chilled melon, then add lemon or lime juice to taste. Beat the egg white until just frothy and whisk into the melon mixture. Freeze in an ice-cream maker for optimum results. Alternatively, pour into a shallow freezer tray and freeze until the sorbet is almost frozen. Mash well with a fork and refreeze until solid.

4. To make the orange sorbet, pour 200 ml (⅓ pint) water into a saucepan and add the sugar. Proceed as for step 2, but add the thinly pared rind of the oranges and their juice. Leave to cool, stir in the orange flower water, then chill. Strain, whisk in the egg white and freeze as in step 3.

5. To make the strawberry sorbet, pour 250 ml (9 fl oz) water into a saucepan and add the sugar. Proceed as in step 2. Meanwhile, wash and hull the strawberries. Place in a blender or food

processor and process until smooth. Pass through a sieve, if liked. Chill.

6. Stir the syrup and balsamic vinegar into the strawberry purée, and beat in the egg white as in step 3. Freeze in the usual way.

NOTE: When making sorbets and ice creams it is best to have all the ingredients chilled before freezing – this speeds up the freezing process. Transfer the sorbets to the refrigerator 30 minutes before serving to soften slightly.

The melon must be as ripe as possible to ensure the intense sweet flavour.

TECHNIQUE

Pass the puréed melon through a sieve into a bowl.

LEMON SYLLABUBS WITH GRAPES

Sweet juicy grapes are steeped in a light, lemon-flavoured syrup, then served topped with a frothy syllabub. Choose seedless varieties of grapes and leave them whole. Or if you happen to find the intensely-scented large Muscat grapes, then halve them to reveal their golden flesh and scoop out the seeds with the tip of a teaspoon.

SERVES 6

450 g (1 lb) seedless green
    grapes
200 ml (7 fl oz) sweet white
    wine
finely pared rind and juice of
    1 lemon
45 ml (3 tbsp) caster sugar
300 ml (½ pint) double
    cream

TO DECORATE
blanched lemon rind shreds
    (see below)

PREPARATION TIME
15 minutes, plus soaking
COOKING TIME
Nil
FREEZING
Not suitable

330 CALS PER SERVING

1. Place the grapes in a bowl with the wine, lemon rind and juice, and the sugar. Stir gently, then leave to macerate for 2-3 hours.

2. Spoon the grapes into tall glasses, then strain the soaking liquid into a bowl. Whip the cream until holding soft peaks, then gradually whisk in the grape liquid until the cream thickens to a floppy consistency.

3. Spoon the syllabub mixture on top of the grapes. Chill for up to 2 hours, or serve at once, decorated with lemon rind shreds.

NOTE: The wine will separate out when the syllabub is left to stand, so if you prefer, serve straight away.

LEMON RIND SHREDS: Finely pare the rind from a small lemon, using a vegetable peeler. Cut into fine strips. Blanch in boiling water for 2 minutes, then drain. Rinse in cold water, drain and dry on kitchen paper.

TECHNIQUE

Gradually whisk the grape soaking liquid into the cream until the mixture thickens to a floppy consistency.

VARIATION

Replace the grapes with strawberries, halve or quarter them if large and flavour with orange rind and juice instead of lemon.

CLOTTED CREAM ICE CREAM

Nothing can compare with the flavour of homemade ice cream, particularly this deliciously rich version with its tempting variations. The perfect complement for ripe flavourful summer fruits, serve it in small scoops as it is very rich!

125 g (4 oz) caster sugar

3 egg yolks

10 ml (2 tsp) cornflour

2.5 ml (½ tsp) vanilla
essence

150 ml (¼ pint) double
cream

400 g (14 oz) clotted cream

TO SERVE

ripe soft fruits (eg
raspberries and
strawberries)

PREPARATION TIME
20 minutes, plus freezing
COOKING TIME
About 10 minutes
FREEZING TIME
About 4 hours

425 CALS PER SERVING

1. Set the freezer to fast-freeze. Put the sugar in a saucepan with 150 ml (¼ pint) water and heat gently, stirring until dissolved. Bring to the boil and boil for 1 minute. Remove from the heat and allow the syrup to cool slightly.

2. Put the egg yolks, cornflour and vanilla essence in a bowl with half of the double cream. Beat until smooth. Heat the remaining double cream in a saucepan with the clotted cream until almost boiling. Pour over the egg yolk mixture, stirring.

3. Return to the saucepan and heat gently, stirring until slightly thickened. Leave to cool, then stir in the syrup.

4. Transfer the ice cream to a freezer-proof container and freeze until semi-frozen, then whisk lightly to break up the ice crystals. Freeze until firm.

5. Transfer the ice cream to the refrigerator about 30 minutes before serving to soften slightly. Serve scooped into individual dishes, with soft fruits.

VARIATIONS

Soft Fruit: Purée 350 g (12 oz) mixed ripe strawberries, raspberries and redcurrants in a blender or food processor, then sieve to remove the pips, Stir into the cream before freezing.

Almond and Amaretto: Reduce the caster sugar to 50 g (2 oz). Stir in 75 g (3 oz) crushed macaroon biscuits and 30 ml (2 tbsp) amaretto liqueur after whisking the partially frozen ice cream.

Creamy Fudge: Reduce the caster sugar to 25 g (1 oz). Grate 75 g (3 oz) cream fudge and stir in after whisking the partially frozen ice cream.

Pear and Ginger: Soak 75 g (3 oz) dried pears in cold water overnight. Drain, chop and add to the sugar syrup. Finely chop 15 g (½ oz) preserved stem ginger and add with the pears after whisking the partially frozen ice cream.

TECHNIQUE

Pour the hot cream onto the egg yolk mixture, stirring constantly.

FROZEN VANILLA YOGURT WITH STRAWBERRY SAUCE

This is a delicious light frozen yogurt. Made with sheep's milk yogurt which is low in fat, it has a mild tangy flavour that combines well with the strawberry and balsamic vinegar sauce. If you wish to serve this during the winter, accompany with cinnamon-flavoured poached apples instead of strawberry sauce.

SERVES 6

FROZEN YOGURT
150 ml (¼ pint) semi-
   skimmed milk
5 ml (1 tsp) powdered
   gelatine
750 ml (1¼ pints) sheep's
   milk Greek yogurt
125 g (4 oz) Greek or wild
   flower-scented honey
2 egg whites
5 ml (1 tsp) vanilla essence
SAUCE
350 g (12 oz) strawberries
5-10 ml (1-2 tsp) balsamic
   vinegar
TO SERVE
225 g (8 oz) blueberries
lavender flowers, to
   decorate (optional)

PREPARATION TIME
35 minutes
COOKING TIME
Nil
FREEZING Suitable

235 CALS PER SERVING

1. Set the freezer to fast-freeze. Warm the milk in a saucepan until hot but not boiling. Remove from the heat and sprinkle over the gelatine, stirring quickly until it dissolves. Let cool slightly.

2. Mix the yogurt and honey together. When the gelatine has cooled to the same temperature as the yogurt, mix the two together.

3. Whisk the egg whites in a bowl until they form soft peaks, then fold into the yogurt mixture with a metal spoon. Stir in the vanilla essence. Freeze in an ice cream machine, according to manufacturer's instructions. Alternatively, turn into a freezerproof container, cover and freeze for 1½-2 hours, until beginning to freeze around the edge. Remove from the freezer, beat well or work in a food processor for a few seconds. Return to the freezer. Repeat twice more at 30 minute intervals, then freeze until firm.

4. To prepare the sauce, purée the strawberries in a blender or food processor. If preferred, pass the purée through a nylon sieve. Stir the balsamic vinegar into the strawberry purée and pour into a jug.

5. Remove the ice cream from the freezer 20-30 minutes before required, to soften. Scoop into chilled glasses,

pour on the strawberry sauce and top with blueberries. Decorate with lavender flowers if wished.

VARIATION

Fold the strawberry purée into the half-frozen yogurt, after the final beating. Use other puréed fruits to flavour the ice cream. Spoon the half-frozen yogurt into individual ramekin dishes, after the final beating.

TECHNIQUE

Fold the whisked egg whites into the yogurt mixture with a metal spoon.

BROWN SUGAR MERINGUES WITH RASPBERRY SAUCE

Generous clouds of meringue are filled with whipped cream and sliced peaches and served on a sharp ruby red sauce. Demerara sugar adds a slight caramel flavour to the meringues and colours them a pretty, pale beige. Use nectarines instead of peaches, or strawberries, if you prefer.

SERVES 6

MERINGUE
4 egg whites
125 g (4 oz) granulated
  sugar
125 g (4 oz) demerara sugar
RASPBERRY SAUCE
450 g (1 lb) fresh or frozen
  raspberries, thawed
30 ml (2 tbsp) lemon juice
icing sugar, to taste
30 ml (2 tbsp) kirsch
TO ASSEMBLE
2-3 ripe peaches
15 ml (1 tbsp) kirsch
300 ml (½ pint) double
  cream

PREPARATION TIME
35 minutes, plus cooling
COOKING TIME
3-4 hours
FREEZING
Not suitable

375 CALS PER SERVING

1. Preheat the oven to 110°C (225 °F) Mark ¼. Put the egg whites in a large bowl and whisk until very stiff but not dry. Gradually whisk in the combined sugars, spoonful by spoonful, allowing the mixture to become very stiff between each addition.

2. Line a baking sheet with non-stick baking parchment. Spoon or pipe about 12 meringues onto the parchment. Bake in the oven for 3-4 hours until thoroughly dried out.

3. Remove the meringues from the oven and leave to cool on the parchment. Carefully lift off when cool and store in an airtight container until required.

4. To make the raspberry sauce, place the raspberries in a blender or food processor with the lemon juice and icing sugar to taste. Work to a purée, then pass through a sieve to remove any seeds. Stir in the kirsch, cover and chill in the refrigerator.

5. Immerse the peaches in a bowl of boiling water for 20 seconds to loosen the skins. Lift out and plunge into cold water to stop further cooking. Peel off the skins. Halve the peaches and remove the stones. Slice neatly and sprinkle with 15 ml (1 tbsp) kirsch.

6. To serve, whip the cream until it just holds soft peaks. Spoon the cream onto six of the meringues. Arrange the sliced peaches on top and sandwich together with the remaining meringues. Place on individual serving plates and pour over the raspberry sauce. Serve immediately.

NOTE: The secret to making these meringues is to whisk the egg whites initially until very stiff and to whisk until stiff between each addition of sugar. Do not add the sugar too quickly, or the meringue will become thin.

TECHNIQUE

Shape the meringue into large ovals, using two tablespoons and place on a baking sheet lined with non-stick baking parchment.

BAKING

FLORENTINES

These enticing chewy morsels are rich with fruit and nuts, and this original version also includes sunflower seeds. After baking, the edges of the florentines are rolled in melted chocolate. As an alternative, spread the chocolate over the backs of the biscuits and mark into wavy lines with a fork.

MAKES 12

25 g (1 oz) glacé cherries
40 g (1½ oz) flaked almonds
60 g (2½ oz) unsalted butter
50 g (2 oz) caster sugar
30 ml (2 tbsp) double cream
25 g (1 oz) sunflower seeds
20 g (¾ oz) chopped mixed
   peel
20 g (¾ oz) sultanas
15 g (½ oz) plain white flour
125 g (4 oz) plain dark
   chocolate, in pieces

PREPARATION TIME
15 minutes
COOKING TIME
8-10 minutes
FREEZING
Not suitable

170 CALS PER BISCUIT

1. Preheat the oven to 180°C (350°F) Mark 4. Lightly grease a large baking sheet. Roughly chop the cherries. Lightly crush the almonds.

2. Melt the butter in a small saucepan. Add the sugar and heat gently until dissolved, then bring to the boil. Remove from the heat and stir in the cream, sunflower seeds, mixed peel, sultanas, cherries, almonds and flour. Beat well until evenly combined.

3. Place heaped teaspoonfuls of the mixture onto the baking sheet, spacing them well apart to allow room for spreading. (You'll probably need to cook half the mixture at a time.)

4. Bake for about 6-8 minutes until the biscuits have spread considerably and the edges are golden brown. Remove from the oven and, using a large plain metal biscuit cutter, push the edges into the centre to create neat rounds. Return to the oven for a further 2 minutes or until deep golden.

5. Leave the Florentines on the baking sheet for 2 minutes to cool slightly, then transfer to a wire rack to cool completely. Cook the remaining mixture in the same way.

6. Melt the chocolate in a heatproof bowl over a pan of simmering water. Stir until smooth. Roll the edges of the

biscuits in the chocolate and place on a sheet of non-stick baking parchment until set. Store in an airtight tin.

NOTE: If the biscuits solidify before you've had the chance to shape them with the cutter, return to the oven for a further 30 seconds.

VARIATION

For added colour, dip half the biscuits in plain chocolate and the other half in milk or white chocolate.

TECHNIQUE

Working quickly bring the spread edges of the biscuits in to the centre, using a large metal cutter. Finish by rotating the cutter in a circular movement to give perfectly round biscuits.

SPICE FINGER BISCUITS

Crisp and light with a slightly chewy centre, these simple finger biscuits have an almost meringue-like texture. The deliciously spicy after-taste is accentuated by the sprinkling of black pepper, although this can be omitted for a more conventional biscuit. Serve with coffee, or as an accompaniment to creamy desserts.

MAKES 16-18

1 egg white
10 ml (2 tsp) cornflour
2.5 ml (½ tsp) ground
    cinnamon
2.5 ml (½ tsp) ground ginger
125 g (4 oz) caster sugar
75 g (3 oz) ground almonds
freshly ground black pepper
    and extra spice, for
    sprinkling

PREPARATION TIME
12 minutes
COOKING TIME
15 minutes
FREEZING
Not suitable

65-50 CALS PER BISCUIT

1. Preheat the oven to 180°C (350°F) Mark 4. Line a large baking sheet with non-stick baking parchment.

2. Whisk the egg white in a bowl until stiff, but not dry. Sift the cornflour and spices over the egg white. Add the sugar and ground almonds and gently stir the ingredients together to form a light sticky paste.

3. Place the mixture in a large piping bag, fitted with a 1 cm (½ inch) plain nozzle. Pipe 7 cm (3 inch) finger lengths onto the baking sheet, spacing them slightly apart. Sprinkle with pepper and a little extra spice and bake for 12 minutes or until crisp and golden. Transfer to a wire rack to cool.

NOTE: If you don't have a suitable piping nozzle, spoon walnut-sized pieces of the mixture onto the lined baking sheet instead.

VARIATIONS

Coriander Biscuits: Substitute ground coriander for the cinnamon and add the grated rind of ½ orange. Sprinkle crushed coriander over the biscuits before baking.
Coconut Biscuits: Replace the spices and ground almonds with 75 g (3 oz) desiccated coconut and add a few drops of almond essence.

TECHNIQUE

Pipe 7.5 cm (3 inch) finger lengths of the mixture onto the lined baking sheet, using a knife to break off the mixture.

LEMON AND CARDAMOM RINGS

Cardamom seeds – crushed to extract their heady fragrance and spicy, lemony flavour – are combined with plenty of lemon zest in these attractive biscuit rings. A deliciously tangy, smooth lemon icing is brushed over the tops of the biscuits after baking.

MAKES ABOUT 14

15 ml (1 tbsp) cardamom
  pods
175 g (6 oz) unsalted butter
50 g (2 oz) caster sugar
225 g (8 oz) plain white flour
finely grated rind of
  2 lemons
20-25 ml (4-5 tsp) lemon
  juice
LEMON ICING
125 g (4 oz) icing sugar
25-35 ml (5-7 tsp) lemon
  juice
TO DECORATE
15 ml (1 tbsp) cardamom
  pods
strips of finely pared lemon
  rind, for sprinkling

PREPARATION TIME
20 minutes, plus chilling
COOKING TIME
10-12 minutes
FREEZING
Not suitable

170 CALS PER BISCUIT

1. Preheat the oven to 180°C (350°F) Mark 4. Lightly grease two baking sheets. Crush the cardamom pods, using a pestle and mortar, to remove the seeds. Discard the pods and lightly crush the seeds.

2. Cream the butter and sugar together in a bowl until pale and fluffy. Beat in the flour, cardamom seeds, lemon rind and enough lemon juice to mix to a smooth paste.

3. Place half of the mixture in a piping bag, fitted with a 1 cm (½ inch) plain nozzle. Pipe a small round of paste onto a baking sheet. Continue piping adjacent small rounds to shape a ring. Repeat with the remaining paste to make about 14 rings. Chill in the refrigerator for about 30 minutes.

4. Bake the biscuits for 10-12 minutes until turning golden around the edges. Transfer to a wire rack to cool.

5. To make the icing, sift the icing sugar into a bowl and mix in enough lemon juice to give the consistency of pouring cream. Brush over the tops of the biscuits. Crush more cardamom seeds, as above, and sprinkle over the biscuits with the lemon rind.

NOTE: Use a lemon zester to pare delicate strips of rind for decoration. Alternatively finely grate the rind.

VARIATIONS

Use grated orange or lime rind and juice in place of the lemon.

TECHNIQUE

Pipe small adjacent rounds of the mixture in circles to form biscuit rings, about 7.5 cm (3 inches) in diameter.

ALMOND FUDGE CRUMBLES

Hidden pieces of crushed almond flakes and chewy fudge marry perfectly in these simple biscuits. Scattered with more crumbled fudge and almonds, they are baked to a cookie-like crumbliness, then served with a dusting of icing sugar. Choose a good quality almond essence to bring out the full almond flavour.

MAKES 24

75 g (3 oz) flaked almonds
50 g (2 oz) vanilla fudge
200 g (7 oz) plain white flour
pinch of salt
2.5 ml (½ tsp) bicarbonate of
 soda
125 g (4 oz) unsalted butter
125 g (4 oz) muscovado
 sugar
1 egg
5 ml (1 tsp) almond essence
TOPPING
25 g (1 oz) flaked almonds
25 g (1 oz) vanilla fudge
icing sugar, for dusting

PREPARATION TIME
10 minutes
COOKING TIME
12 minutes
FREEZING
Suitable

130 CALS PER BISCUIT

1. Preheat the oven to 190°C (375°F) Mark 5. Lightly grease two baking sheets. Crumble the almonds into small flakes. Finely dice the fudge.

2. Sift the flour, salt and bicarbonate of soda into a bowl. Add the butter, cut into small pieces, and rub in using the fingertips. Add the sugar, egg, almond essence, flaked almonds and fudge and mix to a fairly firm dough.

3. Turn onto a lightly floured surface and roll into a cylinder, 23 cm (9 inches) long. Cut the dough into 24 rounds. Place the rounds, slightly apart, on the baking sheets.

4. Lightly crumble the almonds and chop the fudge for the topping. Scatter over the biscuits and press down lightly to adhere. Bake the biscuits for about 12 minutes until turning golden around the edges. Leave on the baking sheets for 5 minutes, then transfer to a wire rack to cool. Serve dusted with icing sugar.

NOTE: Use a slab of vanilla or 'cream' fudge, or individually wrapped sweets.

VARIATIONS

Coffee and Walnut Crumbles: Add 15 ml (1 tbsp) finely ground espresso coffee to the dry ingredients and substitute finely ground walnuts for the almonds.

Apple and Raisin Crumbles: Use raisin fudge and substitute chopped dried apples for half of the almonds.

TECHNIQUE

Cut the cylinder of dough into 24 equal-sized pieces.

CHOCOLATE SOFT CENTRES

These crackled, crumbly biscuits consist of a crisp chocolate 'case' which cleverly conceals a velvet smooth chocolate centre. When served freshly baked the filling literally melts in-the-mouth; if served cool it hardens slightly to an equally delicious fudge-like texture.

1. Lightly grease a large baking sheet. Cream the butter and sugar together in a bowl until pale and fluffy. Beat in the egg yolk. Sift the cocoa powder and flour into the bowl and mix to a firm dough, using a round-bladed knife.

2. Turn out onto a lightly floured surface and knead lightly. Chill in the refrigerator for 30 minutes.

3. Preheat the oven to 190°C (375°F) Mark 5. Roll a third of the dough out thinly on a floured surface and cut out 18 circles, using a 4 cm (1½ inch) cutter. Place on the prepared baking sheet and press a chocolate square into the centre of each one.

4. Roll out the remaining dough and cut out 18 larger circles, using a 5 cm (2 inch) cutter. Lay these over the chocolate bases, securing the edges to enclose the chocolate filling.

5. Bake for 10 minutes or until the biscuits have spread and risen. Leave on the baking sheet for 5 minutes, then transfer to a wire rack to cool. Serve dusted with cocoa powder.

NOTE: The larger circles of dough will crack slightly as you position them over the bases.

VARIATION

Use milk or white chocolate squares to fill the biscuits instead of plain chocolate.

TECHNIQUE

Lay the larger circles of dough over the chocolate bases, moulding and easing them to fit.

WHITE CHOCOLATE BROWNIES

Deliciously moist, laden with chocolate and crusted in a glossy coat of sugar, chocolate brownies are one of the most adorable teatime treats! This white chocolate version, packed with hazelnuts and generous chunks of creamy white chocolate, make an exciting and equally enticing alternative.

MAKES 12

175 g (6 oz) shelled
   hazelnuts
500 g (1 lb 2 oz) white
   chocolate
75 g (3 oz) butter
3 eggs
175 g (6 oz) caster sugar
175 g (6 oz) self-raising
   white flour
pinch of salt
5 ml (1 tsp) vanilla essence

PREPARATION TIME
20 minutes
COOKING TIME
30-35 minutes
FREEZING
Suitable

490 CALS PER BROWNIE

1. Preheat the oven to 190°C (375°F) Mark 5. Grease and line a baking tin measuring 22 × 29 cm (8½ × 11½ inches) across the top and 19 × 27 cm (7½ × 10½ inches) across the base. (Or use a tin with similar dimensions.)

2. Roughly chop the hazelnuts. Roughly chop 400 g (14 oz) of the chocolate and set aside. Break up the remaining chocolate and put into a heatproof bowl with the butter. Place over a pan of simmering water until melted. Leave to cool slightly.

3. Whisk the eggs and sugar together in a large bowl until smooth, then gradually beat in the melted chocolate mixture. Sift the flour and salt over the mixture, then fold in with the hazelnuts, chopped chocolate and vanilla essence.

4. Turn the mixture into the prepared tin and level the surface. Bake for 30-35 minutes until risen and golden, and the centre is just firm to the touch. Leave to cool in the tin. Turn out and cut into 12 squares. Store in an airtight container for up to 1 week.

NOTE: When cooked, the mixture will still be very soft under the crust; it firms up during cooling.

VARIATIONS

Use any other roughly chopped nuts instead of the hazelnuts. Almond, walnuts, pecans and brazil nuts are suitable.

TECHNIQUE

Gradually beat the melted chocolate mixture into the eggs and sugar; the consistency will become quite firm.

DOUBLE CHOCOLATE MUFFINS

Homemade muffins have a deliciously light texture that crumbles into soft, airy pieces of sponge when eaten freshly baked. This dark, chocolatey version is richly flavoured with melted chocolate; additional chunks of dark and white chocolate are folded in before baking, too. These give wonderfully smooth, melt-in-the-mouth bites of pure delight!

MAKES 14

300 g (10 oz) plain chocolate
125 g (4 oz) white chocolate
375 g (13 oz) self-raising
flour
15 ml (1 tbsp) baking
powder
65 g (2½ oz) cocoa powder
75 g (3 oz) light muscovado
sugar
1 egg
1 egg yolk
10 ml (2 tsp) vanilla essence
90 ml (6 tbsp) vegetable oil
375 ml (13 fl oz) milk
icing sugar or cocoa
powder, for dusting
(optional)

PREPARATION TIME
15 minutes
COOKING TIME
25 minutes
FREEZING
Suitable

370 CALS PER MUFFIN

1. Preheat the oven to 220°C (425°F) Mark 7. Line 14 deep bun tins or muffin tins with paper muffin cases. Break up 175 g (6 oz) of the plain chocolate and melt in a heatproof bowl set over a saucepan of simmering water.

2. Roughly chop the remaining plain and white chocolate. Sift the flour, baking powder and cocoa powder into a bowl. Stir in the sugar.

3. In another bowl, beat together the egg, egg yolk, vanilla essence, oil, melted chocolate and milk. Add to the dry ingredients with the chopped chocolate and stir the ingredients together quickly until the flour is only just incorporated; do not over-mix.

4. Spoon the mixture into the paper cases, piling it up in the centre. Bake for 25 minutes until the muffins are well risen and craggy in appearance. Transfer to a wire rack and dust lightly with icing sugar or cocoa powder, if desired. Serve warm or cold.

NOTE: Unlike small sponge cakes, the muffin mixture should virtually fill the cases before cooking to achieve the traditional shape.

VARIATIONS

Add 5 ml (1 tsp) ground cinnamon or mixed spice when sifting together the dry ingredients.

TECHNIQUE

Spoon the muffin mixture into the paper cases, piling it up slightly in the centres.

CARROT CAKE WITH MASCARPONE TOPPING

In this carrot cake, brazil nuts replace the more familiar walnuts and mild, creamy mascarpone provides a delicious smooth frosting. The crowning glory is a rich decoration of fried carrot shavings – crisp, golden and lightly sugared. You could, of course, apply a sprinkling of chopped toasted nuts instead.

MAKES 8-10 SLICES

350 g (12 oz) carrots
125 g (4 oz) brazil nuts
225 g (8 oz) unsalted butter
  or margarine, softened
225 g (8 oz) caster sugar
175 g (6 oz) self-raising
  white flour
5 ml (1 tsp) baking powder
2.5 ml (½ tsp) ground allspice
4 eggs
grated rind of 1 orange
15 ml (1 tbsp) orange juice
50 g (2 oz) ground almonds
FROSTING
250 g (9 oz) mascarpone or
  low-fat cream cheese
5 ml (1 tsp) finely grated
  orange rind (optional)
30 ml (2 tbsp) orange juice
30 ml (2 tbsp) icing sugar
TO DECORATE
1 large carrot
oil, for frying
icing sugar, for dusting

PREPARATION TIME
25 minutes, plus cooling
COOKING TIME
35-40 minutes
FREEZING
Suitable: Cake only

735-570 CALS PER SLICE

1. Preheat the oven to 180°C (350°F) Mark 4. Grease and base-line two 18 cm (7 inch) base measurement moule à manque tins or sandwich tins. Dust the sides of the tins with flour and shake out the excess. Peel and finely grate the carrots. Coarsely chop the Brazil nuts and lightly toast them.

2. Cream the butter or margarine and sugar together in a bowl until pale and fluffy. Sift the flour, baking powder and allspice into the bowl. Add the eggs, orange rind and juice, and the ground almonds; beat well. Stir in the carrots and brazil nuts.

3. Divide the mixture between the tins and level the surfaces. Bake for 35-40 minutes until risen and firm to touch. Transfer to a wire rack to cool.

4. For the topping, beat the cheese, orange rind if using, orange juice and icing sugar together in a bowl until smooth. Use half to sandwich the cakes together. Spread the remainder over the top of the cake, swirling it attractively.

5. For the decoration, peel the carrot and pare into long thin ribbons, using a swivel vegetable peeler. Dry the carrot ribbons on kitchen paper. Heat a 1 cm (½ inch) depth of oil in a frying pan until a

piece of carrot added to the hot oil sizzles on the surface. Fry the carrots, in two batches, until they shrink and turn golden. Drain with a slotted spoon and dry on kitchen paper.

6. Scatter the carrot pieces over the top of the cake and dust with icing sugar. Chill until ready to serve.

NOTE: It is important to thoroughly dry the carrot ribbons before frying to ensure a crisp result.

TECHNIQUE

Fry the carrot ribbons, half at a time, in the hot oil. When shrivelled and turning golden, lift out with a slotted spoon and transfer to kitchen paper to dry and crisp.

CHOCOLATE GÂTEAU WITH BRANDIED PRUNES

Under the disguise of a smooth, cream coating lies a wickedly rich cake to tempt all chocolate lovers. Moist plump prunes, steeped in a brandy flavoured syrup, are layered between the dark chocolate sponge rounds.

75 g (3 oz) bitter chocolate

175 g (6 oz) unsalted butter, softened

300 g (10 oz) light muscovado sugar

3 eggs

300 g (10 oz) plain white flour

5 ml (1 tsp) bicarbonate of soda

10 ml (2 tsp) baking powder

150 ml (¼ pint) soured cream

FILLING

175 g (6 oz) no-need-to-soak dried prunes

5 ml (1 tsp) vanilla essence

2.5 ml (½ tsp) cornflour

90 ml (6 tbsp) brandy

TO DECORATE

450 ml (¾ pint) double cream

250 ml (8 fl oz) crème fraîche

cocoa powder, for dusting

PREPARATION TIME
35 minutes, plus cooling
COOKING TIME
25-30 minutes
FREEZING
Suitable: Stage 3

475 CALS PER SLICE

1. Preheat the oven to 190°C (375°F) Mark 5. Grease and base line three 20 cm (8 inch) sandwich tins. Break up the chocolate and heat very gently in a saucepan with 150 ml (¼ pint) water until melted. Cool slightly.

2. Cream the butter and sugar together in a bowl until pale and fluffy. Gradually beat in the eggs, a little at a time, adding a little of the flour to prevent curdling. Sift together the remaining flour, bicarbonate of soda and baking powder.

3. Stir the chocolate into the creamed mixture, then fold in the flour and soured cream. Divide between the prepared tins and level the surfaces. Bake for 25-30 minutes until firm to touch. Turn out and cool on a wire rack.

4. For the filling, roughly chop the prunes and place in a saucepan with 90 ml (3 fl oz) water, and the vanilla essence. Bring to the boil, reduce the heat and simmer gently for 5 minutes. Blend the cornflour with 15 ml (1 tbsp) water, add to the pan and cook, stirring, for 1 minute until thickened. Remove from the heat and add the brandy. Leave to cool.

5. For the decoration, whip the cream until just holding its shape. Fold in the crème fraîche.

6. Spread the prune filling on two of the sponges, then cover with a little of the cream. Assemble the three layers on a serving plate and cover with the remaining cream, swirling it attractively. Serve dusted with cocoa powder.

NOTE: The prune filling, once cooled, should be very moist, with juices still visible. Add a little extra liqueur or water if it has become dry.

TECHNIQUE

Using a palette knife, spread the cream over the top and sides of the cake until evenly covered. Swirl attractively with tip of knife.

LIGHT CHOCOLATE FUDGE CAKE

This stunning white chocolate cake is a great favourite with chocolate lovers! Light sponge rounds are sandwiched together with whipped cream, flavoured with tiny pieces of white chocolate and lemon juice for a pleasantly contrasting lemony tang. The entire cake is covered with an irresistible white chocolate fudge icing and scattered liberally with chocolate shavings.

MAKES 12 SLICES

50 g (2 oz) white chocolate
4 eggs
125 g (4 oz) caster sugar
finely grated rind of 1 lemon
125 g (4 oz) plain white flour
FILLING
50 g (2 oz) white chocolate
150 ml (¼ pint) double
  cream
25 ml (5 tsp) lemon juice
ICING
175 g (6 oz) white chocolate
125 g (4 oz) unsalted butter
60 ml (4 tbsp) milk
175 g (6 oz) icing sugar
TO FINISH
chocolate shavings (see
  page 8)
cocoa powder or icing
  sugar, for dusting

PREPARATION TIME
35 minutes, plus cooling and
chocolate shavings
COOKING TIME
30-35 minutes
FREEZING
Suitable: Open freeze, then wrap
loosely in foil.

385 CALS PER SLICE

1. Preheat the oven to 180°C (350°F) Mark 4. Grease and line a 19 cm (7½ inch) round cake tin (see note). Finely grate the chocolate.

2. Put the eggs, sugar and lemon rind in a large heatproof bowl over a pan of hot water and whisk until the mixture has doubled in volume and is thick enough to leave a trail on the surface when the whisk is lifted. Remove the bowl from the pan and whisk until cool.

3. Sift the flour over the mixture, then sprinkle with the grated chocolate. Fold in lightly, using a large metal spoon. Turn into the prepared tin and bake for 30-35 minutes until just firm to the touch. Turn out and cool on a wire rack.

4. For the filling, chop the chocolate into small pieces. Whip the cream until it just holds its shape. Stir in the chocolate and lemon juice.

5. Split the sponge horizontally into 2 layers and sandwich together with the filling. Place on a serving plate.

6. For the icing, break up the chocolate and put into a pan with the butter and milk. Heat gently until dissolved, then stir until smooth. Beat in the icing sugar.

7. Allow the icing to cool, then beat until it forms soft peaks. Spread over the top and sides of the cake. Scatter lavishly with chocolate shavings. Serve dusted with cocoa powder or icing sugar.

NOTE: If you do not have a 19 cm (7½ inch) cake tin, use a 20 cm (8 inch) one instead. The sponge will be slightly more shallow.

TECHNIQUE

Using an electric whisk, beat the cooled icing until it forms soft peaks.

TIERED FRUIT GÂTEAU

Tiering a gâteau brings a refreshing informality to any special occasion. In this creation, light sponge layers are sandwiched together with macerated soft fruits and a hazelnut praline cream. Pretty chocolate collars surround the layers, while glazed soft fruits and herb flowers provide the elaborate decoration.

MAKES 24 SLICES

LARGE CAKE
6 eggs
175 g (6 oz) caster sugar
175 g (6 oz) plain white flour
SMALL CAKE
2 eggs
50 g (2 oz) caster sugar
50 g (2 oz) plain white flour
FILLING
350 g (12 oz) strawberries
175 g (6 oz) raspberries
30 ml (2 tbsp) rosewater
40 g (1½ oz) caster sugar
TO FINISH
175 g (6 oz) shelled
    hazelnuts
150 g (5 oz) caster sugar
900 ml (1½ pints) double
    cream
350 g (12 oz) plain chocolate
900 g (2 lb) soft fruits, such
    as strawberries, rasp-
    berries, blueberries, red
    and blackcurrants
105 ml (7 tbsp) redcurrant
    jelly
herb flowers (optional)

PREPARATION TIME
1½ hours, plus cooling
COOKING TIME
45-50 minutes
FREEZING
Suitable: Without glazed fruits

425 CALS PER SLICE

1. Preheat the oven to 180°C (350°F) Mark 4. Grease and base-line a 28 cm (11 inch) and a 15 cm (6 inch) round cake tin. Dust with flour and shake out excess.

2. For the large cake, whisk the eggs and sugar together in a very large heat-proof bowl over a pan of hot water until the mixture is thick enough to leave a trail. Remove bowl from pan and whisk until cooled. Sift flour over mixture and fold in lightly. Turn into the large tin and bake for 20-25 minutes until just firm. Cool on a wire rack. Make the small cake in the same way and bake for 15-17 minutes.

3. Slice the strawberries and toss in a bowl with the raspberries, rosewater and sugar. Gently heat the hazelnuts and sugar in a heavy-based pan with 15 ml (1 tbsp) water until sugar dissolves, then cook to a deep brown caramel. Immediately pour onto an oiled baking sheet. Leave to cool and harden, then coarsely crush. Whip the cream until just peaking, then fold in the praline.

4. Halve the cakes horizontally. Sandwich the large cakes together on a platter with two thirds of the fruit filling and a little praline cream. Sandwich the small cake with the remaining fruits and a little more cream. Cut a strip of greaseproof paper, 5 cm (2 inches) longer than the circumference of the large cake and 2 cm (¾ inches) deeper. Repeat for the small cake.

5. Spread remaining praline cream over cakes, then carefully position the small cake, off-centre, on the large one. Chill.

6. Melt the chocolate in a bowl over a pan of simmering water. Spread over each greaseproof strip, right to the long edges and 1 cm (½ inch) from each end. Leave until the chocolate has thickened slightly, then carefully wrap the small strip around the small cake. Wrap the long strip around the large cake (another pair of hands is useful at this point!). Chill for 5-10 minutes until set, then carefully peel away the paper.

7. Decorate the gâteau with the soft fruits. Melt the redcurrant jelly with 15 ml (1 tbsp) water and brush over the fruits. Apply the herb flowers.

TECHNIQUE

Position the small chocolate strip around the small cake, pressing gently to fit.

SYRUPY SEMOLINA HALVA

Grainy semolina, baked to form a firm sponge base for citrus fruits saturated in spicy syrup, evokes the flavour of near eastern patisserie! Allow the sponge to steep for several hours or overnight in the thick syrup so that the syrup is thoroughly absorbed. Serve accompanied by thick yogurt and strong black coffee.

125 g (4 oz) unsalted butter, softened

125 g (4 oz) light muscovado sugar

grated rind of 1 orange

grated rind of 1 lemon

30 ml (2 tbsp) lemon juice

2 eggs

175 g (6 oz) semolina

5 ml (1 tsp) baking powder

125 g (4 oz) ground almonds

30 ml (2 tbsp) poppy seeds

TO FINISH

2 oranges

2 lemons

300 g (10 oz) caster sugar

300 ml (½ pint) freshly squeezed orange juice

2 cinnamon sticks, halved

PREPARATION TIME
30 minutes
COOKING TIME
30 minutes
FREEZING
Suitable: Cake only

1. Preheat the oven to 220°C (425°F) Mark 7. Grease and base-line a shallow 23 cm (9 inch) square baking tin. Cream the butter and sugar together until pale and fluffy.

2. Add the orange and lemon rind, lemon juice, eggs, semolina, baking powder, ground almonds and poppy seeds. Beat well until evenly mixed, then turn into the prepared tin and level the surface. Bake for about 20 minutes until slightly risen and turning golden. Remove from the oven and leave to cool in the tin. Peel off the paper, then return to the tin.

3. To finish, finely pare the rind from 1 orange and 1 lemon in strips using a citrus zester. Cut away all the white pith from both oranges and lemons, then thinly slice the fruit. Place the sugar in a heavy-based saucepan with the orange juice, cinnamon sticks and pared fruit rind. Heat gently, stirring until the sugar dissolves, then bring to the boil and boil for 3 minutes.

4. Remove the pared fruit rind and cinnamon from the syrup with a slotted spoon and reserve. Pour just over half of the syrup evenly over the surface of the cake. Scatter the fruit slices, pared rind and cinnamon sticks on top.

5. Return the remaining syrup to the heat and cook for another 5 minutes or until thickened and beginning to caramelise. Pour evenly over the fruit and leave for several hours before cutting. Store in an airtight plastic container for up to 4-5 days.

NOTE: If preferred, you can arrange the decorative fruits in lines to make cutting easier.

TECHNIQUE

Beat the cake ingredients together until thoroughly mixed; the consistency will be fairly thick.

STICKY ORANGE FLAPJACKS

Coated in buttery syrup and golden baked to a chewy, sticky perfection, porridge oats are transformed into a classic teatime favourite. Nutty sunflower seeds and finely pared orange zest are included in this simple recipe – to provide an interesting new twist.

MAKES 18

2 small oranges
250 g (9 oz) unsalted butter
250 g (9 oz) caster sugar
175 g (6 oz) golden syrup
425 g (15 oz) porridge oats
30 ml (2 tbsp) sunflower
seeds
45 ml (3 tbsp) fine-shred
orange marmalade

PREPARATION TIME
10 minutes
COOKING TIME
25-30 minutes
FREEZING
Suitable

300 CALS PER FLAPJACK

1. Preheat the oven to 180°C (350°F) Mark 4. Grease a baking tin measuring 22×9 cm (8½×11½ inches) across the top and 19×27 cm (7½×10½ inches) across the base. (Or use a tin with similar dimensions.)

2. Using a citrus zester, finely pare the rind from the oranges in strips. Place in a heavy-based saucepan. Add the butter, cut into pieces, with the sugar and syrup. Cook over a moderate heat, stirring until the butter has melted. Remove from the heat and stir in the oats, until evenly coated in syrup.

3. Turn the mixture into the prepared tin and level the surface. Sprinkle with the sunflower seeds. Bake for 25-30 minutes until turning deep golden around the edges; the mixture will still be very soft in the centre. Leave in the tin until almost cold.

4. Heat the marmalade in a small saucepan with 15 ml (1 tbsp) water until syrupy. Brush evenly over the flapjack. Turn out onto a board and cut into 18 bars. Store in an airtight container for up to 1 week.

NOTE: To weigh syrup, first measure out the sugar quantity and leave it in the scales bowl, making a small well in the centre. Add additional weights for the required quantity of syrup and spoon the syrup into the well. Both sugar and syrup will then slide cleanly into the saucepan.

VARIATIONS

Fruit and Nut Flapjacks: Omit the orange rind, sunflower seeds and marmalade. Add 125 g (4 oz) luxury mixed dried fruit and 75 g (3 oz) chopped and toasted mixed nuts with the oats.

Pear and Cinnamon Flapjacks: Omit the orange rind, sunflower seeds and marmalade. Add 5 ml (1 tsp) ground cinnamon with the sugar, and 150 g (5 oz) roughly chopped dried pears with the oats.

TECHNIQUE

Place the citrus zester against the orange skin and draw firmly towards you to remove the rind in fine strips. Repeat all over the skin.

CITRUS ECCLES CAKES

Flaky, light and oozing butter, these delicate lattice-topped pastries are a far cry from some dry and heavy shop-bought versions. In this recipe they are filled with currants, citrus peel and muscovado sugar, and drizzled with melted butter after cooking. For maximum enjoyment serve with that freshly baked lingering warmth.

MAKES 20

PASTRY

175 g (6 oz) firm unsalted
  butter

225 g (8 oz) plain white flour

pinch of salt

5 ml (1 tsp) lemon juice

FILLING

175 g (6 oz) currants

50 g (2 oz) chopped mixed
  peel

50 g (2 oz) muscovado sugar

finely grated rind of
  2 lemons

TO FINISH

beaten egg, to glaze

caster sugar, for dusting

50 g (2 oz) unsalted butter

PREPARATION TIME
35 minutes, plus chilling
COOKING TIME
12-15 minutes
FREEZING
Suitable

160 CALS PER CAKE

1. To make the pastry, cut the butter into small dice. Sift the flour and salt into a bowl. Add the butter, lemon juice and 100 ml (3½ fl oz) iced water. Using a round-bladed knife mix to a soft dough, adding a little extra water if it is too dry.

2. Knead lightly, then roll out on a lightly floured surface to an oblong, about 30 cm (12 inches) long and 10 cm (4 inches) wide. Fold the bottom third up and the lower third down, keeping the edges straight, then give the pastry a quarter turn. Repeat the rolling, folding and turning four more times. Wrap in greaseproof paper and leave to rest in the refrigerator for 30 minutes.

3. For the filling, mix the currants, mixed peel, sugar and lemon rind together in a small bowl.

4. Preheat the oven to 220°C (425°F) Mark 7. Lightly grease two baking sheets. Roll out half of the pastry on a lightly floured surface to a 50 × 20 cm (20 × 8 inch) rectangle. Cut in half lengthways, then cut each strip into five equal pieces.

5. Using the tip of a knife make three 2 cm (¾ inch) cuts, 5 mm (¼ inch) apart down the centre of one piece of pastry. Make three more rows of cuts either side of the first row so that when the pastry is pulled apart slightly it creates a lattice. Repeat with remaining pieces of pastry. Brush edges with beaten egg.

6. Set aside half of the filling. Divide the remainder between the latticed pastries, placing it in the centres. Bring the edges of the pastry up over the filling, pinching them together to seal. Invert onto one baking sheet, so the latticed sides face upwards.

7. Repeat with the remaining pastry and filling to make ten more pastries. Brush the pastries with beaten egg and sprinkle lightly with sugar. Bake for 12-15 minutes, until golden. Melt the butter and pour a little into each Eccles cake, through the lattice. Serve warm.

CHERRY AND ALMOND CAKES

Replace currants, peel and lemon rind with 125 g (4 oz) chopped glacé cherries, 50 g (2 oz) chopped blanched almonds and 125 g (4 oz) grated almond paste.

TECHNIQUE

Make rows of cuts in the pastry 5 mm (¼ inch) apart and stagger the rows to shape the lattice.

SAFFRON SCONES

With its golden colour, wonderful aroma and intriguing taste, regal saffron gives an exciting lift to the humble scone. Serve warm with melting butter or generous scoops of thick clotted cream. Slices of juicy melon and mango would make the perfect accompaniment.

MAKES ABOUT 12

½-1 sachet or 2.5-5 ml
  (½-1 tsp) saffron strands
  (see note)
150 ml (¼ pint) milk
  (approximately)
225 g (8 oz) self-raising
  white flour
pinch of salt
5 ml (1 tsp) baking powder
40 g (1½ oz) firm unsalted
  butter or margarine
30 ml (2 tbsp) caster sugar
beaten egg, to glaze

PREPARATION TIME
15 minutes, plus infusing
COOKING TIME
10-12 minutes
FREEZING
Suitable

110 CALS PER SCONE

1. Preheat the oven to 220°C (425°F) Mark 7. Lightly grease a baking sheet. Roughly break up the saffron strands and place in a saucepan with half of the milk. Bring just to the boil, then remove from the heat and leave to infuse for 20 minutes.

2. Sift the flour, salt and baking powder into a bowl. Add the butter, cut into small pieces, and rub in using the fingertips until the mixture resembles fine breadcrumbs. Stir in the sugar.

3. Stir in the saffron milk and half of the remaining milk. Mix with a round-bladed knife to a soft dough, adding the rest of the milk if the mixture is too dry; it should be soft and slightly sticky.

4. Knead lightly and roll out to a 2 cm (¾ inch) thickness. Cut out rounds, using a 5 cm (2 inch) cutter. Place on the baking sheet and brush the tops with the beaten egg. Bake for 10-12 minutes until well risen and golden brown. Transfer to a wire rack to cool. Serve split, with butter, or clotted cream and fruits.

NOTE: Use either ½ or 1 sachet saffron strands, depending on the strength of flavour required. As with any recipe using baking powder, scones should be baked immediately as the baking powder is activated as soon as it comes into contact with liquids.

ORANGE AND ROSEMARY SCONES

Replace the saffron with the finely grated rind of 1 orange and 15 ml (1 tbsp) finely snipped rosemary leaves. Do not heat the milk before mixing.

TECHNIQUE

Roll out the dough to a 2 cm (¾ inch) thickness and cut out rounds, using a 4 cm (1½ inch) pastry cutter. Re-roll trimmings and cut out more rounds.

ALMOND AND APRICOT ROULADE

This irresistible moist roulade is flecked with grated marzipan and drizzled with amaretto liqueur, giving a superb almondy flavour. In perfect contrast, fresh ripe apricots and crème fraîche are encased inside. The roulade is best made a day in advance and filled shortly before serving, preferably with strong dark coffee.

MAKES 8 SLICES

ROULADE
25 g (1 oz) flaked almonds
125 g (4 oz) white almond paste
5 eggs, separated
150 g (5 oz) caster sugar
5 ml (1 tsp) vanilla essence
45 ml (3 tbsp) plain flour
45 ml (3 tbsp) amaretto de Saronno liqueur
FILLING
6 ripe apricots
300 g (10 oz) crème fraîche
caster or icing sugar, for dusting

PREPARATION TIME
20 minutes, plus standing
COOKING TIME
20 minutes
FREEZING
Not suitable

380 CALS PER SLICE

1. Preheat the oven to 180°C (350°F) Mark 4. Grease a 33×23 cm (13×9 inch) Swiss roll tin and line with greased non-stick baking parchment. Scatter the flaked almonds evenly over the paper. Grate the almond paste.

2. Whisk the egg yolks with 125 g (4 oz) of the sugar until pale and fluffy. Stir in the vanilla essence and grated almond paste. Sift the flour over the mixture, then lightly fold in.

3. Whisk the egg whites in another bowl, until stiff but not dry. Gradually whisk in the remaining sugar. Using a metal tablespoon, carefully fold a quarter of the egg whites into the almond mixture to loosen, then fold in the remainder.

4. Turn into the prepared tin and gently ease the mixture into the corners. Bake for about 20 minutes or until well risen and just firm to the touch. Remove from the oven and cover with a sheet of non-stick baking parchment and a damp tea-towel. Leave until cool, or overnight if possible.

5. Remove the tea-towel and invert the roulade (and paper) onto a baking sheet. Peel off the lining paper. Sprinkle another piece of baking parchment with caster sugar and flip the roulade onto it. Drizzle with the amaretto liqueur.

6. Halve and stone the apricots, then cut into small pieces. Spread the roulade with the crème fraîche and scatter with the apricots. Starting at one of the narrow ends, roll up the roulade. Transfer to a plate and dust with caster or icing sugar to serve.

NOTE: The roulade will probably crack during rolling – this is a characteristic!

VARIATIONS

Replace the apricots with strawberries or raspberries. Brandy or Grand Marnier can be used instead of the amaretto.

TECHNIQUE

Starting from one of the narrow ends, carefully roll up the roulade, using the paper to help.

CHOCOLATE LEAF GÂTEAU

For this stunning gâteau a light, chocolate genoese is split and generously filled with a white chocolate and Cointreau-flavoured cream, then topped with a glossy dark chocolate cream icing and crowned with chocolate leaves. Use a variety of well-defined leaves to make the decoration – for optimum effect.

MAKES 14 SLICES

50 g (2 oz) unsalted butter
5 eggs
150 g (5 oz) caster sugar
125 g (4 oz) plain white flour
25 g (1 oz) cocoa powder
FILLING
200 g (7 oz) white chocolate
300 ml (½ pint) double
  cream
75 ml (5 tbsp) Cointreau or
  other orange-flavoured
  liqueur
ICING
225 g (8 oz) plain dark
  chocolate, in pieces
225 g (8 oz) double cream
TO DECORATE
75 g (3 oz) bitter chocolate
75 g (3 oz) plain dark
  chocolate
75 g (3 oz) milk chocolate
selection of clean, dry
  leaves, such as rose, large
  mint, lemon geranium
  and small bay leaves

PREPARATION TIME
1½ hours, plus cooling
COOKING TIME
30 minutes
FREEZING
Suitable: Before icing

560 CALS PER SLICE

1. Preheat the oven to 180°C (350°F) Mark 4. Grease and line a 23 cm (9 inch) spring-release cake tin. Melt the butter in a saucepan; leave to cool slightly.

2. Put the eggs and sugar in a large heat-proof bowl standing over a pan of hot water. Whisk until pale and creamy, and thick enough to leave a trail on the surface when the whisk is lifted.

3. Remove from the heat and whisk until cool. Sift together the flour and cocoa powder, then fold half into the egg mixture using a metal spoon. Pour the butter around the edge of the mixture and lightly fold in. Gradually fold in the remaining flour and cocoa.

4. Pour into the tin. Bake for about 30 minutes until well risen, just firm to touch and beginning to shrink from sides of tin. Turn out and cool on a wire rack.

5. To make the filling, finely grate the white chocolate. Whip cream with the liqueur until thickened but not peaking. Fold in the chocolate. Split the sponge horizontally and sandwich together with the cream. Invert onto a wire rack so that the flat base is now the top.

6. For the icing, place the chocolate in a heavy-based saucepan with the cream. Heat gently until chocolate is almost melted. Remove from heat and stir until smooth and glossy; let cool slightly.

7. Position a large plate or tray under the wire rack holding the cake. Pour the icing onto the cake. Using a palette knife, ease the icing down the side until the cake is completely covered. Carefully transfer to a serving plate.

8. For the chocolate leaves, break up the bitter chocolate and place in a heat-proof bowl over a pan of hot water and leave until melted. Repeat with the plain and milk chocolate; keep separate.

9. Using a paintbrush, paint the under-sides of the leaves with the different melted chocolates, taking it just to the edges. (You'll need about 15 of each shade). Leave in a cool place or refrigerate until set. Carefully peel the leaves away from the chocolate. Press the chocolate leaves gently around the sides of the gâteau to decorate.

TECHNIQUE

Once all of the icing has been poured over the top of the cake, ease it down the side, spreading with a palette knife.

COCONUT GÂTEAU WITH LIME AND KIRSCH

This beautiful white sponge is made using a meringue base into which the dry ingredients and flavourings are folded. Lime zest speckles the sponge and a kirsch syrup gives a moist kick. Freshly toasted coconut shavings and syrupy lime slices add both sweetness and tang to the rich cream coating.

MAKES 10-12 SLICES

7 egg whites
good pinch of salt
5 ml (1 tsp) cream of tartar
10 ml (2 tsp) vanilla essence
300 g (10 oz) caster sugar
finely grated rind of 2 limes
50 g (2 oz) freshly grated
  coconut, or desiccated
  coconut
125 g (4 oz) plain white flour
TO ASSEMBLE
4 limes
50 g (2 oz) caster sugar
60 ml (4 tbsp) kirsch
125 g (4 oz) piece fresh
  coconut, or coconut
  shreds
450 ml (¾ pint) double
  cream
45 ml (3 tbsp) icing sugar
175 g (6 oz) Greek-style
  yogurt

PREPARATION TIME
45 minutes, plus cooling
COOKING TIME
30 minutes
FREEZING
Suitable: Cake only

515-430 CALS PER SLICE

1. Preheat the oven to 160°C (325°F) Mark 3. Grease and base-line two 20 cm (8 inch) sandwich tins. Whisk the egg whites in a large bowl until just holding their shape. Add the salt and cream of tartar and whisk until stiff but not dry. Gradually whisk in the sugar, a little at a time, whisking well between each addition until stiff and very shiny. Whisk in the lime rind with the last of the sugar.

2. Add the coconut, then sift in the flour and lightly fold in until just incorporated. Divide between the tins and level the surfaces. Bake for 30 minutes until the surfaces are pale golden and crusty. Leave to cool in the tins.

3. For the decoration, finely pare the rind from two of the limes in shreds, using a sharp knife. Remove the peel and white pith from all 4 limes; thinly slice the flesh. Dissolve the sugar in 150 ml (¼ pint) water in a small heavy-based pan over a low heat. Add the lime slices and shredded rind and cook gently for 1 minute. Drain with a slotted spoon and reserve. Leave the syrup to cool.

4. Stir the kirsch into the cooled syrup. Split each cake in half horizontally and drizzle each layer with the syrup. If using fresh coconut, cut away the skin, then pare the flesh using a swivel vegetable peeler. Lightly toast the parings or coconut shreds until turning golden.

5. Whip the cream with the icing sugar until just peaking, then fold in the yogurt. Place one cake layer on a serving plate and spread with a little of the cream mixture. Arrange a quarter of the lime slices on top and sprinkle with a little of the coconut shavings. Repeat the layers twice, using up half the cream and most of the coconut and lime slices. Top with the final cake layer.

6. Spread the remaining cream all over the cake. Decorate the top with the remaining lime slices and coconut, and the pared lime rind. Chill in the refrigerator until ready to serve.

TECHNIQUE

Using a metal tablespoon, carefully fold the flour and coconut into the meringue mixture until just incorporated.

Hazelnut meringue GÂTEAU

Tiers of lightly spiced meringue – laced with two-tone chocolate pieces – form a delicious case for lightly whipped cream and a hazelnut praline. For a lighter gâteau, replace half of the cream with thick Greek-style yogurt or fromage frais. You can also increase the amount of spice if you prefer a more intense flavour.

MAKES 10 SLICES

MERINGUE
125 g (4 oz) shelled hazelnuts

5 egg whites

250 g (9 oz) caster sugar

2.5 cm (½ tsp) ground mixed spice

75 g (3 oz) white chocolate chopped

75 g (3 oz) plain chocolate, chopped

TO ASSEMBLE
75 g (3 oz) shelled hazelnuts

125 g (4 oz) caster sugar

300 ml (½ pint) double cream

cocoa powder, for dusting

PREPARATION TIME
40 minutes, plus cooling
COOKING TIME
About 1½ hours
FREEZING
Not suitable

630 CALS PER SLICE

1. Line 2 baking sheets with non-sticking baking parchment. Draw a 23 cm (9 inch) circle onto one sheet, using a plate as a guide. On the other sheet, draw a 17.5 cm (6½ inch) circle. Turn the paper over. Preheat the oven to 140°C (275°F) Mark 1.

2. To make the meringue, lightly toast the hazelnuts, then chop roughly. Whisk the egg whites in a bowl until stiff but not dry. Gradually whisk in the sugar, a tablespoon at a time, whisking well between each addition until the meringue is stiff and very shiny. Whisk in the spice with the last of the sugar. Carefully fold in the chopped hazelnuts and white and plain chocolate.

3. Spoon the meringue onto the circles, then spread neatly into rounds. Bake for about 1½ hours until dry and the undersides are firm when tapped. Turn the oven off and leave the meringues to cool in the oven.

4. For the praline, lightly oil a baking sheet. Put the hazelnuts in a small heavy-based pan with the sugar. Place over a gentle heat, stirring until the sugar melts. Continue cooking until the mixture caramelises to a rich golden brown colour, then pour onto the baking sheet. Leave to cool and harden.

5. Place the praline in a polythene bag and beat with a rolling pin until very coarsely crushed.

6. Carefully transfer the largest meringue round to a serving plate. Whip the cream until softly peaking, then spread over the meringue. Scatter with the praline. Cover with the smaller meringue round and dust the top of the gâteau with cocoa powder.

NOTE: Remember to switch the baking sheets around halfway through cooking the meringue rounds, to ensure an even result.

TECHNIQUE

Spread the hazelnut meringue onto the prepared baking sheets, just to the edges of the marked circles. Swirl the edges of the large meringue and the whole surface of the smaller meringue with a palette knife.

GINGERBREAD NATIVITY

This spicy gingerbread stable with its simple figures is easier to make than it looks – especially if you follow the step-by-step guide (overleaf) and use the template outlines provided. If it seems like too much work, try making tree decorations instead. Simply stamp out stars, trees etc, using suitable cutters and make a small hole in the top of each one – to enable a ribbon to be threaded through after baking, for hanging on the tree.

MAKES I NATIVITY

**350 g (12 oz) plain white
  flour**
**5 ml (1 tsp) bicarbonate of
  soda**
30 ml (2 tbsp) ground ginger
**15 ml (1 tbsp) ground
  cinnamon**
2.5 ml (½ tsp) ground cloves
125 g (4 oz) butter
**175 g (6 oz) soft light brown
  sugar**
60 ml (2 tbsp) golden syrup
1 egg (size 4)
CARAMEL
125 g (4 oz) caster sugar
30 ml (2 tbsp) water
TO DECORATE
**twiglets or lean straw
  matting**
**demerara and/or other
  brown sugars, for
  sprinkling**
a little glacé or royal icing
food colourings
**edible gold leaf or lustre
  powder**
few toffees or flat sweets

PREPARATION TIME
About 2 hours, plus drying
COOKING TIME
8-10 minutes
FREEZING
Suitable: Uncooked gingerbread
dough only

1. Cut out templates for the stable (see pages 186-7). Line two baking sheets with non-stick baking parchment. Preheat the oven to 190°C (375°F) Mark 5.

2. Sift the flour with the bicarbonate of soda and spices into a large bowl. Rub in the butter until the mixture resembles fine breadcrumbs. Stir in the sugar.

3. Warm the syrup very slightly and beat in the egg. Cool slightly, then pour onto the flour mixture. Beat with a wooden spoon to a soft dough. Bring together with your hands and knead until smooth. Cut off one third of the dough, wrap in cling film and reserve.

4. On a lightly floured surface, roll out the other piece of dough to a 5 mm (¼ inch) thickness. Using the stable templates and a sharp knife, cut out each shape. Carefully transfer to the baking sheets, straighten any edges and chill for 15 minutes. Knead the trimmings into the reserved dough, re-wrap and chill to make the figures later.

5. Bake the stable pieces for 8-10 minutes or until golden brown. Leave to cool and harden for 10 minutes on the baking sheet, then transfer to a wire rack to cool completely.

6. To make the caramel, dissolve the sugar in the water in a heavy-based pan over a low heat, then boil to a pale caramel. Immediately dip the base of the pan in cool water to stop further cooking. Use this caramel to join the edges of the stable together and to cement it to a cake board. Join the roof to the stable. Stick twiglets or straw matting to the roof, if liked. Sprinkle sugar(s) in and around the stable.

7. Using the templates (on pages 188-9), cut out the figures and carefully place on the baking sheets. Bake as before, checking after 8 minutes. Cool as before (use any remaining dough to make biscuits).

8. Decorate the figures with gold leaf or lustre powder, and coloured glacé or royal icing. Allow to dry before assembling around the stable. Use a toffee or sweet and a little icing to cement the base of each figure to the board.

TECHNIQUE

To make the caramel, cook the sugar syrup to a pale golden colour.

GINGERBREAD NATIVITY

The gingerbread nativity is fun to make – especially if you have children to help you! The following step-by-step guide shows you how to make and assemble the stable, and how to decorate the figures. Use edible decorations, unless you make it known that the nativity is not to be eaten.

1. Cut out templates for the stable (see right), using greaseproof paper or cardboard. Line two baking sheets with non-stick baking parchment.

2. Roll out the larger piece of gingerbread dough to a 5 mm (¼ inch) thickness. Using the templates and a sharp knife, cut out one of each shape.

3. Trace the outlines of the figures (overleaf) to make templates for Mary, Joseph, Baby Jesus, Angel Gabriel, Star of Bethlehem, Kings and Shepherds. Roll out the remaining dough and place the templates on the dough. Cut out using a sharp knife. Remember to cut 3 kings and 2-3 shepherds.

4. Carefully transfer the shapes to the baking sheets without destroying the shapes. Straighten any edges and chill for 15 minutes.

5. Bake the pieces of gingerbread in a preheated oven at 190°C (375°F) Mark 5 for 8-10 minutes or until golden brown. Leave on the baking sheet for 10 minutes, then transfer to a wire rack to cool completely.

6. Use the caramel to join the edges of the stable together and to cement it to a covered cake board. Dip the edges in the caramel and push them together or use a spoon to coat the edges. Remelt the caramel as necessary by sitting the pan in a saucepan of boiling water until it liquifies again. Join the roof to the stable with the caramel.

7. Stick twiglets or clean straw matting to the roof, or leave plain if preferred. Scatter different shades of sugar around the stable to resemble sand and earth.

9. Decorate the characters with glacé or royal icing. Allow to dry before assembling in and around the stable.

10. Cement a toffee or flat sweet to the base of each figure with a little icing or caramel so that it will stand upright. Stick suitable sweets onto the Kings to resemble their gifts.

STABLE TEMPLATES

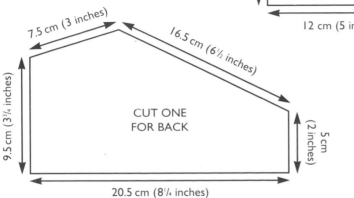

8. Give Baby Jesus, Mary, Joseph and the Angel gold halos, and the Kings and Star of Bethlehem a bit of gold too! Stick gold leaf on with a little beaten egg white or apply gold lustre powder.

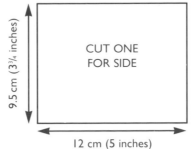

CUT ONE
FOR SIDE

5 cm
(2 inches)

12 cm (5 inches)

CUT ONE
FOR SIDE

9.5 cm (3¾ inches)

12 cm (5 inches)

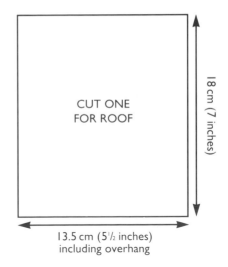

CUT ONE
FOR ROOF

18 cm (7 inches)

13.5 cm (5½ inches)
including overhang

CUT ONE
FOR BACK

7.5 cm (3 inches)

16.5 cm (6½ inches)

9.5 cm (3¾ inches)

5 cm
(2 inches)

20.5 cm (8¼ inches)

CUT ONE
FOR ROOF

9 cm (3½ inches)
including overhang

13.5 cm (5½ inches)
including overhang

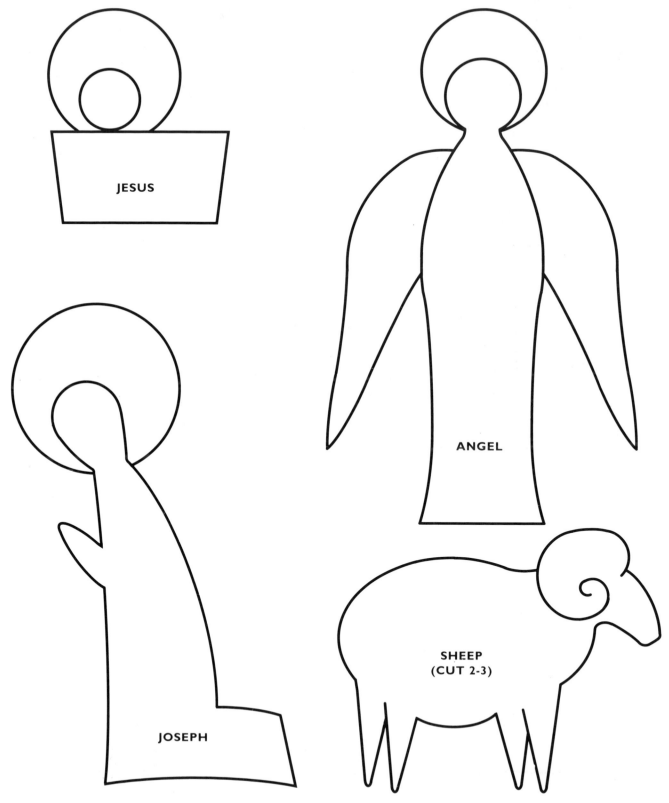

JESUS

ANGEL

JOSEPH

SHEEP
(CUT 2-3)

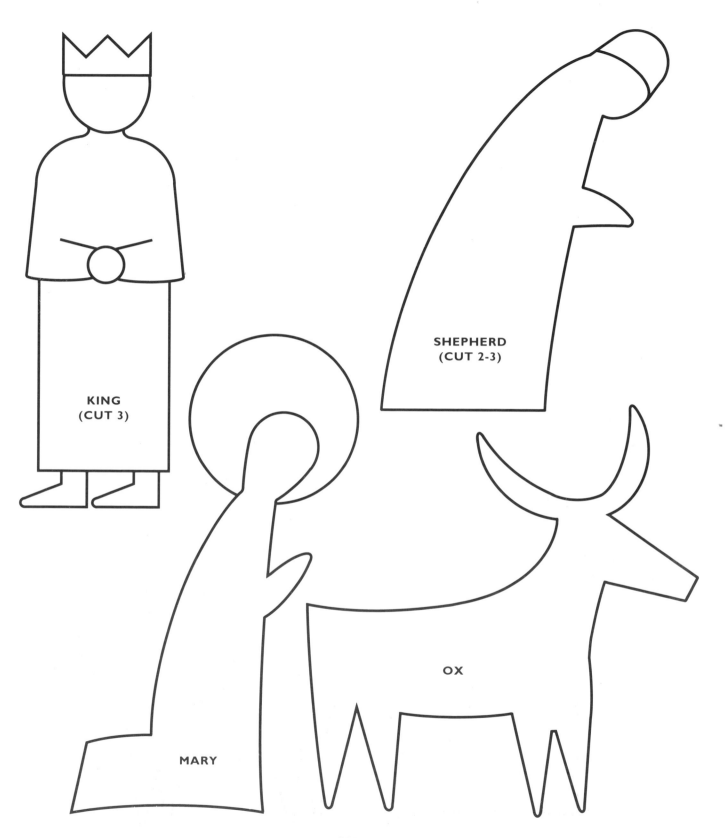

KING
(CUT 3)

SHEPHERD
(CUT 2-3)

MARY

OX